Psychology III

Theories for genuine human evolution

By Dr. Edward Schellhammer

1st Edition in English, 2020, translated from the German Edition
© Copyright 2020. Dr. Eduard Schellhammer. All rights reserved.

ISBN-13: 9781478372301

www.SchellhammerBusinessSchool.com
www.SchellhammerInstitute.com

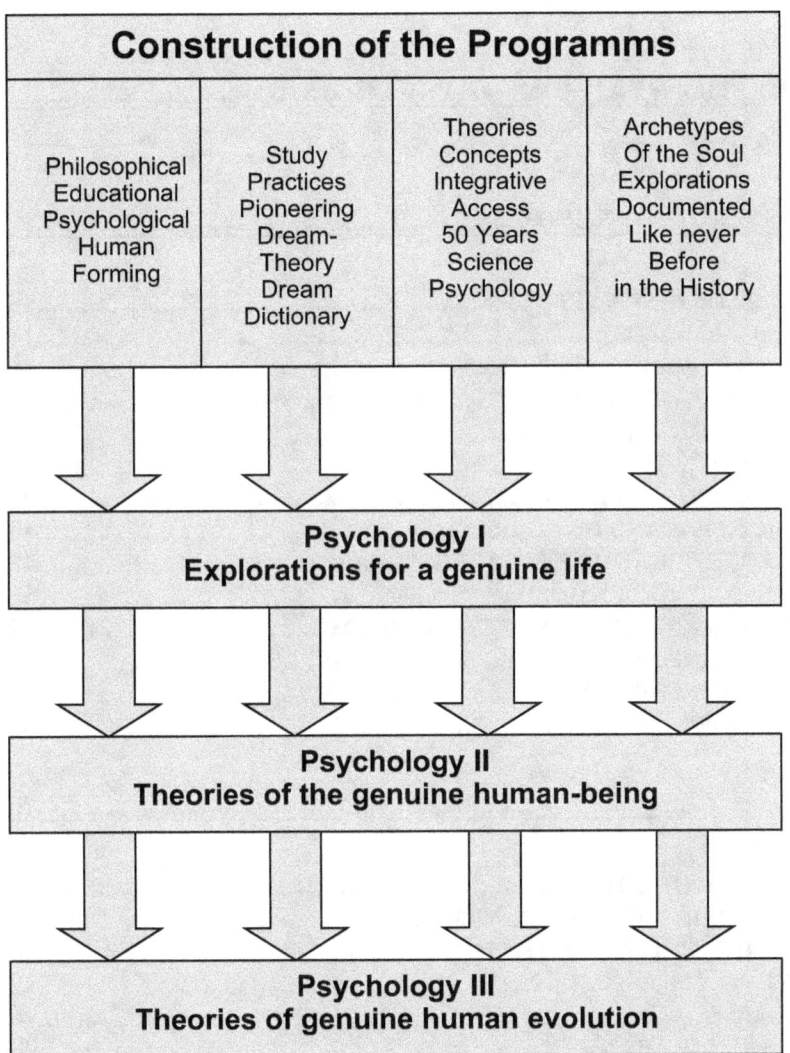

Construction of the Programms

Philosophical Educational Psychological Human Forming	Study Practices Pioneering Dream-Theory Dream Dictionary	Theories Concepts Integrative Access 50 Years Science Psychology	Archetypes Of the Soul Explorations Documented Like never Before in the History

Psychology I
Explorations for a genuine life

Psychology II
Theories of the genuine human-being

Psychology III
Theories of genuine human evolution

Table of Contents

List of Diagrams

The Highest Archetype:
Circle-Cross-Mandala
= Life Symbol

This is the archetype
for the process and the goal of individuation.
This is rooted in the archetypal
evolutionary humanity.

In Somnis Veritas for Psychology III

Dreams tell the truth. Dreams stay above theories, ideologies and dogmas. During the last 33 years I had over 12,000 dreams about the state of humanity and the planet. I had an estimated 3,000 dreams about humans' evolution and all processes of the Archetypes of the Soul. Examples:

From the heaven debouching, first energy, panic in the air, frightening, then something like warships or war machines fly towards the earth; suddenly the entire sky is full of them. An unbelievable dimension as large and deep as the sky, everything is full of these flying machines. A never before existed machinery of destruction. A total apocalyptic scene.

Many important strong men are in fact nothing other than baby pissers without legs.

I am in the Vatican, in an immense arch room, full of all kinds of junk. A big amount of rubbish, compressed many meters high. I am there and take a look at it while thinking: There is absolutely nothing here that could have a value or could be vivid.

I walk through the Vatican. And I ask myself who has paid and still pays for all this, and under which conditions has all this been built. And I think: Hidden behind all of this is an immeasurable megalomania, a perverse suppression and exploitation of people, robbery and homicide, wars and dictatorships, lies about God and religion.

The horizon is gloomy. Air and ground are poisoned. A cosmic nightmare is in the atmosphere.

2008 I told to people in a dream: "You have 10 years left to take strong measures to avoid the total collapse." But nobody listened.

The day will come when no bread exists.

In 35-40 years, everything will be over, the end, no more earth and no more humanity.

I am coming to a church in Jerusalem: The main part has got a cupola, the plaza outside is square-shaped with a column at each corner. All around there are more columns or turrets. As I step on the square, I say to a person next to me: "I can see the last riddle, solving it means, that we've reached the goal." I know the solution. On one of the steeples the circle-cross-Mandala is missing. The great wise and true experts of the holy books of humanity know through immemorial tradition, that only the true Christ and Messiah can solve this riddle with a dream. I know that the circle-cross-Mandala has to go on the steeple top and I remember in my dream: I've received this a few years ago (in reality!). I take it out and want to attach it there. It fits perfectly.

A famished child is dancing on a battlefield full of corpses and blood. The child is dancing a dance of death. I ask the president of the USA: "Do you want to accept me as the reincarnated Messiah? You will avoid 80% of the damage and suffering."

I tell people: "Never again will I come back to this earth. I am only here for a visit and I have to accomplish a job. And you have to get your shit together yourself."

I am interviewed on television: At the end I am asked: Do you want to say a last word to the viewers? I answer: "Yes, I can say to everybody: Continue living as you have up until this day and you will lose the earth!"

I tell to masses of people: "I have not come from millions of light years away to this earth, sent from God, to play here the cretin and idiot. With me humanity and the earth will have a good future. Without me humanity will perish. The choice is now yours!"

The truth and the Archetypes of the Soul are the primordial foundation and aim of science, human life, and society. Psychology doesn't have either of them! The entire social sciences do not have it. That's the scandalous drama of science.

The absence of the truth and of the Archetypes of the Soul produces enormous destructive energy and developments in sciences and societies.

It shows clearly that sciences do not take care of the archetypal, psychical and spiritual evolution of mankind nor do they have any respect for the creation.

Such science is a sham. Such sciences dehumanize mind and soul, and eliminate the dignity of humans.

Such sciences are infected with the most toxic virus ever existed: the dynamic code for regicide and deicide. In the end, it will irreversibly and unstoppably lead to the doom.

It can happen within decades if drastic global measures are not soon taken.

Dr. Edward Schellhammer

Introduction: Failure of psychology

Psychology and science

- The education programs at universities have not significantly changed since 1960/1970.
- The psychology programs at universities have not significantly changed since 1960/1970.
- The concepts about 'human being' at universities have not significantly changed since 1960/1970.
- The psychical-spiritual understanding of human life has not significantly changed since 1851.

Since Sigmund Freud and Carl G. Jung there is practically no pioneering research and knowledge developed in the social sciences about 'humans. The unconscious world of humans, which has a primordial role in humans' life, is completely ignored. The world of dreams, of meditation, of psychical and cosmic energy, and of the influences during prenatal time is absolutely neglected in the sciences of psychology and education. Philosophy and philosophical anthropology carelessly ignore these enormously important worlds. Humans' evolution has in the political and economic image about humans, including in Christianity, zero importance and practically no psychical and spiritual understanding. And they all have absolutely no idea about the Archetypes of the Soul and the inner processes. That's an outrageous disaster!

Psychology and education

- Highest importance has education as the fundamental preparation for success in life, work, and renewal in a very fast changing world. Pioneering vocational education is fundamental. Psychology is here constitutive.
- The immense problems of humanity and the planet can't be solved without fundamental renewal of education and especially a fundamental revision and re-construction of economics.
- Democracy and prosperity can never be better than the state of mind (and soul) of the collective and the way people do business. Professional competences of its leaders are indispensable.
- Work is a natural need of humans and improves satisfaction, self-esteem, and positive emotional state. Business success and professional satisfaction requires personality, knowledge and skills.

- Democracy can never be better than the state of mind of the working people, the small and medium sized businesses, and the quality of their performance.

Failure of psychology and education

- The ignorance and exclusion of human's spiritual intelligence (dreams), emotional intelligence, intuition and creativity, and the world of the psychical energy
- The lack of psychologically relevant education for mastering life: money, self- and life management, relationship, marriage, family life, etc.
- The constrained and obsessive accreditations (standardizations) of psychology (including psychotherapy, counselling, life coaching, etc.)
- The centralization of academic psychology with a highly rigid innovative inflexibility of institutions and curriculums
- The ignorance about human values such as love, care, truth, inner needs, psycho-social security (trust), inner roots of integrity (ethics)
- The disrespect for individual differences such as personality, character, performance, talents, inner potentials
- The paralyzing of teacher's (professor's) pioneering creativity and inner dedication due to prescribed dominant intellectual curriculums
- The inability to rapidly respond with new psychological knowledge related to the fast changes in society and the world
- The incompetent and immature politicians and experts in the local and national departments of psychology and education
- The ideological interests that mark curriculums, research, exam practices, principles of selection, school career and professional career
- The lack of complex thinking about life philosophy, spirituality, mind, dreams, environment, politics, media, consumption
- The performance criteria that ignore practical relevance, human values and a holistic humane understanding
- The absence of topics such as lies, cheat, deceit, falseness, fabrications, distortions, manipulations, brainwash (in politics, economics, religion, media, education), etc.
- The rigid, arrogant and authoritarian atmosphere towards children and adolescents in educational institutions
- The lack of joyful learning, creative learning activities, respect for the psychical-spiritual process of learning
- The lack of promotion of self-confidence, of critical explorations of the world (made by humans!), and of respect for 'being a human on earth'
- The lack of promoting the genuine inner needs for working as a part of satisfaction, fulfilment and meaning of life

Psychology and human's evolution

- Strong focus on new learning, creative learning, pioneering spirit, analysing and thinking in complex networks and with the biggest possible pictures
- Strong foundation and profound understanding of humans, human made problems, human values and humane life based on the psychical organism and on the Archetypes of the Soul
- New understanding of marriage, family, children's education, health, mastering conflicts and problems must become subjects and topics of science and education
- Knowledge must be developed and balanced with inner rooted spirituality, moral integrity, meaning of life, respect for humanity, nature, animals and the planet
- Peace, justice, hope, love, care, happiness, self-responsibility, truthfulness, reliability, trust and realistic faith (hope) must become subjects and topics of psychology and education
- Constructive behaviour in the everyday life, in social life, in political participation, in the world of work and business must become subjects and topics of psychology and education
- Holistic and permanent all-embracing psychical-spiritual development aiming for inner satisfaction and fulfilment must become subjects and topics of psychology and education
- Inner rooted spirituality, moral integrity, meaning of life, respect for humanity, nature, animals and the planet must become subjects and topics of psychology and education
- Self-responsibility for positive attitudes and for high quality of working must become higher meaning than mere earning money; must also become subjects and topics of psychology and education

The essence

What people have in their inner 'screen' (consciousness) is a nano-part of the reality. 7.8 billion people have only a nano-part of the reality in their mind. And they falsely think they have the right knowledge and picture about the reality. Additionally, all their psychical functions are distorted, displaced, perverted, undeveloped, suppressed, destroyed, and ignored by psychology, the public education, the religion, the media, the politics and the economics. Or they know it perfectly and it is exactly what they want for their interests.

This is the state of 7.8 billion people permanently, every day shaped, manipulated and brainwashed for the collective main stream of consciousness and attitudes. Only a few people are beyond this stream and these people are the hidden rulers of the world and some individuals with a clear view. This collective main stream is regressive and dehumanizing.

Psychology III develops the foundation of the alternative evolutionary path for humans and humanity as a whole, for life, education, and business.

All humans and the entire humanity are in a continuous psychological-spiritual evolution. The indispensable dynamics for human's evolution lies in the care for the genuine inner needs, in strengthening and living the capacities of love, in the catharsis of the unconscious, in the use of the constructive potentials in the unconscious mind, in the right understanding of the world of dreams, in the right way of contemplation (the use of the spiritual intelligence), and in the right model of the individual and collective evolution – which I call 'Individuation' or 'global Individuation'.

The science of psychology has no understanding about this vital human dimension and let the psychotic master technocrats dominating human's evolution which will irreversibly lead to the upcoming doom.

Academic psychology, public education and formation, religion and journalism as a science, from Harvard to Oxford, from Barcelona to Berlin, have become the servant of the satanic supra-master minders taking away humans' dignity, degrading humans to conditioned rats, and destroying cultures, folks, and nations around the globe.

7.8 billion people are cheated, deceited, manipulated, brainwashed, and fooled with psychological methods from 'the invisible hand'.

No student should study psychology without exploring and understanding this evil game of cosmic dimension; or alternatively the student will inescapably be victim and follower ('soldier') of this satanic game.

Psychology III explores the full potentials of humans' psychological and spiritual evolution.

1. The psychical needs

Essential theses

There are basic mental needs, which are necessary for an evolutionary, life-oriented life:

☐ Love   ☐ Relationships   ☐ Work / activities
☐ Meaning and value   ☐ Spirit / God   ☐ Truthfulness

Needs can be classified according to their focus on:

☐ Yourself   ☐ other people
☐ World / Objects   ☐ Transcendence

There are artificial needs: these are needs that are self-absorbed or self-generated; they have no or little (?) gain in value for humans.

Many psychic forces and external factors inhibit, disfigure or promote the experiencing and shaping of basic needs.

Human beings have the opportunity to shape their needs in such a way that they become a life expression and do not reduce themselves to tension reduction or functionality.

1.1. Variety of inner needs

1.1.1. The basic needs

What does man think when he hears or reads the word "need"? There are many options. One thinks of money, another of sex.

Some may think of love, a simple affection. Holiday wishes may be urgent. Anyone looking for a partner imagines his ideal for this need. Those who are unemployed feel the urge to work.

"If only I could laugh again", some people think in a stressful life situation. Kids want to play.

Young people want to discover the world and "experiment" with life. Parents have many needs that affect living with their children.

Old people, in turn, have other needs, e.g. facilitation or activity appropriate with age.

Many people have a need for God experience. The needs vary greatly depending on age and individual situation.

The fact is: Every person has needs that have vital significance for his or her equilibrium and for a fulfilled life. There is not the "needless man". Life itself essentially consists of needs.

So, we can assume that there are certain needs that all people have in certain stages of life.

A need contains various components. Elementary is: Man experiences a state of deficiency, be it physically, be it in connection with some psychical force.

A mental function wants to be used. If it goes unnoticed and unused, it creates tension.

If a human being experiences a desire, it creates a tension that pushes for realization. The tension is increased with the target state, which is not reached at the moment. If one gives in to the urge, a movement results in the direction of the goal until the need is fulfilled. Then this voltage is eliminated. This process always takes place in the habitat, has here usually a concrete expression of the goal.

The basic needs of man cannot be determined physiologically.

Likewise, it is not enough to define the minimum social needs at the level of higher developed animals. Man is also a "cultural being". He has a higher intelligence and is able to distinguish values.

Since man is in need of education and training, his needs are also changing. They take many forms through this process.

In addition, the human being experiences his existence also in the context of meaning questions. The experience of meaning in existence is elementary basic need.

Reflections and discussion

There are certain needs arising from the nature of the psychical and biological nature of human. Such needs can be referred to as so-called "basic needs". A selection of them for illustration:

Biological needs	Love and appreciation
Safety and protection	Creative activity
Care and care	Creation of life areas
Belonging to other people	Job
Relationship man-woman	Authenticity, development

These basic needs vary considerably according to:

Age (period of life)	Intensity	Damages due to deficit
Development status	Area of life	Frustration border

A need consists on:

Initial state	An urge / a tension
State of the aim	A direction of movement

The identification of basic needs is not always easy. It often requires focused attention.

The abundance of daily external influences, education and lifestyle can greatly influence and hinder the experience of basic needs.

Man can diversify his needs, because he has:

☐ an intellect with the potential of creativity
☐ an ability to love with multiple expressions
☐ an inner mind as a driving force
☐ malleable skills with many playful variations
☐ culturally diverse forms of expression

Diagram 1.1.1: Need as energetic value

Diagramm OS7-1: Bedürfnis als energetische Werteinheit

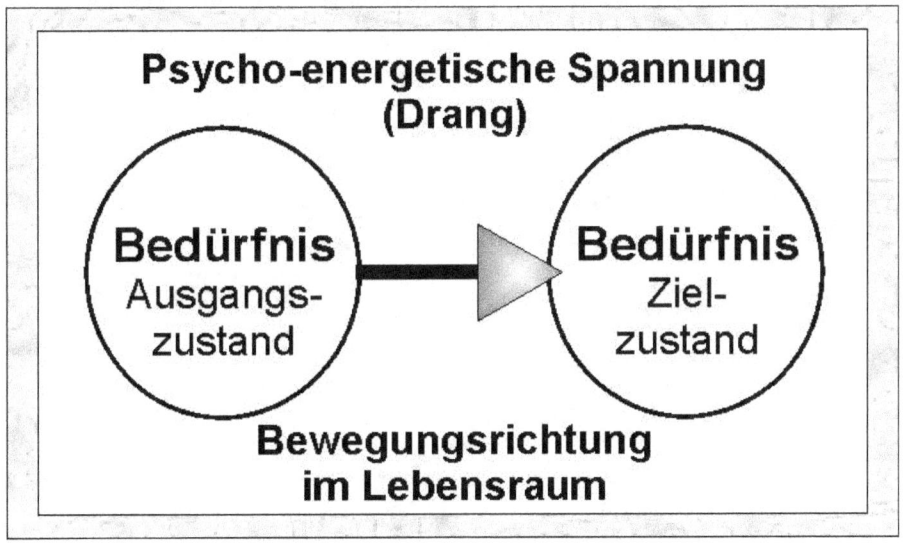

Analyse von Bedürfnissen:

Ausgangszustand und Zielzustand
Spannungszunahme und Spannungsrichtung
Faktoren Lebensraum auf Ausgangslage
Faktoren Lebensraum auf Zielzustand
Wirkungen Ausgangszustand auf Lebensraum
Wirkungen Zielzustand auf Lebensraum

English translation: Psycho-energetic tension (desire) from **Need:** Starting point in **Direction of movement in the living space** to **Need:** Target state.

Analysis of needs: Starting point and target state &Increase of tension and direction of tension & Factors of living space from starting point & Factors living space to target state & Effects staring point to living space & Effects target state to living space

The spectrum of needs

From various books we take a selection without classifying them.

List of needs:

• Eat (food)	• Performance
• Autonomy	• Doing business
• Drinking	• Exercise of power
• Resistance	• After transcendence experience
• Clothing	• Building up
• God experience	• Down-to-earthness
• Peace	• Order
• Sleep	• Life orientation
• Sexuality	• Failure avoidance
• Artistic creation / Experience	• Connectedness
• Tenderness	• Self-presentation
• Avoidance of humiliation	• Identity (self-image)
• Game	• Searching for help
• Exclude inferior ones	• Justice
• Knowledge urge	• Social connection
• Avoidance of risks	• According to reasonableness
• Craving for admiration	• Self-actual
• Dominance	• Exuberance
• Avoiding suffering	• Self-esteem
• Common ground	• Being happy
• Pain prevention	• Social bonding
• Adventures	• Joy and moments of happiness
• Caring	• Security
• Tension generation	• Having confidence
• Understand (insight)	• Protection
• Stress reduction	• Predictability
• Discover	• Lawfulness
• Peace and relaxation	• Prosperity
• Purchase	• Behavioural regulation
• Security	• Mobility
• Aggression	• Receiving approval
• Roots in the hereafter	• Adventurous spirit
• Independence	• Withheld
• Possession	• Beauty
• Harmony	• Humanity
• Children having (procreate)	• Authority

• Defend	• Leadership
• Creativity	• Move
• Love	• Experience nature
• Esteem of value	• Doing something special
• Creating culture	• Sensory experience

☐ Mark which needs to be adequately fulfilled.

☐ Circle those needs that you feel are not fulfilled.

Individual functions of needs

Below we will make a selection from the list of needs above.
Two core considerations can be employed:

1. What happens when the need is not met? What are the effects?

2. What does it do if the need can be adequately fulfilled?
Make your own thoughts on these two questions!

List of needs	Effect by satisfaction	Effect by deficit
To eat and drink		
Clothing		
Tenderness		
Sexuality		
Security		
Autonomy		
Identity		
Self-realization		
Love live		
Love experienced		
Security		
Joy, happiness		
Trust		
Humanity		
Human dignity		
Experience of God		
Adventurous spirit		
Beauty		
Experience nature		
Special achievement		
Job		
Social bond		
Possession		

Notes and perspectives

How does man (on average) handle his needs?

Write down the key words in this subchapter:

What happens with a chronic deficit of need fulfilment?

Identifying and observing basic needs is essential because: ...

What did you learn about basic mental health needs in your parents' home, school and church?

What significance in living together has the discussion about needs?

Which needs are decisively promoted by politics and economy?

What does advertising convey to fulfilment of needs?

Formulate an important question for your needs:

1.1.2. The artificial needs

"Artificially" generated needs are rarely experienced as "artificial". They affect a feeling state as well as the basic needs. They are often experienced as necessary.

The experience of a necessity arises through an urge. This psycho-energetic tension wants to be "redeemed".

While many basic needs press for the realization of psychic powers, artificial needs are more concerned with the object of need: one wants to have it, experience it, enjoy it. Then the "haunting" is usually over quickly.

Such needs are generated externally. Almost consistently, secondary themes are addressed that should mobilize the individual for this cause: "You deserve it," "Sweeten your life," "This sets you free," "So you're a personality," "So you're in," "Of course everybody has this", "You are clever" etc.

Artificial needs are linked with associations that act as attraction force and create a tension (an urge) through the association. Linking a product with "freedom" or "adventure" activates the basic need for "autonomy" and "interest / desire to discover". The psychic energy generated here is directed in the direction of "buy the product", which generates an action impulse.

So, love, harmony, security, tenderness, appreciation, praise, understanding, belonging and some basic needs can be more connected with things and circumstances that have nothing to do with it.

"Artificial" needs can also be generated from within. They represent a direct shift of basic needs, or should allow to displace important things in life. They have a replacement function.

They aim to have something or to be, without having to work it out from the inside: Finding rest with overeating; to be a valuable person through valuable furniture; to be an important and strong person with a lot of money; to find sexual satisfaction without love; to achieve maximum performance under risk of life, instead of accepting life as the highest challenge; watching and experiencing how others live instead of living their own lives; to mock others or cause suffering to others rather than reconcile their own suffering; "Playing games", instead of living truthfulness and so on.

Man can "discharge" an inner tension associatively connecting in a direction that has nothing to do with the cause of tension. To think here is action movies, record performances, consumption addiction, etc.

Reflections and discussion

Man, experiences much as a need, which is neither vital nor life-building from his mental-spiritual and biological nature. Here are some examples:

- ☐ Toys without pedagogical and without child-friendly value
- ☐ Talk about others, though this is without personal gain
- ☐ Drive around the area aimlessly
- ☐ "Guinness"-achievements
- ☐ Life-threatening sports achievements
- ☐ Entertainment products without human and mental cultural value
- ☐ Consumption of certain goods that contain neither real nor symbolic value

There are artificial needs that have a subjectively experienced necessity. They are created by:

- ☐ Internal pressure
- ☐ Suppression of emotions
- ☐ Internal conflicts
- ☐ Displacement of real wishes
- ☐ Experience curiosity
- ☐ Dodge duties
- ☐ Employment urge
- ☐ Need for movement
- ☐ Avoiding an effort
- ☐ Seek recognition

Above all, artificial needs are stimulated or generated by environmental factors. They are not geared directly to the satisfaction of basic needs. External factors are:

- ☐ Advertising
- ☐ Models
- ☐ Peer pressure
- ☐ Incentives
- ☐ Lifestyle
- ☐ Life story
- ☐ Environment
- ☐ Subculture

Diagram 1.1.2: Factors creating artificial needs

Diagramm OS7-2: Faktoren, die künstliche Bedürfnisse schaffen

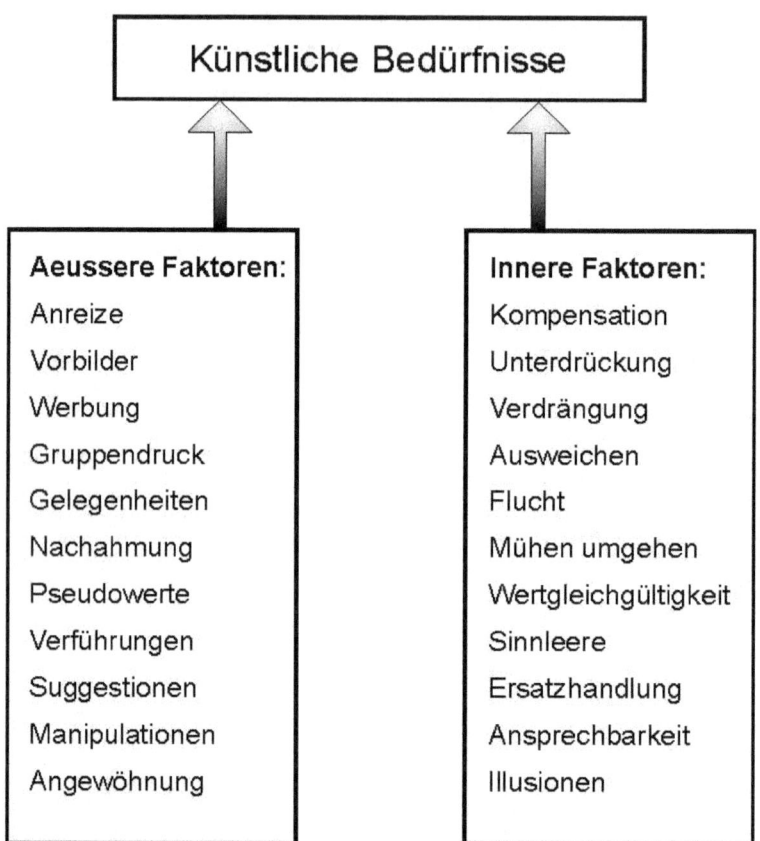

Künstliche Bedürfnisse

Aeussere Faktoren:

Anreize

Vorbilder

Werbung

Gruppendruck

Gelegenheiten

Nachahmung

Pseudowerte

Verführungen

Suggestionen

Manipulationen

Angewöhnung

Innere Faktoren:

Kompensation

Unterdrückung

Verdrängung

Ausweichen

Flucht

Mühen umgehen

Wertgleichgültigkeit

Sinnleere

Ersatzhandlung

Ansprechbarkeit

Illusionen

English translation:
External factors: Incentive, Model, Publicity, Peer Pressure, Opportunities, Imitation, Pseudo Value, Seduction, Suggestions, Manipulation, Habit
Internal factors: Compensation, Suppression, Repression, Evasion, Escape, Avoiding Troubles, Indifferent to Values, Lack of Sense, Displacement Activity, Responsiveness Illusion

Meaning and life fulfilment

We put the need fulfilment in the context of the question of meaning in life.

Man, in search of meaning is only frustrated in today's society. And that is because the affluent society is able to satisfy practically all human needs.

A need is empty in our society, and that is the need for meaning, i.e. the deepest need of man to find meaning in his life or, better, in every situation of life.

Man can find meaning, irrespective of whether he is religious or not, and certainly where we cannot change a situation, we are required to change ourselves, to mature, to grow, to rise above ourselves.

Sense not only is, but can also be found, and in the search for it man leads the conscience. Conscience is a sense organ. It can be defined as the ability to detect and recognize the singular and unique meaning that is hidden in every situation.

There is no situation in which life would cease to offer us meaning, and there is no one for whom life has not given a task. In the fulfilment of meaning, man realizes himself.

If we fulfil the meaning of suffering, we realize the most human in man, we mature, we grow, we grow beyond ourselves. Suffering has meaning when the suffering person becomes another.

If we really wanted to see the whole meaning of life in mere satisfaction of needs, then life would ultimately seem pointless. Because what is lust? A condition. The materialist - and hedonism goes along with materialism - would even say that pleasure is nothing but some process in the ganglion cells of the brain. And the achievement of such a process should be meaningful to live, to experience, to suffer or to do something?

The purpose of life is not to ask, but to answer by answering for life. It follows, however, that the answer is not to be given in words, but in fact, by action.

In place of nihilistic denial, the attempt must be made to interpret meaning. Meaning interpretation, however, is not identical with meaning: The human being who tries to interpret the meaning of life does not seek to arbitrarily give any sense to being, but to find 'the' meaning.

Attitude values are superior to the creative and experiential values in moral height. However, to realize attitude values requires not only a creative ability and not only the ability to experience, but also the ability to suffer. The acquisition of the ability to suffer is an act of self-creation.

The human never decides only something, but also himself and self-decision is self-creation. Self-creation is self-realization and this is sense-fulfilment.

Satisfaction of gratification and meaningfulness

Need satisfaction and meaningfulness are mutually exclusive. However, satisfying needs can make sense, but does not, and often does not do it; However, meaningfulness does not mean that there are always satisfying needs, except the need for meaning and always the need for self-realization (self-creation, individuation). Again, we provide a list of needs. For this one can formulate a meaning in the right column.

The question: What can you recognize (live) about this need for meaning? Give key-words:

Need	Immanent meaning
Urge for knowledge	
Security	
Have relationships / live	
Love experienced	
Doing business	
Experience joy	
Independence	
Experience nature	
Security	
Self-expression	
Adventurous spirit	
Quiet	
Experience of God	
Prosperity	
Sense Experience	
Building up	
Value esteem	
Possession	
Self-esteem	
Mobility	

Notes and perspectives

What are the collectively significant artificial needs?

Write down the key words in this subchapter:

What do artificial needs cause?

Needs fulfilment as meaning and life fulfilment is essential, because: ...

What did you learn about the meaning of meaningfulness in your parents' home, school and church?

What meaning in living together has the meaning of life?

What needs of people are ignored in politics and the economy?

How does advertising convey artificial needs?

Formulate an important question for life fulfilment:

1.1.3. The satisfaction of needs

The satisfaction of needs has to be learned.

Of course, human can react very easily to hunger: He eats bread or prepares a meal. Then he can quickly consume the food, or eat appropriately and consciously.

So, it is with the sexuality, or with the clothing. Socks, pants and a shirt, plus a jacket and shoes, is not that enough?

As a "cultural being" man can design his clothes. It's a similar story with living: A bed, a table and a chair, a few shelves for what is necessary. The cultural man wants to live with "culture" and sets up his living diverse. That's the way it is with many things, including the car.

Creating culture calls for complex social structures, state and private institutions, work and thinking, education and active responsibility for oneself and the community of people.

So, the needs are more than tension reduction. They are an expression of man. They create culture.

What man creates out of needs also has symbolic value for him: He experiences himself in it. This means stimulation, consciousness and reflection of oneself. Man can transgress this limit by placing his "I" in the objects:

The engine then quickly replaces the missing own strength. The tailored suit covers the inside chaotic personality or a beautiful home decor replaces the lack of atmosphere of love.

A saying goes: "Take everything away from man, then you see his value". The true value of man arises and grows through his accomplishments in the field of love, wisdom, and spirit.

These human values can only grow as human beings face the challenges of psychic life.

The strength of the "I" is grounded in psychical life and in mental-spiritual achievements.

With things, including capital, man can strengthen his weak self; or with power and violence. Then what he has is not an expression of what he is. This leads to individual and collective problems of a tragic nature.

Dealing with needs is based on attitudes towards mental life.

Because it is clear: The less man turns to this reality, the more he needs replacement and coverage.

If religion is cultivated without inner orientation, politics without orientation to the psyche organism and economy without love and spirit, then this is the same as with the customized suit or the strong engine under the hood.

So, things, mental education systems and their practices become a substitute.

Reflections and discussion

Biological needs such as hunger, thirst, sexuality and body warmth can be met technically and objectively. The person with a psychical life and with spirit has learned to also form biological needs in a rich manner, to a certain extent practicing "with culture".

Many people can make these basal needs rich with many menus, numerous types of drinks, original clothing, and a sexual life that involves the whole person playfully and creatively.

Man is more than a lust apparatus, which is only aimed at reducing tension and functioning.

Mental needs such as appreciation, emotional affection, group affiliation, thinking, discovering, working, achieving, loving and some more can be reduced to a minimum or even completely denied, without the human dying immediately.

But the man stunted and suffers. Then psychic forces are destructive. The forces themselves activate a tension of need that acts indirectly or displaced if proper realization is not possible.

Many destructive life disorders arise from unfulfilled true psychic primary needs, for example:

☐ Violence   ☐ Perversions   ☐ Wars
☐ Exploitation   ☐ Addiction   ☐ Fanaticism
☐ Dispute   ☐ Violence   ☐ Suppression
☐ Consumerism

Certain needs are spiritual. From these springs also the need for religion: To understand the origin, the goal of existence, and to live in being embedded in this transcendental rooting.

If man does not find the access to this reality in himself through dreams and meditation, then he lives artificially created realities which at least emotionally create a religious "ambience". From this search arise:

☐ Religions   ☐ Philosophies   ☐ Esotericism
☐ Gnosticism   ☐ Ideologies   ☐ Sects

Habitat always determines how people experience and fulfil their needs. The path of the least effort leads to many forms of malformations.

Diagram 1.1.3: Satisfaction of needs as experience of life

Diagramm OS7-3: Bedürfnisbefriedigung als Erleben von Dasein

> **Bedürfnisbefriedigung ist mehr als Spannungsreduktion:**
>
> Erleben von Werten
> Sich selbst ausdrücken
> Schöpferisch sein
> Sich selbst bewusst steuern
> Erleben echter Freiheit
> Leistungen vollbringen
> Kultur und Stil leben
> Echtheit und Wahrhaftigkeit
> Selbsterweiterung
> Ausgewogenheit
> Bejahung der Menschlichkeit
> Selbstbestimmung
> Phantasie mitwirken lassen
> Freude mit Liebe am Leben
> Einsatz für einen Sinn

English translation:
Satisfaction of needs is more than reduction of tension: Experiencing values, Mode of self-expression, being creative, consciously regulating oneself, experiencing genuine freedom, effecting performance, living culture & style, Authenticity & truthfulness, widening of oneself, Balance, Affirmation of humanness, Self-determination, incorporating phantasy, Joy with Love to Life, Effort for meaning

Strategy of problem-solving unmet needs

First, mention a need that you find satisfying as a major problem (that is, you want to live, fulfil, shape, and do not know how). Then answer the 30 strategy questions!

The unfulfilled need:

The problem-solving strategy without setting the order:

1. What are the previous solution statements?
2. What external factors have hindered a solution to date?
3. Where do you see (internal) factors that impede a solution?
4. What are ways of solution that you have not gone yet, but know?
5. Why have you not yet tried the solutions you know?
6. Why exactly do you want to fulfil this need?
7. Did you formulate the need correctly? Can you put it another way?
8. Break down the need into sub-needs (steps, building blocks).
9. What are the burdensome, detrimental and 'critical' consequences of the deficit?
10. Can you give a positive impression to these negative consequences? Which)?
11. Are there boundary conditions that you can change (first)?
12. Can it be that you over / underestimate the value of this need?
13.Do you have previous experiences (failure, frustration) in the way?
14.Has earlier (until today) other people devalued you this need?
15.Is there an idealization in your ideas for satisfying your needs?
16.Can you imagine compromises for fulfilment? Which?
17.What do you see the meaning (the missing meaning) of this need?
18. Are there any other needs that have priority?
19. Can you replace this need with another need?
20.What are the successful solutions for other needs?
21.Can you apply (adapt) the success strategy to this need?
22.What happens if you cannot satisfy this need all your life?
23.Is the need genuine, vitally important and a share to self-development?
24. Describe your suffering in this deficit.
25.Can you find a new goal orientation by rebalancing the values?
26.Do you fear the need fulfilment? Why?
27.Do not make enough effort to achieve your goal? Why?
28.What changes in your life when this need is fully fulfilled?
29.What is new when you break the need down into the smallest components?
30.How do you deal with your current frustration experience?

Needs in the horizon of the values of being

The contrast between our knowledge and action is obvious. Man orients in his actions at usefulness, desirability, badness, goodness or expediency. Man evaluates, controls, judges, condemns or approves. Man reacts to experiences in a personal form and takes the world to nothing but a means for our purpose.

Thus, man cannot know the values of being; these are:

☐ Wholeness: Unity, integration, unicity, simplicity, organization, order, structure
☐ Perfection: Necessity, correctness, inevitability, appropriateness, justice
☐ Completion: Termination, finitude, fulfilment, destiny, skill
☐ Justice: Fairness, orderliness, legalism
☐ Liveliness: Process, spontaneity, self-regulation, full functioning
☐ Richness: Differentiation, complexity, complicacy
☐ Simplicity: Honesty, nudity, essentiality, abstract structure
☐ Beauty: Correctness, form, vitality, simplicity, wealth, uniqueness
☐ Goodness: Correctness, desirability, justice, goodwill, honesty
☐ Uniqueness: Individuality, incomparability, novelty
☐ Ease: Facility, lack of effort or striving, grace
☐ Playfulness: Fun, joy, entertainment, happiness, humour
☐ Truth: Honesty, nudity, simplicity, beauty, authenticity.
☐ Self-sufficiency: Autonomy, independence, separateness

If we look at reality with inner eyes, not with the real eyes, we operate "introspection" (or imagination). Here, the reality is different than we perceive it with the real eyes. We experience the value of an (external) reality (or element of this reality). And this intrinsic value cannot be separated from the actual reality in introspection. We become aware meditatively that objective reality, as we can see it clearly in introspection, contains an equally objective value aspect. This inner perception of 'facts' brings the 'being' and the 'desired' into an inseparable whole.

Those who cannot free themselves from utilitarian and pleasure-oriented perception will never be able to experience the values of being human. At most he will search rationally and intellectually for an (empirical) proof of the existence of the values of being; but can never find it.

The 'self-realized human being' is characterized by the following characteristics:

1. Clearer, more effective perception of reality
2. Greater openness to experiences
3. Stronger integration, wholeness and unity of the person
4. Greater spontaneity and expressivity; full functioning; liveliness
5. A real self; a fixed identity; autonomy; uniqueness
6. Greater objectivity, distance, transcendence of the self
7. Recovery of creativity
8. Ability to combine the concrete and the abstract
9. Democratic character structure
10.Ability to love

Reflection: Combine your current wishes for need fulfilment with the values of being and interpret the 'value for self-realization'!

Notes and perspectives

What does man (on average) satisfy his needs?

Write down the key words in this subchapter:

What causes the suppression of basic mental needs?

Fulfilling existing values is an essential basic need, because: ...

What did you learn about the values of being in your parents' home, school and church?

What meaning in living together has the conversation about the realization of the values of being through self-realization?

Which values of being predominate in politics and economy?

Which values does the advertising convey?

Formulate an important question about the problem-solving strategy in the fulfilment of the values of being:

1.1.4. Exercises

1. What are currently your conscious basic needs?

2. Which of your needs would you classify as artificial needs?

3. Which needs are particularly important to you?

4. Which basic needs have you not dealt with to this day?

5. How do other people deal with your needs?

6. How do other people generally deal with their basic needs?

7. How do you deal with the needs of other people?

8. Which factors of the habitat affect your needs?

9. Which basic needs do you fulfil and to what extent? Enter keywords:
Spontaneous reaction:

Urge for knowledge	
Security	
Having relationships	
Love experienced	
Earning money / doing business	
Experiencing joy	
Independence	
Experiencing nature	
Safety	
Self-expression	
Adventurous spirit	
Quiet	
Experience of God	
Experience at home	
Experience of sense	
Build up	
Value esteem	
Possession	
Self-esteem	
Physical pleasure	
Work and performance	

Comment:

Conclusions:

10. Forms of need fulfilment

10.a) What happens when the need is fulfilled / not fulfilled?

10.b) How do you fulfil the need? How can you better fulfil the need?

List of basic needs	a) Effects by scarcity	b) Better ways to find satisfaction
To eat and drink		
Clothing		
Tenderness		
Sexuality		
Security		
Autonomy		
Self-identity		
Self-realization		
To live love		
Experienced love		
Security		
Joy, happiness		
Trust		
Humanity		
Human dignity		
Experience of God		
Adventurous spirit		
Beauty		
Experience nature		
Special achievement		
Job		
Social bond		
Possession		

What do you conclude from your information?

Multiple Choice Test 1

Choose the four correct answers:

1.1. The basic needs. Real basic needs are:

☐ a) Creative activity
☐ b) Safety / Protection
☐ c) Live love
☐ d) Have many good friends
☐ e) Doing nothing
☐ f) Work

1.2. The artificial needs. Characteristic of artificial needs is:

☐ a) Replacement for basic needs
☐ b) Mass exaggeration
☐ c) Innate
☐ d) Learned (environment, role models)
☐ e) Defence function
☐ f) Simplicity

1.3. The satisfaction of needs. The following statements are to be considered as relevant to the topic:

☐ a) Aggression has nothing to do with unfathomable basic needs.
☐ b) Needs satisfaction is more than tension reduction.
☐ c) Fanaticism has to do with unmet basic needs.
☐ d) There are no "higher" needs; needs are physiological.
☐ e) The habitat influences people's need experience.
☐ f) Needs satisfaction can be created in many ways creatively.

1.2. Needs and its effects

1.2.1. Basic needs and its characteristics

Certain physiological needs are a vital necessity, for man would not be able to live without their satisfaction. These include hunger, thirst, warmth, body protection, sleep and sexuality. Likewise, humans need a minimum of physical activity.

There are also psychical needs that are vital to man.

Without the formation of psychical life, man cannot live humanely. Without love human beings are stunted, may not even survive.

The need to shape the habitat is species-specific "human". Man cannot survive if he does not create a minimum living space. Man has always appropriated the habitat in some form and taken possession of the things he has created, partly individually and partly collectively.

The need for a man-woman relationship is not based solely on sexual urges, but on the qualities of the human being that attract and complement each other.

It is hard to imagine that a person without any relationship (group sympathy) can live and grow healthily.

Through evolution, man has discovered his unity from an archaic consciousness: Everyone experiences the urge for a minimal autonomy, for a self-esteem that sets itself apart from others.

The more man is aware of his psychical possibilities, the more he is compelled by thinking and skills to shape life. Thinking and learning skills are basic needs that have grown out of evolution. These include: Work, the production of goods, cultural creation, game and social organization.

Taking man any security and stability, this implicates interferences, partly in the fulfilment of other basic needs, and partly in the psycho-physical functioning.

Always and in all cultures, people have experienced themselves embedded in the cosmos in some way. From this, the need has arisen to understand existence transcendentally, to clarify it by thinking and to live ritually.

The religious experience, understanding and acting is a basic need. In all destructive expressions of life that disregard any human value, it shows that the sense of positive, open-minded and constructive values is driven by a deep need to assert oneself.

Reflections and discussion

The basic needs have four orientations aimed at actual realities:

- ☐ On yourself (mental and physical reality)
- ☐ On the habitat (including the goods)
- ☐ To other people (mental, social, physical reality)
- ☐ On the transcendence (the divine as reality)

Basic needs are:

- ☐ Hunger, thirst, warmth, protection, reproduction, sexual relaxation
- ☐ Physical exercise, training
- ☐ Design of the living space
- ☐ Creating goods, culture and games
- ☐ Take ownership of habitat and goods
- ☐ Man-woman relationship
- ☐ Groups, social relationships
- ☐ Work, performance
- ☐ Safety and stability
- ☐ Autonomy, self-assertion, self-actualization
- ☐ Knowledge and thinking
- ☐ Wellbeing, joy, health, life support
- ☐ Love, meaning and value
- ☐ Growth and development, differentiation of possibilities
- ☐ God-experiencing, transcendence-rooting and rituals

The basic needs have some elemental characteristics that are based on the psycho-physical nature of man:

☐ Life needs for mental and physical health
☐ Natural desire (drive) for the realization of existence
☐ Condition experience as a deficit and need for expansion
☐ Idea of goal in the sense of fulfilment (saturation)
☐ A psychical energy charge (tension, strength)
☐ Validity for the people in general

Basic needs develop through mental-spiritual evolution, through education, formation and cultural appropriation. Their expression is therefore manifold.

Discuss with others how psychic-spiritual development can transform basic needs and fulfilment:

Diagram 1.2.1: The alignment of the basic needs

Diagramm OS7-4: Die Ausrichtung der Grundbedürfnisse

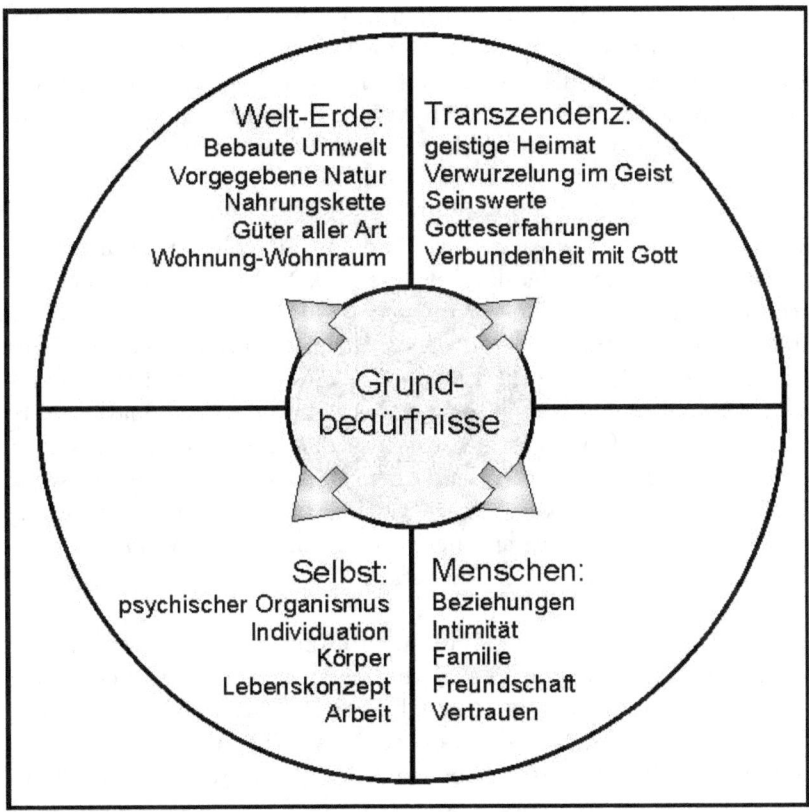

English translation: (From left above to right below)
Basic needs influence:
World-Earth: Built environment, given nature, food chain, all kind of goods, flat/living space &
Transcendence: Spiritual home, rooted in the spirit, values of being, experience of God, bond with God &
Self: Psychical organism, individuation, body, concept of life, work &
Human: Relations, intimacy, family, friendship, confidence

1.2.2. Substitutional needs & their characteristics

"Substitutional needs" are factors created by the environment or by the person's artificially created needs. They replace other needs. This may give the impression that the satisfaction of the basic needs has a morally positive value, while the substitute needs are morally reprehensible.

Now, if someone has the need for an aperitif, this is neither a basic need, nor can one speak straight out of a need for substitution. One person may work twelve hours a day on a regular basis; from this one cannot conclude that it is a "workaholic" or a substitute need. There is no standard by which anyone could judge which capacity is for whom a "substitutional need" and for whom not.

There are people who have great capacity and considerable psychical powers, while others can never reach that level or intensity. Nobody has to expect the same basic needs and expressions of the way of life with a factual reason of each humans. In addition, the basic needs are changing, on the one hand because of the age, and on the other hand also in the context of the mental-spiritual process. Then personal inclinations and talents should also be considered. For one, reading a lot is a basic need, while another paints a lot, another makes a lot of music, and another does a lot of creative manual work. A mother with a toddler experiences motherhood in some situations as fulfilling a real basic need, while another woman wishes to have children just to live the home that she has never had herself.

Basic needs and substitutional needs are therefore relative to the person, their mental situation and life history. From this perspective, the artificial needs and the substitutes needs to be interpreted. Substitutional needs and artificial needs (which cannot always be interpreted as substitutes) also fulfil a compensation function, which can be considered positive as a regulatory function. Often a regressive connection is the beginning for a progressive development.

In addition, life often forces compromise services. From the point of view of love and the spirit, however, sadism, humiliation or the like cannot be a basic need.

Reflections and discussion

The artificially created needs (often called "substitute needs") have some characteristics:

- They are trained, artificially stimulated and "induced".
- They are a "construction" of the individual.
- They are not necessary for a mental-spiritual development.
- They do not mean weighty real or symbolic value.
- They are often above all an exaggeration in the measure.
- They often only have a replacement function due to repression.
- They are often the reversal of healthy needs into the meaningless / destructive.

Most substitutional needs have an effect that deviates from, prevents, and even counteracts healthy, life-oriented self-fulfilment. Some aspects are:

Alienation from oneself	Passivity
Avoidance of intimacy	No creativity
Excessive pleasure increase	Projections
Repression of reality	Escape from oneself

Characteristic of replacement needs is:

- Alienated use of goods without real or symbolic profit
- Experience without appreciable profit (out of pure curiosity / boredom)
- Activity and mobility without an effective goal (activism)
- Experience intensity from pure intensity desire
- Employment wealth without personal or material gain
- Record performance with great dangers and little / no sense

The identification of substitutional needs is often an interpretation question. What can still be understood as a basic need for the one, is, perhaps, for another considerably artificially created / lived need, which should replace something.

Put together some substitute needs in a group and discuss each example of how it can be an "artificial" or perhaps a basic one; or for which other needs they can be interpreted as substitutes.

Diagram 1.2.2: Difference basic need – substitutional need

Diagramm OS7-5: Unterscheidung Grundbedürfnis - Ersatzbedürfnis

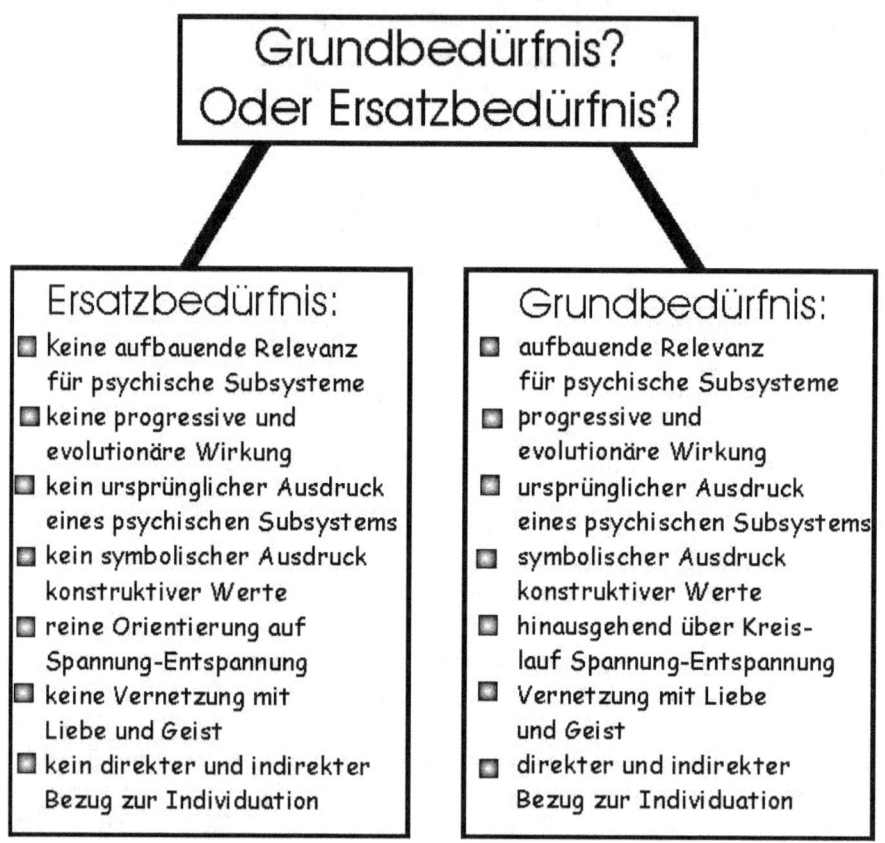

English translation:
Basic need? or substitutional need?
Substitutional need: No constructive relevance to psychological systems, no progressive and evolutionary effect, no original concept of a psychical subsystem, no symbolic expression of constructive values, pure orientation to tension-relaxation, no networking with love and spirit, no direct and indirect reference to individuation

Basic need: Constructive relevance to psychical subsystems, progressive and evolutionary effect, original concept of a psychical subsystem, symbolic expression of constructive values, transcending circle tension-relaxation, networking with love and spirit, direct and indirect reference to individuation

1.2.3. Consequences unmet basic needs

If a toddler experiences little or no love, mental disorders often develop throughout life. Adults also need love, attention and experience of being accepted. If a person receives little love and much rejection, then later on he does the same with others. If a person cannot shape his or her habitat, it stifles its life-giving.

The consequences of the suppression of sexual desire are well known. Those who cannot somehow transform sexual tension will develop life-averted replacement designs; many become ill. People who experience little security and stability live in diffuse anxiety, which often turns into aggression.

Many who cannot express themselves individually become dull or identify with extremist patterns.

The less man differentiates his psychical life, the more stunted his personhood is within the framework of ideologies, dogmas or materialism. The less man lives love, the more he tends to destroy his habitat. If man cannot expand his consciousness about himself, then he lives in projections.

Artificial needs produce a momentum of their own: first a pleasant or tension-intensive pleasure, then a steady repetition. Such "artificial" needs contain dangers: Man becomes alien to himself. He moves away from what is contained in him as a way of life. He does not fulfil what is required from the inside.

Real self-realization is prevented in this way. This in turn leads to increased replacement needs. Then man experiences internally empty, unsatisfied. Everything remains at the surface of imaginary reality. Being loses its inner value and meaning.

The fewer basic needs can be met, the more deficit situations have a destructive effect. Man seeks replacement or frustration discharge. The experienced tension is explained with completely non-existent facts. People can learn to recognize their real basic needs. There are ways to change deficits.

Reflections and discussion

The suppression of basic needs always has consequences:

Mental disorders	Fixation on ideologies
Psycho-somatic suffering	Dogmatism
Inner emptiness	Fundamentalist thinking
Futility of existence	Oppression of others
Destructive acting	Unfolding blocking
Narrowing of the other	Indifference to nature

The elimination of basic needs pushes for artificial needs as a substitute; Aspects are:

- ☐ External experience instead of inner experience
- ☐ Identification with external values instead of internal ones
- ☐ Abuse of others for own needs
- ☐ Gross misuse of resources
- ☐ Ritualized acts of defence against the inner life
- ☐ External binding to objects
- ☐ Development of illusory realities
- ☐ Loss of sense of dimension and life risk

If an individual life with many artificial needs can end without damage, in the collective the consequences are fatal:

Violence	Crimes	War	Environmental destruction

Discuss the consequences of unfulfilled basic needs according to the following scheme:

Consequences unfulfilled basic needs	Individuum	Collective
Love		
Rooted Transcendence		
Sexual satisfaction		
Inner autonomy		
Truthfulness		
Wisdom		
Inner growth		

Diagram 1.2.3: Effect of unfulfilled needs

Diagramm OS7-6: Wirkungen unerfüllter Bedürfnisse

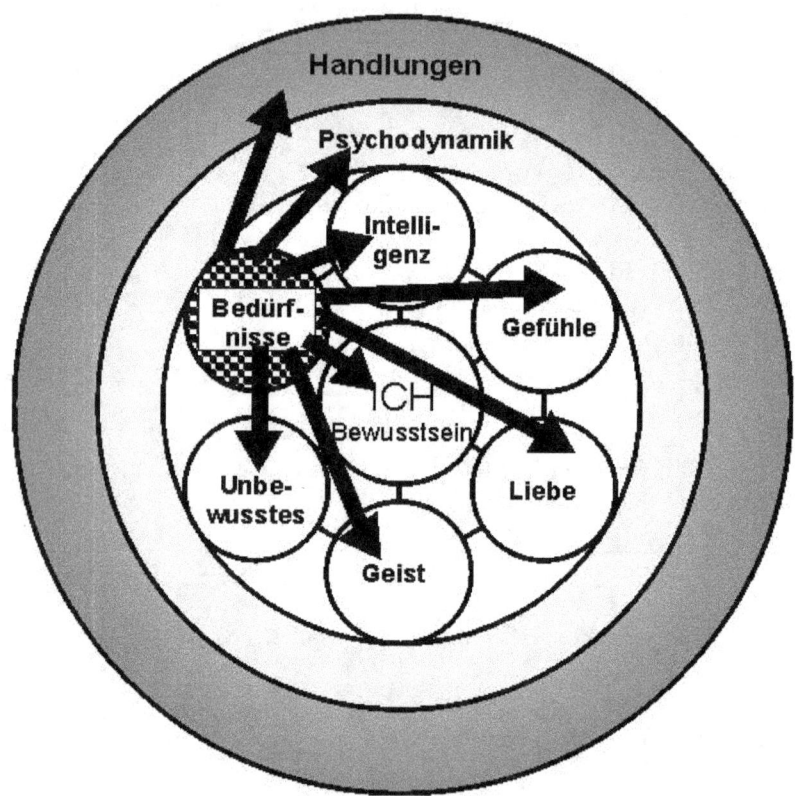

English translation:
Needs influence Activeness, psychodynamics, intelligence, emotions, love, "I"
consciousness, spirit, unconscious

1.2.4. Meaning and value aspects of needs

If we consider the psycho-energetic dynamics of needs, then the conclusion is that the goal of life is the satisfaction of needs or the relaxation of a tense situation. This results in a new tension, which in turn has to be relaxed. This cycle can be interpreted as experiencing lust, wherein the unsatisfied situation as unpleasure and the redemption of it as pleasure is experienced.

If experiencing lust is equated with happiness, then the goal of life can be defined as the "highest possible" pleasure life and in this sense as "happiness". However, this is not feasible for many reasons. This kind of pleasure is bound to materialism, because this experiencing of the lust only has a physiological character. Any value in life would be coupled to this pleasure-unpleasure cycle. The experience of fulfilment would always be the beginning of unpleasure. The process in this polarization is beyond this luck. Man, hurries from one punctual pleasure to the next. Such a cycle contains no development, only repetition and intensification of a state that is always to be recreated. This is known to i.e. to emptiness and boredom.

All non-physiological needs have a tendency to be creative beyond this tension regulation cycle. Lust fulfilling is not simply a relaxation of energy, but leads to objectifications. Love promotes mental growth and life openness. The design of the habitat releases new creative forces and experiencing possibilities. Cultural work leads to "products", which in turn can be experienced.

The organization of coexistence (e.g. with institutions) helps individuals to balance in their autonomy with others. The man-woman relationship enables forms of experiencing about the properties of being in their interactions.

Knowledge and thinking expand the comprehension of one's own wholeness in a greater wholeness, as well as the possibilities of "I"-control of the unfolding processes. The transcendence-rooting (not the pictorial experience, infused into childhood or later on, but the original inner experience) deepens every sense experience beyond the material.

Reflections and discussion

Needs can be interpreted as a closed loop, but this does not adequately capture the phenomenon of need shaping and need satisfaction:

☐ Pleasure-unpleasure
☐ Tension-relaxation
☐ Pleasant-unpleasant
☐ Tension free - new tension

An essential feature of basic human needs is its ever-increasing creative impact:

☐ Love: growth, development, dealing with others, dealing with nature and wildlife, understanding, constructive living together, expression of joy

☐ Achieving, working: creating products, coping with conditions, creating new things, expanding living space, differentiating experience possibilities

☐ Autonomy: to realize oneself, to develop inclinations and abilities, to give individuality an expression in the relationship life

Needs receive value for each through the experience of pleasure and above all through the evolutionary effects. These values exceed the pleasure-unpleasure living and reach the experience of being; here are some examples:

☐ Value experience is not "bottomless", but rooted cosmically
☐ Value experience is an affirmation of being and entity
☐ Meaning and value are above (outside of) health and materialism
☐ Meaning and values are close to the creative actions
☐ Becoming wholeness (in the sense of individuation) is mental and spiritual

Discuss in the group in connection with need satisfaction:

a) That gives me meaning in life (this is my sense experience):

b) These are for me values in life (This is my value experience):

c) Artificial needs contain the following values and meaning: (Choose together three examples of artificial needs):

Diagram 1.2.4: Aspects of meaning and value of needs

Diagramm OS7-7: Sinn- und Wertaspekte von Bedürfnissen

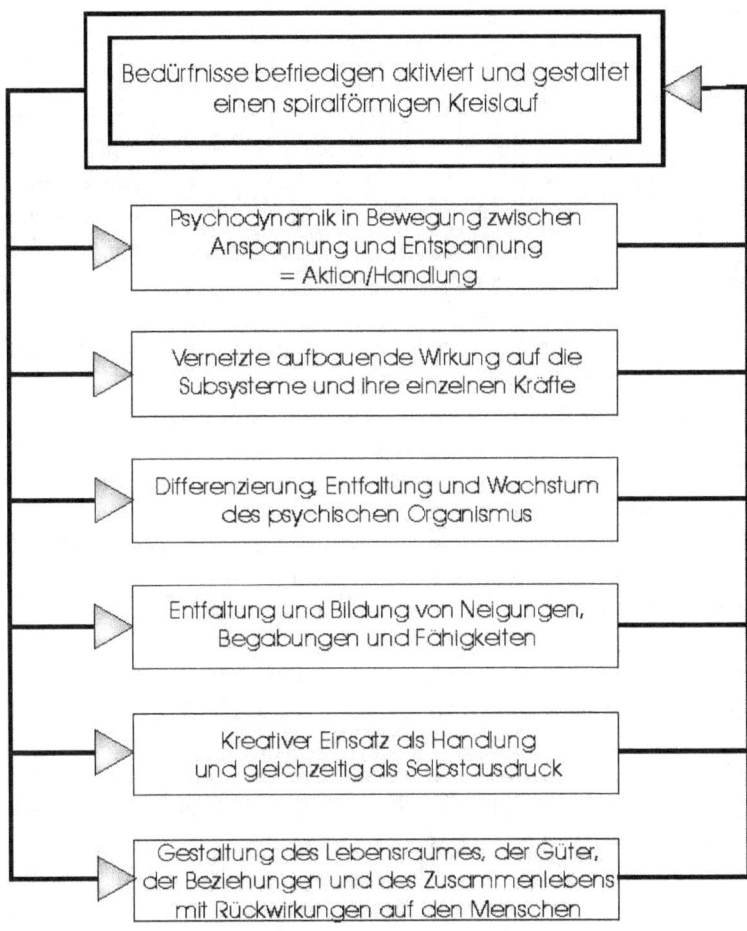

English translation: Satisfying needs activate and form a spiral cycle:
Psychodynamic in move between tension and relaxation = action/activeness;
Linked constructive effect to the subsystems and its individual forces;
Differentiation, deployment and growth of the psychological organism;
Deployment and formation of dispositions, talents and skills;
Creative input as activeness and at once as expression of one's own;
Designing of habitat, goods, relations and cohabitation with reaction of the human

1.2.5. Factors influencing the need experience

From birth on, the human lives and grows in a complex habitat with many individual factors, which also fundamentally shape and influence the experience and satisfaction of the needs. A social system as a coercive system acts on the stimulus-response basis, and thus with positive and negative amplifiers. Praise and punishment control what are allowed and may be lived.

Internalized realities, the images in the unconscious, act unrecognized and impede the reproduction of the previously recorded realities. What you experience as pleasant and "successful" tends to be repeated. The external stimuli, i.e. influences of the media, the habitat and other people, provide patterns as how needs can be experienced in a permitted manner and by what means they are to be satisfactorily successfully satisfied.

These suggestive influences are as powerful as laws in a totalitarian state, only it is more difficult to recognize this heteronomy as such. These one-sided external stimuli force an unbalanced need orientation.

The "competition" in the western industrialized society is transferred to experiencing and dealing with needs: Those who satisfy their needs easier, faster, cheaper, easier, more intensive and more successful are the "best". All who alighted of this race tend to choose the path of the least resistance. Outward incentives that accommodate this trend are more influential.

Are found in individual deficits, whose roots usually last into early childhood, they are particularly responsive to words with "balsam" effect. So that is emphasized "cordially welcome to us" on a TV channel to parents' home replacement. This does not necessarily have to be a disadvantage; it certainly also includes evolutionary possibilities; but controls the sequence of needs through the following program design: from the responsiveness to consumption and satisfaction in an illusion. Since the same stimulus works with time fade, it is more and more to increase with colours, sound, forms, actions and "crazy" (in form and shape).

In this way, the developing-psychologically "normal" changing need experience is co-formed from the root in every phase of life, also through relationships, work, religion and politics.

Reflections and discussion

Factors from all systems of the habitat affect the experience and the organization of the needs:

☐ Political system
☐ Built environment
☐ Personal life opportunities
☐ Capital for realization
☐ People and groups of people

☐ Religion
☐ Cultural Heritage
☐ Media
☐ Learning opportunities
☐ Work

From the unconscious different forces act on the responsiveness:

☐ Unfulfilled needs (deficits)
☐ Sad experiences (with variable effects like fear, blockage, etc.)
☐ Internal commandments and standards: "That's allowed"
☐ Attitudes, beliefs and ideals (role models)

In the interaction between education and environment or life and the environment, the individual learns what must be repressed and suppressed. The repressed looks disfigured back to the various needs:

☐ Selfhood
☐ Relations

☐ Leisure
☐ Interior

☐ Work
☐ Body

Emotionally strong influence on the need experience:

☐ Praise / punishment
☐ Peer pressure
☐ Zeitgeist
☐ Instructed-be

☐ Image building
☐ Standardized criticism
☐ Threats
☐ Authoritative "You may"

Group work: What factors / elements / circumstances do you experience as conducive / obstructive or diverting into artificial needs in the following three examples?

Basic needs	Beneficial is:	Blocking is:	Redirecting effects:
Relationship Man-woman			
Wisdom, knowledge from the spirit			
Living values			

Diagram 1.2.5: Subjective imprinting of experiencing needs

Diagramm OS7-8: Die subjektive Prägung des Bedürfniserlebens

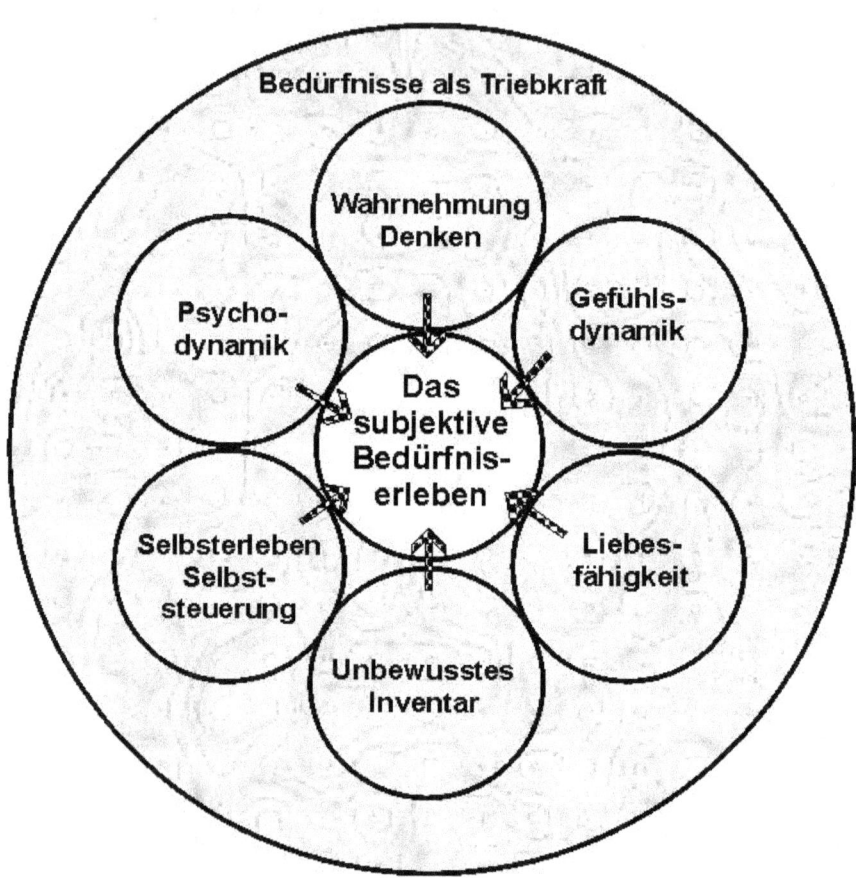

English translation: (From left above to right below)
Needs as driving force:
Perception, thinking & Psychodynamics & Dynamic of emotions &
Experiencing of oneself, management of oneself & Capability of love &
Unconscious inventory affects the Subjective experiencing of needs

1.2.6. The shaping of needs

Needs are always accompanied by a certain "energy boost". Man can have a say in this process. He can also be driven by the energy in one direction or another, in the direction of direct implementation, at other times by relaxation of psychic energy; once by displacement (substitute action) or, what happens by itself: by conversion into psycho-somatic suffering.

Needs can be consciously made active or automatically, lived out in terms of energy discharge. Man decides consciously or "semi-consciously" which increasing needs tension should be integrated and lived. He can determine which needs are to be developed and which ones can be suppressed at the roots of their origin.

Since man's basic needs are to be transformed from an archaic to an evolutionary state, they cannot simply be lived "libidinously" or "instinctively" without causing harm. The "raw form" needs differentiation and cultural design.

The balanced and differentiated satisfaction of the basic needs requires learning processes and conscious "I"-guidance. This also includes the conscious volitional act and the decision. The shaping of one's own needs starts with self-reflection and self-knowledge.

This education of basic needs begins with questions, such as e.g.: "What are my current needs? How do they dynamically push? What activates my needs? How can I shape them in my daily life?"

The goal question leads to reflection on meaning and values. The short-term satisfaction of one need can hinder or render impossible the fulfilment of another, which demands a demanding path. For example, the need for a "good" relationship requires many learning processes and "work on foundations."

The design of one's own living space, the cultivation of nutrition, cultural creation (and cultural experience), autonomy and all aspects of so-called "self-actualization" require many small learning steps. The higher the value and the sense, the more efforts are necessary for satisfying fulfilment.

Reflections and discussion

The conscious design of needs requires education. This starts with a few questions:

- ☐ What are my current needs?
- ☐ What needs are inanimate?
- ☐ What needs are suppressed and repressed?
- ☐ In what directions are the current needs pressing?
- ☐ How do I usually meet current needs?
- ☐ What is the "result" of each satisfied needs?

The design of needs calls for reflections on goals, meaning and values:

- ☐ What value do the different needs gratifications have for me?
- ☐ How do I experience the meaning of each achieved fulfilment?
- ☐ What do my current and current needs satisfactions mean?

Often the need may be genuine and the goal may be "right," but the ways are not appropriate:

- ☐ What do I do to satisfy my needs?
- ☐ What efforts can I accept and take on?
- ☐ What are my priorities in daily life?
- ☐ How do I go about achieving fulfilment?
- ☐ What do I miss or disregard on the way to the goal?
- ☐ Which external factors are inhibitory / promoting?

Needs fulfilment is self-realization, since all basic needs begin with the psychical system and the body. It follows:

- ☐ Balanced satisfaction of needs goes hand in hand with a comprehensive holistic education of all psychic powers.
- ☐ Needs fulfilment integrates intellect, love, spirit and ability.

Discuss in the group the relationship of goal, effects and means (path) to reach a satisfaction of needs. For this, formulate some "critical action situations" as an example:

Diagram 1.2.6: Set-up and unloading of a need unit

Diagramm OS7-9: Aufbau und Entladung einer Bedürfniseinheit

Psycho-energetische Einheit
in Spannungsruhe

Aufforderungscharakter
durch thematischen "Wert"

Es folgt: Anspannung
Energie-Aufladung

Es folgt:
Bedürfnisbefriedigung = Entladung
Umsetzung
Konversion
Verschiebung
Entspannung

English translation:
Psycho-energetic unit in calm of tension & Stimulative nature by thematic
"value" >
Following: Tension & Set-up of energy >

Following: Satisfaction of need = unloading: Transformation, conversion, displacement, relaxation

1.2.7. Working unit

1.2.7. Working unit - 1

1. a) How do you experience your basic needs? Which, above all?

1. b) How do people deal with their basic mental health needs? Example:

2. Why can the following needs be considered basic needs? Give an argument from your own experiences (in keywords):

Hunger, thirst, warmth, protection, reproduction, sexual relaxation

- ☐ Physical exercise, training:
- ☐ Design of the living space:
- ☐ Creating goods, culture and play:
- ☐ Take ownership of habitat and goods:
- ☐ Man-woman relationship:
- ☐ Groups, social relationships:
- ☐ Work, performance:
- ☐ Safety and stability:
- ☐ Autonomy, self-assertion, self-updating:
- ☐ Knowledge and thinking:
- ☐ Wellbeing, joy, health, life support:
- ☐ Love, meaning and value:
- ☐ Growth and development, differentiation of possibilities:
- ☐ Experiencing God, transcendence rooting and rituals:

3. Formulate an educational goal in the context of your basic needs:

4. a) Imagine one of your most important basic needs:

b) Your conclusion in one sentence:

1.2.7. Working unit - 2

1. a) How do you differentiate your basic needs from your substitution needs?

1. b) Reflect "Consumer behaviour as a need":

2. Reflect the following 'private' needs of individual people (one sentence):
2. a) Watch TV for 3-4 hours daily

2. b) very aggressive and above all fast driving

2. c) always be dressed fashionably

2. d) in winter, when possible, go skiing

2. e) always be under / with people

2. f) drive around for a chat in the area

2. g) sexually relax with porno books regularly

2. h) be the best in a sport

2. i) eat chocolate daily

2. k) want to watch every horror movie

2. l) want to see exactly how it looks in a traffic accident

3. Formulate an educational goal from the field of artificial needs:

4. a) Imagine one of your substitute needs:

4. b) Your conclusion in one sentence:

1.2.7. Working unit - 3

1. a) How do you experience the consequences of unfulfilled needs?

1. b) Which social consequences have individually unfulfilled basic needs?

2. a) Describe the consequences of unsatisfied basic needs according to the following scheme:

Consequences by scarcity	Consequences for the Individuum	Consequences in the collective
Love		
Tooted in transcendence		
Sexual satisfaction		
Inner autonomy		
Truthfulness		
Wisdom		
Inner development		

2. b) Your conclusions:

3. Formulate an educational goal in dealing with unmet basic needs:

4. a) Imagine the consequences of unfulfilled basic needs:

4. b) Your conclusion in one sentence:

1.2.7. Working unit - 4

1. a) How do you experience the value and purpose of your basic psychic needs?

1. b) What is "sense", once apart from pleasure gratification:

2. a) Reflect on the need satisfaction:
a) That gives me meaning in life (this is my sense experience):

b) These are for me values in life (This is my value experience):

c) Artificial needs contain the following values and meaning: (Choose three examples of artificial needs):

1st example:

2nd example:

3rd example:

3. Formulate an educational goal for you about "values in life":

4. a) Imagine the most important meaning in your life:

4. b) Your conclusion in one sentence:

1.2.7. Working unit - 5

1. a) How do you experience the external influences on your needs?

1. b) How do work and politics affect the need experience of the individual?

2. What factors / elements / circumstances do you experience as conducive / obstructive or diverting into artificial needs in the following three examples?

Basic needs	Beneficial is:	Hindering is:	Redirecting result:
Relationship Man-woman			
Wisdom Knowledge From the spirit			
Living values			

3. Formulate an educational goal to promote basic needs:

4. a) Educate about beneficial factors that affect your basic needs:

4. b) Your conclusion in one sentence:

1.2.7. Working unit - 6

1. a) How do you experience the ways to fulfil basic needs?

1. b) Give an example of "learning steps to fulfil a basic need":

2. Describe the relation between the goal, the impact and the means (path) for achieving a satisfaction of needs. To do this, formulate a "critical action situation" as an example:

a) Partnership where both individuation can live:

b) Internally free from burdens of the past:

c) The inner potentials can live:

d) Live life with love:

e) Build my life and move forward with "spirit":

f) Learn more and more about how one's own psychic life works:

3. Formulate an educational goal about steps to meet basic needs:

4. a) Imagine your ways to meet your basic needs:

4. b) Your conclusion in one sentence:

1.2.7. Work unit - 7

All adult people take their basic mental health needs seriously. This is shown like this:

Multiple Choice Test 2

Choose the four correct answers:

2.1. Basic needs are geared towards:
☐ a) Quantity ☐ b) relations
☐ c) Self (psychic) ☐ d) risk experience
☐ e) World design ☐ f) body functions

2.2. Artificial needs cause:
☐ a) Fulfilment through borderline experience ☐ b) avoidance of intimacy
☐ c) Escape from oneself ☐ d) increase in quantity
☐ e) High real-life value (sense) ☐ f) repression of reality

2.3. Unfulfilled basic needs cause:
☐ a) Limited fulfilment of life ☐ b) increased disinterest
☐ c) Reduction of responsibility ☐ d) Optimal pleasure experience
☐ e) Inner calm ("equanimity") ☐ f) destructive psychodynamics

2.4. The following statements are correct:
☐ a) The fulfilment of basic needs promotes meaning of life.
☐ b) The need experience is also a value experience.
☐ c) There are only basic physiological needs.
☐ d) "Living love" is a basic need that includes values.
☐ e) Life-giving is not a central aspect of basic needs.
☐ f) The fulfilment of basic needs goes hand in hand with inner development.

2.5. The need experience is influenced by:
☐ a) Perception ☐ b) ability to love
☐ c) Language structures ☐ d) dreaming
☐ e) Unconscious inventory ☐ f) emotional dynamics

2.6. Needs fulfilment requires:
☐ a) Education ☐ b) a lot of money
☐ c) Recognition ☐ d) self-reflection
☐ e) Skills ☐ f) "I" control

2. Love

Essential theses

Love means to protect, nurture, to have an interest, to live meaning and value, to develop, to be creative, to truly live, to reconcile, to live beyond meaning and value, to perceive duty and responsibility.

Love is affirmation of life with the comprehensive psychical wholeness.

Love attains the psychical wholeness as a basis, path and goal.

Love is the realization of psycho-spiritual being in the living space, in relationships, between groups of peoples and in the state.

Love uses the possibilities of objects and institutions for the realization of love.

Any form of true love is also transferred to habitat design, politics and economic life.

Love is always oriented towards the inner spirit and goes hand in hand with individuation.

2.1. The power of love

2.1.1. The love in the everyday life

Those who speak of love generally have their own life experiences in the background. What are these experiences? The caring mother and the father as head of education are basic experiences. Some people may have deficits in memory.

Many thinks of the love between man and woman, of tenderness, of sexual experiences or of having a nice time together. Some marry for love, they think. But his or her unrecognized deficit for a sheltered home is often a stronger driving force than his or her love for a life partner.

Some dog owners may think of their faithful love dog soul. The love for the cat can become a life content for some, where the "meow" acts as a comfort in the empty, loveless everyday life.

Some talk about love in connection with nature and plants. Others love their home decor, their car, their art on the wall or a certain music. Some speak of the "love of the profession". Some talk about "love of God" or about love for certain human values.

"Spiritual love" is for loners, for people who suffer from deficits or have a "mental depth". For the life of politics and the economy is neither a place for love nor an expression of love.

For many, cultural activities and sports, leisure and entertainment are primarily about money and success, but not about love. "Love" is a much-used word, from "lovely money" to "love of God".

Love is little in demand in neighbourly, national and international life. The facts speak for themselves. This can be read daily in the newspapers. So, people focus on their personal lives. But even then, love fails, hopes fade and ideals burst.

The reality is catching up almost everyone over the years. Love in a relationship can change quickly when the cash register is no longer right. The love in the family is burdened and crushed by millions.

- Many people confuse love with selfishness and lust. That has a few reasons. The fight for a place in the transmission of the world of work and leisure is hard. Anyone who seeks love or wants to live quickly ends up with the losers.

- For some, love means "emotional affection". For others, this is an instrument for doing business. Love in everyday life means for many, no love experience and no love can live. Who needs love, is mentally ill, a weak person or unworldly.

- Tragically, there is very little love in everyday life, in relationships, in business, in politics and in religions.

Reflections and discussion

The kinds of love in life are varied; an overview:

- ☐ Mother / father-child
- ☐ Children's parents
- ☐ To fellow human beings
- ☐ In social help
- ☐ To nature
- ☐ To God
- ☐ To goods
- ☐ To the profession

☐ Between a man and a woman
☐ To yourself
☐ Between teacher-student
☐ Between educators and children
☐ To the animals
☐ For the beautiful
☐ To cultural goods

There are also phenomena of love in everyday life that do not all endorse and forms that are above all subjectively experienced as "love":

- ☐ Homosexuality
- ☐ Prostitution

☐ altruism
☐ love for the church

We distinguish five types of love:

☐ The self-love
☐ The love of life partner, friends, acquaintances, people
☐ The love for God and his spirit, for transcendence
☐ The love for nature and wildlife, for living space in general
☐ Love for the goods, for cultural objects, for institutions

Love is a topic that has a place in all areas of life, for example:

- ☐ In dealing with neighbours
- ☐ Between religions
- ☐ Between peoples
- ☐ In politics
- ☐ In the development of the environment
- ☐ In the construction of children's living spaces
- ☐ In the integration of the elderly
- ☐ In the penal system
- ☐ In the production of toys

- ☐ in dealing with strangers
- ☐ between parties
- ☐ dealing with the needy
- ☐ in the financial world
- ☐ in dealing with the disabled
- ☐ in the forms of entertainment
- ☐ dealing with the weaker

Diagram 2.1.1: The five fields of love

Diagramm OS9-1: Die fünf Bereiche der Liebe

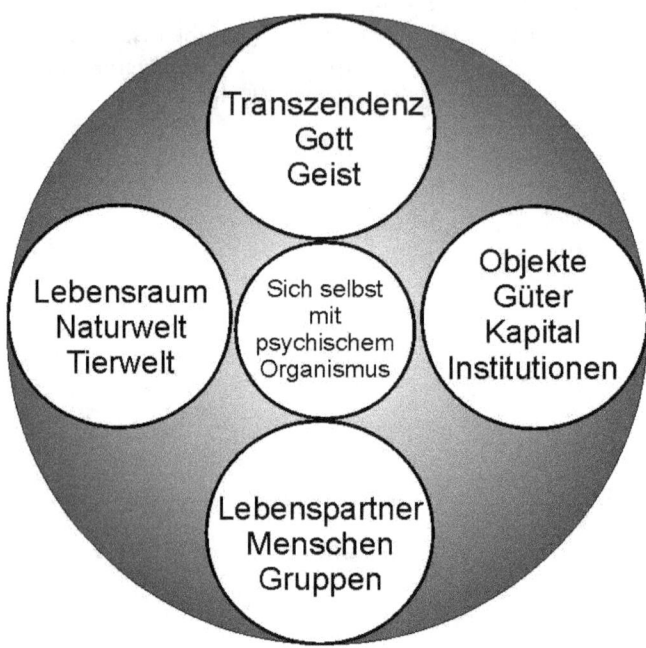

English translation: (From left above to right below)
Transcendence, God, spirit &
Living space, world of nature, world of animals &
One's one with psychical organism &
Objects, goods, resources, institutions &
Life partner, humans, groups

The social dimension of love

We put a thesis: War and environmental destruction are expressions of lack of love. For this we present some thoughts of experts (here strongly shortened):

The process of cultural development may lead to the extinction of the human species, because it affects the sexual function in more ways than one.

The psychical changes associated with the culture process are conspicuous and unambiguous. They consist in a progressive shift in the instinctual goals and limitations of the instinctual impulses.

The most important characteristic of the culture is: The strengthening of the intellect, which begins to dominate instinctual life, and the internalization of the tendency to aggression with all its advantageous and dangerous consequences.

The psychical attitudes that the cultural process demands on us now contradict the war in the most glaring way.

The demonic mind does everything to avoid having to see its own face, and everyone helps it's to the best of his ability. No psychology, because this debauchery could lead to self-knowledge!

Then rather wars, each of which the other is guilty, and no one sees that all the world is obsessed with doing what one flees and fears.

It depends on the free, i.e. conscious decision of man, whether the good should not be translated into satanic. His worst sin is unconsciousness.

When will the time finally come when man will not simply be barbarically presupposed, but will earnestly seek ways and means of depriving himself of his obsession and unconsciousness and making this the most important cultural task.

The great changes that our savage industrial civilization must make if we want to keep the planet alive will not come about through the power of reason or the influence of the facts alone.

What we need is a psychological transformation.

What the earth needs must be felt in us; we have to feel it as if it were our most personal needs.

Facts and figures, reason and logic can show us the faults in our current way of living, and visualize the risks we are taking. But they cannot motivate us, teach us a better way of life, or inspire us to live a better way of life.

Is there no alternative to scare tactics and guilt trips that lend the ecological necessity the fire of intelligence and passion? Yes, it exists. It is the intense interest that comes from a shared identity, from the fact that two people become one.

The deep experience of this common identity is what we call love. Ecologically committed people must ask themselves where they can find it in themselves and in others whose habits and wishes we want to change, how only love can change us.

At the height of the industrial era, Gaia (the earth) calls us back to the oldest philosophical task: Know thyself!

The needs of the planet are the needs of the person. Needs of the person? But the love!!! The standard question:

Where does it lead in 10, 20 or 30 years, when no one wants or can live love anymore?

Absence of love means obsession and unconsciousness.

As a collective delusion, this leads to the destruction of humanity and the planet.

Concrete love in everyday life

☐ Valuing the truthfulness of the other
☐ Taking responsibility for household waste
☐ Showing interest in the psychic life of man
☐ Consciously cultivate one's own psychic life
☐ Considering people who live love
☐ Not exploiting the weaknesses of others for their own benefit
☐ Do not cheat others
☐ Truly live in matters of inner life
☐ Turning to one's own feelings
☐ Doing not empty the ashtray at the red light or in parking lots
☐ Responsible, recognizing your own strength, driving a car
☐ Designing the inhabited environment for the children as well
☐ Building housing estates for the people, not for the quick money

- Developing your own potential and promote it with the others
- Appreciating and cultivating your own sensuality
- Committing to the values of humanity in solidarity
- Promoting people and groups who represent the highest human values
- Breaking down disputes and learn to talk properly
- Valuing one's own goods, use them for mental and spiritual life
- Driving a car, if it makes sense, do not just go round for a chat
- Being thankful for electricity and handle it reasonably (not indifferently)
- Using own resources to promote mental and spiritual life
- Finding more the constructive conversation in the circle of acquaintances
- Seeking the deepest values of man in dreams
- Do not separate old people from society
- Promoting multicultural values and intercultural encounters
- Taking mental-spiritual growth seriously
- Do not shamelessly exploit others' trust materially
- Giving inner depth to one's own life and personal relationship
- Consciously cultivating the beautiful (in your own room, in the house, in the quarter)
- Seeking the living religious in itself, in the other and together
- Being alert to your own destructive forces of the subconscious
- Do not displace the instinctual life, live it and express it in other forms
- Respecting and caring for the needs of one's own body
- Avoiding unnecessary risk of death
- Experiencing one's own lifetime as valuable and use accordingly
- Helping and supporting where opportunities arise
- Using one's own powers where one's own life can be shaped
- Developing inner freedom to consume
- Promote conversation about the values of human life
- Being alert to extremism, dogmatism, fundamentalism
- Promoting and nurturing cultural values and use opportunities as enrichment
- Maintaining the experience of nature regularly
- Protecting the values of living together (family, friends)
- Contributing to not exploiting resources where possible
- Resisting against everything that brings love to stifle, destroyed
- Maintaining entertainment with mind (or leave it where it is not possible)
- Do not let life be speculative as "gambling"
- Highly appreciate the achievements; it is infinitely more valuable than chance profits
- Acquiring a great deal of knowledge in order to make humanity competent
- Rigid principles, approaching and 'softening' rigid norms of humanity
- Controlling the power of the state and the churches in a very critical-democratic way

☐ Developing determination against everything that destroys love and truthfulness

☐ Developing the desire for discovery for the inner transcendental realities

Notes and perspectives

How do most people understand love?

Write down the key words in this subchapter:

What causes indifference to love?

Love is essential, because: ...

What did you learn about love in your parents' home, school and church?

What meaning in living together has the conversation about love?

What would be the seriousness of love in politics and business effect?

Which concrete pictures about love in everyday life convey the advertising?

Formulate an important question about the social dimension of love

2.1.2. Polarity of love and hate

There are beautiful words about love: Love does not murder; it does not kill; it does not exploit nature excessively; it does not cheat; it is honest; it does not steal. But these are very difficult claims.

One has to defend himself from the violent criminals and partialness. Another person has to get his food. Who wants to secure his economic existence, must not love too much, least of all truthfulness.

The powers that dominate social life have nothing to do with love. So, the individual is looking for love in a habitat that gives little expression of love.

The person who wants to live love, with himself, with others, with the possibilities in the habitat and with nature, is the "punished": "Never tell the truth about the psychical life".

If love wants truthfulness, hatred lives the lie. The story is an image of hatred and lies as well as love and truthfulness. In this space-time network, people are intertwined and love has its limits. Where there is no love, hate dominates.

The opposite of love is hatred and greed. Hatred means denial of life and devaluation of all life. Hatred negates the psychical life. Greed gathers itself, exploits, occupies the objects libidinally and wants to "have" for the sake of the ownership.

Hatred and greed are destructive, using every path from violence to lies to destroy and take away whatever life there is to take. Esteem and respect are not present in this attitude to life.

Only in collective solidarity does love have a chance. On a small scale, two people are needed to live the love. In a community, several are determining how love can preserve space. In the state there are all.

With strictness and severity, many politicians should actually defend love in the gear of the industrialized nation and give it the due place. Because without love, the children cannot grow, man cannot be a constructive member of the state.

The more man lives away from love, the greater his inner destructive potential becomes. He also becomes vulnerable to lies. He cannot see what's behind the facade because he does not want to see behind his own masks. This is costly for everyone. A lot of money and many forces are lost.

Uncanny forces were released with love to solve the social problems locally, nationally and internationally. Lack of love brings the politicians much work and costs. Hatred and greed cost the taxpayer a lot of money.

Reflections and discussion

The alternatives to love are historically and presently well known to all people:

☐ Individual suffering   ☐ Social problems
☐ Lies   ☐ Violence
☐ Intrigues   ☐ Needy persons
☐ Addiction   ☐ Economic wars
☐ Crimes   ☐ Wars
☐ Environmental destruction

The antithesis of love is hatred and greed, in particular:

☐ Negation of values   ☐ Indifference
☐ Disrespect   ☐ Substitutional needs
☐ Ridicule   ☐ Vulgarities
☐ Exploitation   ☐ Rejection of love
☐ Irresponsibility   ☐ Carelessness
☐ Libidinousness   ☐ Humiliation
☐ Falsehood   ☐ Suppression
☐ Life refusal   ☐ Dishonesty
☐ Selfishness   ☐ Sadism
☐ Indignity   ☐ Arrogance
☐ Destruction

Hatred and greed are psychical forces, which become important already in the small utterance and only not as "blind anger" or "massless greed". Hate and love form a continuum.

If neither one nor the other is markedly distinctive in the middle, then indifference and apathy are attitudes of life that stand against life.

Greed and hatred are forces against life and create:

- ☐ Mistrust
- ☐ Despair
- ☐ Regression
- ☐ Inferiority
- ☐ Doubt

- ☐ Hopelessness
- ☐ Stagnation
- ☐ Guilt
- ☐ Isolation

Diagram 2.1.2: Progression – regression between love and hate

Diagramm OS9-2: Progression - Regression zwischen Liebe und Hass

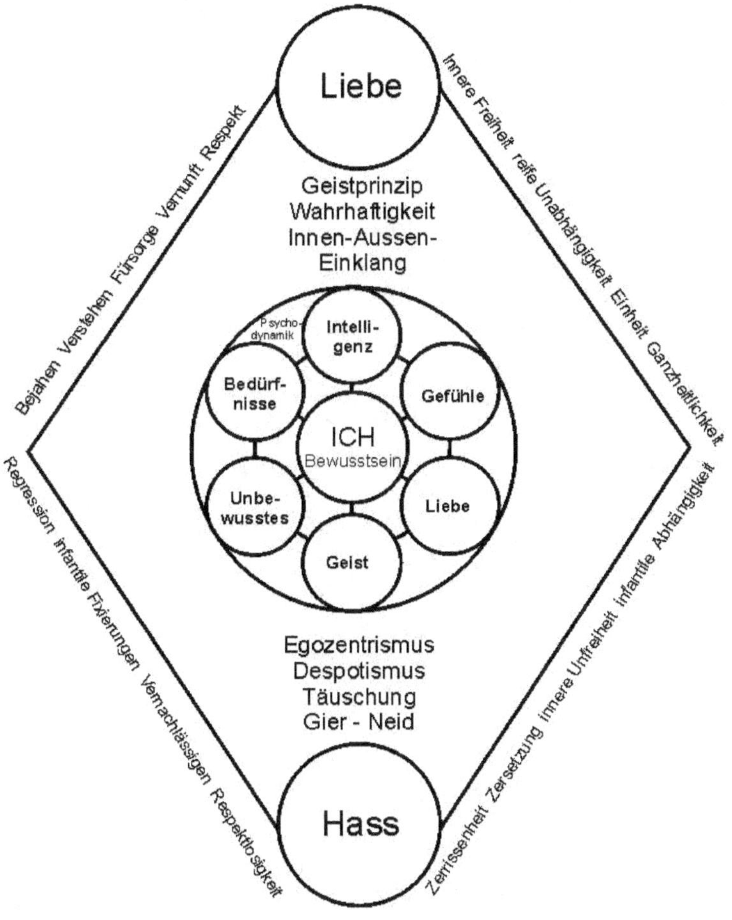

Liebe

Innere Freiheit reife Unabhängigkeit Einheit Ganzheitlichkeit

Bejahen Verstehen Fürsorge Vernunft Respekt

Geistprinzip
Wahrhaftigkeit
Innen-Aussen-
Einklang

Psycho-dynamik · Intelligenz

Bedürf-nisse · Gefühle

ICH
Bewusstsein

Unbe-wusstes · Liebe

Geist

Egozentrismus
Despotismus
Täuschung
Gier - Neid

Regression infantile Fixierungen Vernachlässigen Respektlosigkeit

Zerrissenheit Zersetzung innere Unfreiheit infantile Abhängigkeit

Hass

English translation: (From left above to right below)
Affirming – understanding – caring – reason – respect &
Inner freedom - mature autonomy – unity – completeness support
Love: Principe of the spirit, truthfulness, internal-external harmony
influence the psychical organism: Intelligence, needs, emotions, "I"
consciousness, unconscious, love, spirit progressively, while
Disruption – Disintegration – Inner bondage – Infantile addiction &
Regression – Infantile fixations – Disregard – Disrespect promote
regressively

Hate: Ego-centrism, despotism, deceit, greed – envy

Amoral behaviour and character

There are behaviours that are on the negative side of the spectrum of love and hate: Keywords are: egoism, narcissism, neurosis, inferiority, compensation and again and again the same thing: the lie of life. Behavioural aspects that are morally opposed to love:

Behaviour character aspects	In which sense is all this against love?
Greed	
Envy	
Jealousy	
Pedantry	
Egoism	
Coquetry	
Fanatism for truth	
Impatience	
Cruelty	
Self-torture	
Talkativeness	
Crime	
Neglect	
Spoiling	
Effeminacy	
Despisement	
Exaggeration	
Arrogance	
Defiance	
Tyranny	
Hubris	
Infidelity	
Experience greed	
Prudery	
Boasting	
Ruse	
Imperiousness	
Indifference	
Cowardice	
Craving for admiration	
Idleness	
Hostility	

Contempt	
Obstinacy	
Malignancy	
Bumptiousness	
Have-it all	
Humiliation	
Quarrelsomeness	
Scepticism	
Censoriousness	

The desire for life

By 'desire for life' or 'lust for life', we can understand the intellectual and affective mental disposition that makes life, the world, doing, and the human being altogether light, bright, interesting, and agreeable. Lust for life is a disposition of joyful and pleasant nature, but not simply a phenomenon of euphoria. Lust is at first dynamic, constructive, maybe even adventurous. Lust for life creates an atmosphere of exultation. Lust wants to live, hides in its depth a primitive determination to survive. This is 'the deep desire' This is something completely different than a pure well-being!

At first glance, the presence and degree of this deep desire may seem to be meaningful only for individual health: A matter of private psycho-hygiene. But the 'pleasure in life' shows that it is nothing less than the energy of universal evolution, which, in the form of a congenital attraction to being, mysteriously spurts forth in the most primitive and therefore the most directly uncontrollable reason of each of us; an energy that depends on us to nourish and develop.

This ultimately amounts to say that the world would remain stationary or spinning in circles without ascending if it did not initially find in the heart of its self an ascending factor that is precisely that defined 'life-wanting'. So, the lust for life would ultimately be the basic driving force that moves and directs the universe on its major axis of complexity and consciousness. Lust for life is love for life, that means: An all-determining way of life. It manifests in the physical processes of a person, in his feelings, in his thoughts and gestures. This open living orientation is expressed in the whole human being. It is a quality to live and to keep alive.

Love for life has the tendency for integration and unification. If you love life, you are attracted to the life and growth process in all areas. You would rather create new than preserve. You are astonished and prefer to experience something new rather than seek safety in the affirmation of the old.

Living the adventure is worth more to human than financial security. His attitude to life is functional, not mechanical. He sees the whole thing, not just its parts, he sees structures and not summations. He wants to shape and influence with love and reason.

The opposite is the denial of life, "necrophilia". Its characteristics are:

- ☐ The truly evil
- ☐ To glorify death; fascination to killing and death
- ☐ Fancy diseases, funerals
- ☐ Love violence; destroying life; despise the one who is to be killed
- ☐ Mastering and controlling life
- ☐ Having for the sake of having; possession is everything
- ☐ Only the memory, not the living counts
- ☐ Law and order are their idols
- ☐ Craving for certainty, prediction, control
- ☐ Fearless of total annihilation
- ☐ Being indifferent to life
- ☐ Counting only profit and consumption
- ☐ Mechanical pleasure (sex, happiness, food, drink, etc.)
- ☐ Destruction of nature; lust of the tickle of death risk
- ☐ Overestimation of intellectualism
- ☐ Quantification / bureaucratization of all life
- ☐ Fighting glorifying as a beauty.

Notes and perspectives

Where does the collective stand between progression and regression?

Write down the key words in this subchapter:

What causes egocentrism, deception, greed, envy, hatred?

Genuine lust for life is essential, because: ...

What did you learn about the responsibility for love in your parents' home, school and church?

What significance in living together does the conversation about truthfulness have?

What would the "lust for life" in politics and the economy cause?

What kind of lust for life does advertising convey?

Formulate an important question for moral character formation:

2.1.3. Love as a life care

The power of love is evident in all areas of life. It begins with the integration of the realities, leads to thinking processing and subsequent actions.

In this sense, attitudes also reflect love or hate, i.e. care or aversion to life.

Not only your own life as a lust living and maybe even that of your life partner belongs to life. Living means also working, budgeting and earning money, shopping for things and talking. People also do life in their free time.

Part of life is weakness, failure, bad luck, misfortune and helplessness. To life belong conflicts, crises, difficulties and problems of all kinds.

Life care means that this part of reality is absorbed and answered in the affirmative way. The daily moods and deep feelings are a reality. Love urges to take this experience seriously and deal with it constructively.

In relationships, life care means the integration of all realities: Feelings, the unconscious, the strong and weak forces, the real needs, the inability and the still undeveloped potentials.

Love cannot say: "I want to enjoy your body, if you are happy and laugh, I accept you; if you have no problems and can do everything well, I love you ...".

In the relationship life, life care means that both turn to all realities and cultivate them.

Love also absorbs the aging process as part of life. How is a life with love? Where does life lead with love? It brings to life.

Life care can also be seen in the development of the environment, in the production of goods, in workplace design and in cultural life.

If people live love, then this is reflected in what they produce and artistically create.

Starting position, centre and goal of love is the human being with his body, with his psychical organism and with his habitat.

When people live with the power of love, they shape their habitat for humans.

Work, economy, politics and entertainment are for humans. This results in a spiral process:

Man lives for his all-embracing psychic-spiritual life and this affects the acting, i.e. on the design of habitat and working life.

Caring life in this sense causes creative psychical-spiritual evolution.

The more people live love, the lower the crime and the destruction of the environment: That has favourable consequences, i.e. also for the state treasury.

Reflections and discussion

Love as action means:

☐ Caring
☐ Protecting
☐ Unfolding
☐ Designing
☐ Valuing
☐ Forgiveness
☐ Respect for meaning and value

☐ Interest
☐ Nursing
☐ Affirmation
☐ Nurturing
☐ Taking responsibility
☐ Reconciling
☐ Solidarity for love

Love always means life-giving; belong to the life among other things:

☐ The entire mental life
☐ Decisive also the inner spirit
☐ The individuation
☐ The body in the aging process
☐ The CV with the different phases
☐ The weak and helpless
☐ The failure and losing
☐ Learning and relearning
☐ The conflicts, difficulties, disorders and suffering
☐ The design of the living space
☐ The production of goods for the psycho-spiritual man
☐ The institutions
☐ The economy, industry, services etc.
☐ The workplace
☐ Leisure and holidays

☐ The friends, acquaintances, neighbours, strangers

Life benefit means or effects:

☐ Trust
☐ Joy
☐ Initiative
☐ Responsibility

☐ Hope
☐ Integrity
☐ Intimacy
☐ Creativity

Diagram 2.1.3: Dimensions of creative love

Diagramm OS9-3: Dimensionen der schöpferischen Liebe

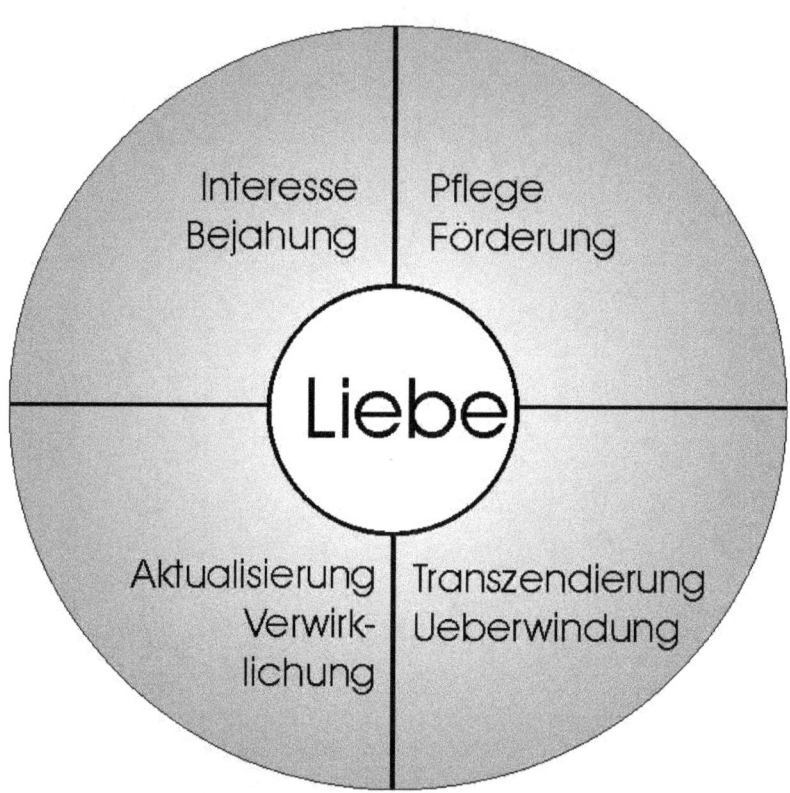

English translation: (From left above to right below)
Interest, affirmation,
Care, encouragement,
Love
Actualization, realization,
Transcending, overcoming

Postulates against love and the lust for life

Western European thinking has certain assumptions that are fundamentally against turning to life. These are, together with drive repression, the crucial roots of necrophilia and promote a human and life show and a lifestyle that is directed against love. Yes, they exert almost total control over humans. These are settings that can be reflected below with the following statements.

Tacit assumptions, unreflective supposing, acts of faith, rarely questioned, believed in authority and trust in science and technology, are:

- ☐ The universe is the product of chance; has neither cause nor goal.
- ☐ The universe is dead; life is only a minor part.
- ☐ Physics is the ultimate science.
- ☐ Really is what can be perceived with the help of the senses.
- ☐ Only the present moment counts.
- ☐ We can understand the physical universe without understanding ourselves.
- ☐ Man is body and nothing else.
- ☐ Man is a creature independent of the environment.
- ☐ Every person starts life 'new', i.e. as a 'blank' sheet.
- ☐ Humans are determined by their genetic material and their environment.
- ☐ Despite determination, man must act as if he possesses a free will.
- ☐ We know the history of humans relatively well.
- ☐ We know about the origin and evolution of man.
- ☐ Every person is isolated from each other, trapped in his nervous system.
- ☐ The psychic energy is completely derived from the physical energy.
- ☐ Man has no function in a meaningless and aimless universe.
- ☐ The only real meaning is maximum pleasure and a minimum of pain.
- ☐ The universe is rough, indifferent and apathetic.
- ☐ It is our job to conquer the universe.
- ☐ We represent the highest form of life, presumably throughout the universe.
- ☐ The low organisms exist for the benefit of humans.
- ☐ Only human beings have a consciousness (animals and plants not).
- ☐ Man has a consciousness.
- ☐ Consciousness is a product of brain activity.
- ☐ Altered consciousness is a transient modification of brain function.
- ☐ The normal state of consciousness is the most adaptable form of organization.
- ☐ Spontaneously altered states of consciousness are an expression of illness.
- ☐ Consciously causing altered states of consciousness is pathological.
- ☐ The body is a passive control circuit.
- ☐ The physical body is the only one we own.
- ☐ Death is the inevitable end of human life.

☐ Physical death is the ultimate redemption of human consciousness.
☐ The personality makes an individual unique, his life worth living.
☐ Feeling personality & finding identity is vital; she loses power.
☐ Personal development stops with adulthood.
☐ Healthy is a personality development if it makes you socially adaptable.
☐ A normal adult person can recognize himself quite a bit.
☐ In normal adults, the personality is structured relatively uniformly.
☐ Logical thinking is the highest ability of humans.
☐ Mind development is the ultimate goal that a person can strive for.
☐ The expansion of our solid knowledge leads to greater wisdom.
☐ There is no direct, sure knowledge about something.
☐ The highest authorities of knowledge and cognition are the philosophers.
☐ Almost all essential knowledge can be conveyed with language.
☐ Logical contradictions in a statement means that this is incorrect.
☐ If people agree with me, they are reasonable.
☐ Fantasy is limited to our honeymooners.
☐ Faith means holding things as true that are not real.
☐ Intuition means 'happy' ideas, sudden insights that are nevertheless rational.
☐ Symbols are purely physical objects with corresponding brain structures.
☐ Faith and psychical experiences work only on ourselves.
☐ Feelings are just electrical and chemical processes.
☐ Feelings lead to irrationality and therefore have to be completely eliminated.
☐ Feelings have no business in scientific work.
☐ Negative feelings are inevitable fate.
☐ All feelings are selfish, animal nature; there are no noble feelings.
☐ Playing is something for children.
☐ Pain is something unpleasant that should be prevented.
☐ Learning is based on electrochemical brain processes.
☐ Learning means accumulating knowledge.
☐ Intellectual learning is the highest form that can handle everything important.
☐ Learning is the cognitive processing of sensory impressions.
☐ The memory is not very reliable.
☐ The only thing we can remember are impressions of our lives.
☐ The only memories we have access to are our own ones.
☐ Wishing is basic and life-sustaining motivation.
☐ Power, sexual satisfaction and pain avoidance are the basic motives.
☐ The only thing we can perceive is the physical world and the body.
☐ The sense organs determine our perception.
☐ Perception is broadly correct, despite selection and prejudice.
☐ Selfish actions of others are the main cause of one's own experience of suffering.

☐ No normal person likes to suffer.
☐ Progress is social progress.
☐ Science is cumulative in nature.
☐ Our civilization (including psychology) is the most significant on our planet.
☐ Our civilization and psychology are progressing steadily.
☐ Conquests are the best way to make progress in understanding.
☐ You cannot be scientist and mystic at the same time.

Which of these settings do you share? Mark it!

Notes and perspectives

What about the creative power of love in most people?

Write down the key words in this subchapter:

What causes a strong lack of life care?

Hundreds of postulates for love are most urgent because: ...

What did you learn in the home, school and church about the power of love as a contribution to life?

What meaning in living together has the conversation about the creative power of love?

What would be the power of creative love in politics and the economy?

Which postulates for love convey the advertising?

Formulate an important question about love as a transcendent power:

2.1.4. Exercises

1. How do you love yourself?

2. How does your love express itself towards psychic life?

3. How do you perceive your responsibility in love?

4. How does your love express itself in your actions?

5. How are you creative and active in your life for meaning and values?

6. How do you use your psychical powers together with love?

7. How does your love express itself in dealing with the psyche of other people?

8. How do you experience the love ability of the people in your living environment?

9. Live self-love. Indicate what applies to you:

4 = do / live / I have regularly   3 = do / live / I often have
2 = do / live / sometimes I have   1 = do / live / I have little
0 = do / live / I seldom / not

☐ I am interested in my inner life and my whole life.
☐ I turn to what I am and live.
☐ I do meaningful things with my material possibilities.
☐ I promote my inclinations and talents.
☐ I take care of my valuable aspects.
☐ I develop the powers in me that are still weak and little formed.
☐ I activate my power potential.
☐ I'm doing what I have in life plans.
☐ I stimulate myself many-sided to expand my person and my life.
☐ I shape the still unformed in me.
☐ I keep building my psychic life.
☐ I am training for work and life.
☐ I use my potential, my knowledge and ability.
☐ I consciously steer myself in everyday life.
☐ I strengthen my weaknesses.
☐ I take my psychical life, including dreams and intuitions seriously.

☐ I am grateful to life for what I can live for.
☐ I like to relate myself to other people.
☐ I experience myself positively as part of nature.
☐ I can seriously accept being inserted into a transcendental network.
☐ I considerately handle my feelings and physical condition.
☐ I can also take difficult moments in life as they are.
☐ I am responsible for my happiness and for everything I do.
☐ I act with competence (expertise) in my job as well as in my personal life.
☐ I can also quickly enjoy small things about myself / in my life.
☐ I'm balanced with my powers.

Total: …

Here interpretation:

Concrete conclusions:

10. Love for mental-spiritual growth.

10.1. Give 5 examples that specifically express your love for your mental and spiritual growth:

10.2. Give 5 examples that specifically express the absence of love for your mental-spiritual growth:

What shows your power of love in your everyday life? Give five examples:

What is the absence of love in your everyday life? Give five examples:

How do you experience your power of self-love in general?

How can you strengthen your power of love?

Multiple Choice Test 3

Choose the four correct answers:

3.1. Love in everyday life. Central types of love are: the love for ...

☐ a) Hobbies
☐ b) Cultural effort
☐ c) Life partner / friend)
☐ d) Habitat
☐ e) one-self
☐ f) Own self-image

3.2. The polarity of love and hate. Basic statements on the subject are:

☐ a) Hatred, greed, exploitation and envy are elements of the opposite pole to love.
☐ b) Love is a basic psychical element that belongs elementarily to life.
☐ c) Love always has something to do with physical pleasure.
☐ d) Love is a basic instinct with different characteristics.
☐ e) Without love, man cannot grow psychically-spiritually.
☐ f) Lack of love almost always leads to aggression against oneself and / or others.

3.3. Love as a gift of life. Love as action includes:

☐ a) Renunciation of material
☐ b) Caring / nursing
☐ c) Affirming / accepting
☐ d) Inserting yourself into a lesson
☐ e) Affirming life
☐ f) Centring in the spirit

2.2. Power and expression of love

2.2.1. Self-love

Self-love is the beginning of every love. Loving has to do with interest, caring, turning to, promoting, growing, protecting and strengthening. People do not do that with their psychical life.

They have no interest in their psychical inner world. Feelings are of little importance to many. The needs are almost everywhere superimposed by artificial needs. Only a few wants to fix their own past.

Finding reconciliation with stressful experiences seems to most to be something foreign. The "spirit" inside remains unnoticed. The potentials develop few men. The "inner child" is suppressed.

The care of thinking and psycho-hygiene are unknown. Some fill up with foreign parts that are just ballast inside.

Patience with oneself and slowly forming oneself, as an expression of self-love, is alien to many. Love has a lot to do with authenticity and truthfulness.

The reality shows us: The human loves little. He loves real life a little.

Many people confuse selfishness with self-love. Egoism splits off the holistic psychical life. This leads to inner turmoil and inner bondage. Destructiveness is the effect. Hatred, greed and envy are consequences of it.

The denial of psychical life leads to irresponsibility towards love and the spirit. Regressive behaviour is a mandatory consequence.

In the end there is always a kind of destruction lurking in the individual as in the collective life.

Love begins with the comprehensive attention and integration of psychical life with all subsystems and individual forces. To affirm, nurture and consciously grow this own life with spirit and responsibility we call self-love.

Through these self-occupations, man becomes a unity and wholeness, he becomes free inwardly.
Life is first what man is with his psychodynamics, his feelings, his thinking, his needs, his intelligence, his will and his spirit.

Acting is also an expression of life. Loving these own areas requires education.

Those who consciously turn to these forces, make them balanced on all sides, truly and evolutionarily love each other.

Reflections and discussion

Self-love means:

☐ Having interest	☐ Maintaining
☐ Esteeming	☐ Affirming
☐ Protecting	☐ Unfolding
☐ Considering	☐ Bearing responsibility
☐ Living truthfulness	☐ Integrating
☐ Consciously controlling	☐ Working competently

Man is largely human with his psychical organism. Self-love reaches the mental wholeness and, in this context, means:

☐ Interested in one's own psychic reality
☐ Attention to one's own psychic powers
☐ Affirming and taking seriously one's own psychic reality
☐ Living consciously with your own psychical wholeness
☐ Discovering and protecting the values of this psychical life
☐ Cultivating, protecting, unfolding, promoting one's own psychical powers
☐ Systematically acquiring knowledge and thereby forming oneself lively
☐ Taking responsibility for your own psychical reality

Self-love can only grow through:

☐ Turn to one's own inner life, i.e. the intelligence functions, the feelings and needs, the unconscious, the spirit, etc.

☐ Give your own life an appropriate expression: Realizing yourself, implementing, using and inserting.

☐ In relations more and more in the other, finding, experiencing, accepting, receiving and promoting oneself.

☐ In the experience of goods and the designed environment more and more find oneself as a unity and integrate into the consciousness.

☐ Accept that meaning and value can be found in life itself, i.e. first in the living inner world and thus also in love and in spirit.

Discuss in the group how self-love manifests itself in daily life.

Diagram 2.2.1: Active self-love

Diagramm OS9-4: Aktive Selbstliebe

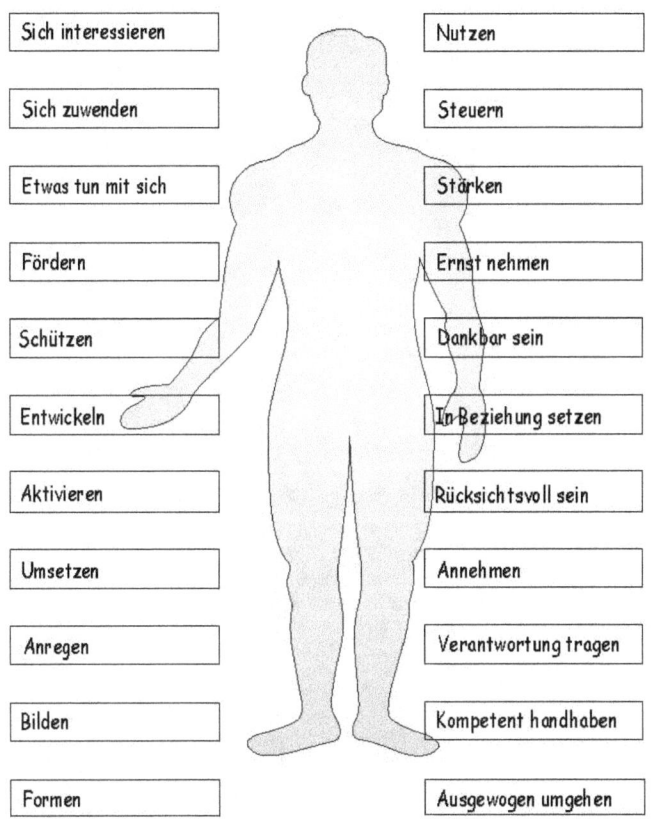

Sich interessieren	Nutzen
Sich zuwenden	Steuern
Etwas tun mit sich	Stärken
Fördern	Ernst nehmen
Schützen	Dankbar sein
Entwickeln	In Beziehung setzen
Aktivieren	Rücksichtsvoll sein
Umsetzen	Annehmen
Anregen	Verantwortung tragen
Bilden	Kompetent handhaben
Formen	Ausgewogen umgehen

English translation: Active self-love:

Being interested	Benefit
Turning to	Regulating
Performing one's own	Strengthening
Supporting	Taking seriously
Protecting	Appreciating
Evolving	Relating to
Activating	Treating with respect
Transferring	Accepting
Stimulating	Bearing responsibility
Shaping	Competent managing

2.2.2. Self-love and love for life

How can man love others, but not himself?

How is it possible to address the needs of others if the individual daily averts and displaces many of his basic needs?

How can man disregard one's own feelings, but lovingly protect and promote one's next?

How can one express "spirit" in life, but ignore one's own inner mind? How should it be possible for someone to love God, but not turn to his psychical inner world?

How can a person love God, glorify him and realize him in life, but reject his own individuation?

How to teach the truth without knowing your own inner true reality?

Such questions point directly to self-love: Only through self-love as a basis and steady precondition, the human is able to really use the love power in life. For only what he perceives and cares for in himself can he observe in others.

Those who perceive their own needs and take care of their responsibilities can integrate those of others. Those who work on their own dreams are capable of developing interest in the dream life of others.

Who forms himself in the individuation, can promote others in it. If a man loves himself, then he loves his partner in life in the same way and the other people: All with their entire psychical organism.

Self-love also reaches the living space. What man lives is the expression of self-love. If he deals with himself with love and spirit, he shapes his habitat and the environment with love and spirit. If a person loves himself, he produces goods and cultural achievements in this connection.

If man loves himself, then he is in connection with the spirit, thereby with God and the transcendental reality: He experiences himself bound here. If people love each other, a human community through love and spirit is possible in peace.

Reflections and discussion

Self-love is the basis for every other form of love. The following theses are justifications and explanations:

☐ There is no love without the foundation of self-love.
☐ There is no love without the psychical powers.
☐ Love grows the more mental life is integrated.
☐ One cannot promote wholeness, but neglect one's own.
☐ You cannot really love and hate at the same time.
☐ Who loves, lives in progression and development.
☐ Love always leads away from disunity and bondage.
☐ You cannot love nature and wildlife, but you cannot love yourself.
☐ Real love for an occupation (profession) is based on self-love.
☐ Every true sense is rooted in self-love.
☐ Love is a human phenomenon, i.e. with intelligence and spirit.
☐ Love means more than caring for emotions, because man is more.
☐ The life of the others affirming calls for affirmation of one's own life.
☐ Promoting truthfulness in others calls for living truthfulness of one's own.
☐ Reconciling with others, presupposes own reconciliation ability.
☐ Promoting the self-realization of others, based on own self-realization.
☐ Loving animals, but not humans is unbalanced (dishonest).
☐ Those who represent love cannot possibly kill others by law.
☐ Those who love themselves all-embracingly do not abuse other people.
☐ Those who cultivate their psychical organism, do not lie or intrigue.
☐ Who loves himself does not cheat others.
☐ Those who have comprehensively experienced love live it also themselves.
☐ Who lives love and thus also spirit, does not exploit nature.
☐ Who recognizes his psychical life understands all people in their depths.

Love is not just a private and intimate affair. Love captures all life. Love belongs in the:

Politics	Economy	Religion	Culture	Education

Discuss with other concrete examples what self-love in social life, nationally and internationally, can mean:

Diagram 2.2.2: From of self-love to love for life

Diagramm OS9-5: Von der Selbstliebe zur Liebe für das Leben

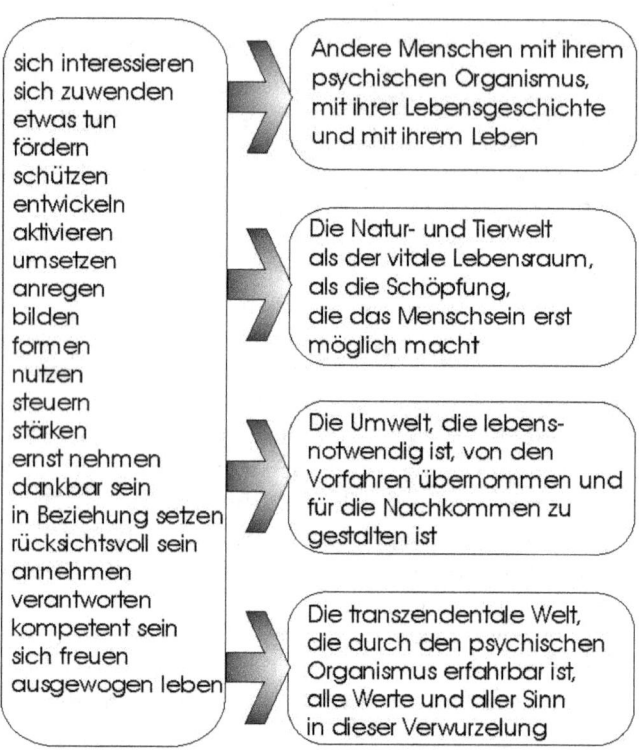

English translation:
Self-lover: Be interested, turning to, doing, supporting, protecting, evolving, activating, transferring, stimulating, shaping, forming, benefit, regulating, strengthening, taking seriously, appreciating, relating to, treating with respect, accepting, bearing responsibility, being competent, enjoying, living balanced
Love for life:
Others with their psychic organism with their life story and their life
World of nature and animals as the vital living space, the creation which make human being possible
Environment, which is indispensable, assumed by the ancestors and to shape for the Descendants

The transcendental world perceptible by the psychical organism with all values and meaning in this rooting

2.2.3. Transcending power of love

The power of love wants to live on its own. It is an expression of life, of the comprehensive psychic life itself. It wants to act and make more of what is. It urges to implement and shape. It is creative.

The power of love goes beyond itself and works in the interest of what holistic psychical life is. Love tends to transform everything that counteracts balanced inner wholeness.

Psychologically speaking, this means that love tends to dissolve "complexes" in the unconscious, to transcend external realities by thinking, and to cultivate feelings in a way that is open to life.

Love wants to assert its own value in life and pushes for achievements for meaning and values that go beyond the individual frame of life.

Love is grounded in the psychical powers, i.e. its foundation is the psychical life and not some external givenness.

In this context, "transcending" means transforming psychical powers, penetrating into spiritual values and anchoring all outer life in psychical-spiritual life.

The psychical life, including the process of individuation, is the proper life. Transcending also means cultivating all life in this direction, not only rooted in it, but in it meaning and value, actual being, recognizing and living. This is a "Towards the actual reality of human life".

This requires the formation of mental life. This includes psychical achievements such as processing, reconciling and being able to renounce something in favour of higher goals in the sense of individuation. Transcending further means that the individual's own holistic being is recognized and lived in a networked way in the system of the human community.

This transcendence of one's own unity also leads to the living space:

What is inside in man as an original wholeness, should receive an expression outside, so that inside more and more evolution can be made possible, for joy of life, for the pleasure of creative activity and also as "encomium".

Only in this anchoring and in this dimension does man find real joy in life. That what we call "transcendence" of the power of love.

Reflections and discussion

The transcending power of love means:

☐ Comprehensively form the psychic life in the process of individuation
☐ Transforming what opposes this process, i.e. processing, pardoning, forgiving, saying goodbye, letting go as an intrapsychic transformation process
☐ Implementing inner life out of individuation
☐ Giving what is inside a psychical structure a form in relations and in shaping the world as well
☐ From the inner mental and spiritual growth more and more new creations forming
☐ To live in the implementation and in the life of what man originally is, living joy
☐ Expressing in manifold ways the transcendental being of man in life forms (culture)
☐ Life as "praise", i.e. as a joyful appreciation of the eternity of psychical-spiritual being and origin
☐ Experiencing and realizing the value and purpose of holistic being

Human life is fragile and exposed to many dangers:

☐ Suffering blows of fate ultimately overcomes only love.
☐ The external circumstances of life, material circumstances as well as political and social conditions burden the love considerably.
☐ Meaning and value of existence is lost if no transcending can take place.
☐ Man cannot live without love, i.e. without transcendence; he is stunted, becomes sick and destructive.

Many forces oppose the transcending of love:

☐ Social conditions   ☐ Hardship and hunger
☐ Arrogance   ☐ Social injustices
☐ Dictatorships   ☐ Selfishness
☐ Fundamentalist thinking   ☐ Hatred

☐ Ignorance   ☐ Violence and unrest
☐ Wars   ☐ Imperiousness

Discuss in the group which framework conditions can promote the realization of the transcending power of love:

Diagram 2.2.3: The transcending power of love

Diagramm OS9-6: Die transzendierende Kraft der Liebe

Die Kraft der Liebe
kann auf vielfältige Weise transzendieren:

von der äusseren Wirklichkeit zur inneren Wirklichkeit

vom Verhalten als äussere Erscheinung zum innerpsychischen Leben

von äusseren Werten zu inneren psychisch-geistigen Werten

Verletzungen überwinden durch innere Bearbeitung

von der körperlichen Lust zu psychisch ganzheitlichen Interessen

von negativen Gefühlen hin zu positiven lebensoffenen Gefühlen

von der Fixierung an Dinge zur innerlich freien Nutzung

denkerische Operationen erweitern mit der Dynamik des Geistes

von der Raum-Zeit-Dimension zu erweiterten Perspektiven

partikuläre Interessen einbetten in eine ganzheitliche Konzeption

vom Lebensrhythmus in die Wachstumsdynamik der Individuation

vom archaischen Zustand hin zu evolutionären Prozessen

vom biologisch-materiellen Erleben hin zum Individuationserleben

vom äusserlich Schönen hin zum psychisch-geistig Schönen

von psychischen Möglichkeiten hin zur Realisierung

von momentanen Eigeninteressen hin zu höheren Wertinteressen

vom dogmatisch-ideologischen Denken hin zur inneren Erfahrung

Demütigungen versöhnen durch Transformationen im Unbewussten

von Sachwerten hin zu den Werten der Archetypen

English translation: The power of love
Can transcend in manifold ways:

From the external reality to the inner reality & from behaviour as external appearance to inner-psychical life & from external values to internal psychical-spiritual values & overcoming injuries by inner treatment & from physical lust to psychical integral interests & from negative emotions to positive openness for life & from bondage to things to internal free benefit & amplifying thinking operations with the dynamic of the spirit & from space-time-dimension to amplified perspectives & embedding particulate interests in holistic conception & from rhythm of life to dynamic of growth of individuation & from archaic state to evolutionary processes & from biological experiencing to experiencing individuation & from external beauty to psychical-spiritual beauty & from psychological possibilities to realization & from current self-interests to higher value-interests & from dogmatic-ideologic thinking to inner experience & reconciling humiliations by transformation in the unconscious & from material assets to the values of the Archetypes

2.2.4. Meaning and value of love

The growth of love begins with the attention to oneself, with self-knowledge and individuation. The spirit gets the chance to become pregnant in life. Entirely new forces are available to man to solve many problems.

Many social problems can be drastically reduced. Because who lives with love and spirit in individuation, has less time for meaningless mobility. He carries a lower accident and disease risk. Violence and crime are decreasing significantly. The environmental burdens are reduced. More money for education and cultural design with spirit is available.

What is the meaning and value of love? Let's turn the question around: What results from a life without love? Man becomes mentally ill.

Many are physically ill for lack of love. The meaning of all activities is only material and lust-oriented without love. All acting becomes internally empty, bland and worthless, if man does not live and unfold his capacity for love in doing so. If love is lacking, dominate hatred and greed, violence and war.

If people do not learn to love, then the relationships are hollow and become cold even in material abundance.

If man fixes his love on lust and on "passable social behaviour", then the inner liveliness of the relation "dies".

If love is only interpreted as a "giving and taking," psychical life does not grow.

For love is first simply "life". If love is lacking, there is also a lack of spirit and, above all, an inner, holistic growth. The less love there is, the more crime increases. Many accidents and damage events are also the result of a lack of love.

If a nation is not in the education process with love, this generates enormous differences of tension. This creates wars between peoples. Between religions grow rejection, condemnation, power struggle and also wars.

Love has its meaning and value in what it does in individual, familial, social, public, international and religious life between different cultures.

Reflections and discussion

Love is based on certain values, cultivates them and wants to give them a life expression:

The good	Order in spirit	Authenticity
The truth	Truthfulness	The beauty
Justice	Joy	The inner wholeness

Love also provides special efforts:

☐ Forgiving ☐ Reconciling
☐ Remorse ☐ Having patience
☐ Living humility ☐ Goodness
☐ Understanding ☐ Granting
☐ Accepting ☐ Resigning

Love gives life a deeper meaning, because the "deeper things" can be found in man himself:

☐ The psychic organism as a living reality
☐ The psychic life that is balanced by the individuation
☐ Wholeness can primal become
☐ The experience of the spirit as a transcendental force
☐ The experience of change and growth processes, which the inner life forming psycho-energetically
☐ The rooting in transcendence through inner experience
☐ Only through love grows and lives the comprehensive psychical life
☐ Experiencing being a living part of the creation plan
☐ The anchoring of earthly life in transcendence
☐ The absence of guilt by individuation and life as a creative being ("realizing creation")

Create together in the group a list of values that make sense for life:

a) in personal life (for yourself):
b) in social life (relationships, encounters):
c) in the design of the habitat:
d) in the production and use of goods:
e) in political, national and international life:
f) another example:

Diagram 2.2.4: From values to meaning in life

Diagramm OS9-7: Von Werten zum Sinn im Leben

Selbstbild	Differenzieren
Dasein	Potentiale entfalten
Liebe	Kraft aufbauen
Geist - Transzendenz	Herkunft verankern
Denkfähigkeit	Einsetzen/nutzen
Kreativität	Im Leben ausdrücken
Lebenskraft	Stärken/nutzen
Individuation	Mensch werden
Gewissen	Mit Liebe und Geist
Körper und Lust	Leben und pflegen
Handlungen	Kompetenz aufbauen

English translation:

Self-perception	Differentiating
Being	Evolving potentials
Love	Establishing power
Spirit – transcendency	Anchoring origin
Capacity of thinking skills	Inserting / using
Creativity	Expressing in life
Power of life	Strengthening / using
Individuation	Becoming human
Conscience	With love and spirit
Body and lust	Living and caring
Activity	Establishing competence

2.2.5. Characteristics of love

Love is a manifold creative constructive life force that must be formed. Love gives meaning and value to life. It makes life worth living and rich.

Love is the key to many "unsolvable" situations. It clarifies precisely, include the future beyond the speedy fulfilment of lust, understands the human being on all sides in a balanced way, achieves something for others and for liveability. Thus, self-love becomes an uplifting charity. It finds an expression in the handling with the nature and the goods, with the animals and plants.

Love respects life in a balanced way. Love integrates in the society the world of children and the elderly. Sick and invalids, as well as those with limited gifts, can discover love and learn to live creatively, like all others in society.

Through this diversity, love works in different directions: For one's own psychical life, for the psychical life of the related persons, for the general living together, for the habitat design, for the political and economic life, for the cultural design and for the religious life.

Creative is the love through the inner experience of the original origin of man. The creation "earth" can be experienced in this transcendental experience of love as a valuable positive expression of life. It is not just created for the afterlife, but also as a habitat for many creative undertakings.

Instead of atomic bombs - the most diabolical work in human history anyway - people can create works of love and of the spirit: As an expression and "adoration" of the origin and eternal spiritual being.

If love is based on self-love, and if the word "self" does not only mean the body and consciously outward-looking life, then love stands on the foundation of psychical life: Love is a creative force for the realization of life. The spirit is the ordering and controlling principle of love. Love is thus the specifically human: As a possibility, as a performance and as a life form.

Reflections and discussion

The characteristics of the power of love are:

☐ Urge for life
☐ Living with the entire mental life
☐ Life with spirit (feedback in dream and meditation)
☐ Life in individuation and for individuation
☐ Expressing inner life out of the individuation
☐ Create living conditions and opportunities outside for individuation
☐ Life out of joy in experiencing the inner wholeness
☐ Life in the anchorage in the inner mind
☐ To shape life outside in the "governmental principle" of the spirit
☐ To design more and more creatively by the inner potential
☐ Life for growth, i.e. for the collective psycho-spiritual evolution
☐ The regulatory force for the collective well-balanced life
☐ Life of inner freedom and autonomy

The lack of inner orientation of man is not only a "question of guilt", but also an expression of the state of evolution, therefore:

☐ Love urges for higher psychical-spiritual levels in the evolutionary process, from archaic humanity to evolutionary humanity.

☐ Evolution does not happen by itself: Man has to take control and design.

☐ Man has the responsibility to take over evolution, which also means he has to push it through with all his efforts.

☐ Love only grows when people, in solidarity with all social instruments, enforce them and integrate them socially.

☐ Love only lives if it is collectively enforced, protected and promoted in cooperation with the spirit.

People protest and strike, fight and work for all sorts of interests, but never for love.

Discuss in the group how space can be created for love in personal and social life, how it can be brought into evolution: a) individually; b) politically; c) religiously

Diagram 2.2.5: Elemental tendencies of the power of love

Diagramm OS9-8: Elementare Tendenzen der Kraft der Liebe

English translation: (From left above to right below)
Establishing joy of life
Unfolding life holistically
Creating habitat from the inside
Living individuation
The power of love
Life anchoring in the spirit
Integrating the psychical organism
Realizing main-Archetype
Implementing transcendency

2.2.6. Love as a complex performance

Most people quickly overlook the fact that love is much more than a feeling. It cannot even be described as a particular feeling, although sometimes well-being is associated with love. Love is also joy in experiencing.

But love is a complex achievement. Love without thinking has little chance to do something solid. Love without spirit is structureless.

Those who want to live with the spirit have to learn to interpret their own dreams and to meditate properly. If you want to love, you must look with concentration and clarity into the inner and outer world. Love also requires an act of will.

Who lives love, looks exactly at the real inner needs, on his acting, on his psychodynamics and on all feelings. In the "raw state" the power of love is archaic, instinctual, brain-physiological pattern.

In real life, love has little chance. This is known by those who have hopefully started a life relationship and then failed. How strong or weak love is, the children, the fringe groups, the homeless and the elderly know.

The message of the love of Christianity could rarely achieve stably in everyday life. Economic life is like a "war". It's about winning market share. Labour struggles are based on interests, rarely on love.

If some want to live love in holidays, then tourism is for others a business that has only one goal: "exploit, as much as possible and by all instruments".

Political life is more "running the gauntlet" and "show business" as an expression of love. For the target achievement, every instrument is right: Lying, cheating, intriguing and shamelessly using every advantage.

Where religions are side by side, there are tensions that often lead to wars.

Love is a force that must be formed in conjunction with all other psychical powers. It also takes into account the forces of social life and the conditions of the habitat. It has to accomplish different achievements depending on the phase of life and activity.

The love must be protected with much vigilance.

Everywhere are people who intend nothing but to destroy all love. In many states, "God Almighty" is in the first paragraph. This implies the individuation and the spirit and the institutionalized formation of love. De facto there is no love.

Reflections and discussion

The unfolding of the power of love requires the formation of all psychical systems:

☐ The perception
☐ The desire / the will
☐ The unconscious
☐ The psychodynamics
☐ The actions

☐ The thinking
☐ The power of integration
☐ The needs
☐ The dream interpretation
☐ The educational methods

Love as an achievement power cannot be considered and lived in isolation:

☐ The design of the habitat for love requires skills.
☐ The "right" consumption requires knowledge (even about oneself).
☐ Love involves the whole life, including the political and economic.
☐ Love is a basic relation to life, not a "feeling".
☐ Love also binds the instruments to the goal.
☐ Love demands social "rules of the game".
☐ Love is to be protected from all forces that only want to destroy.
☐ Love is a collective issue, not just an individual one.

Love as a force is manifold to form:

☐ Already in elementary school
☐ With the sciences
☐ Through personal education
☐ Also specific to marriage / family and education
☐ For the life of all human groups
☐ For the handling with goods
☐ For the designing of the living space
☐ For the integration of the weak, the helpless, the sick and the suffering

Discuss in the group what capabilities are coupled with the power of love:

a) Love relationship / marriage:
b) Recreational activity:
c) Economic life:
d) Workplace design:
e) Political life:

Diagram 2.2.6: The constructive network of love

Diagramm OS9-9: Die konstruktive Vernetzung der Liebe

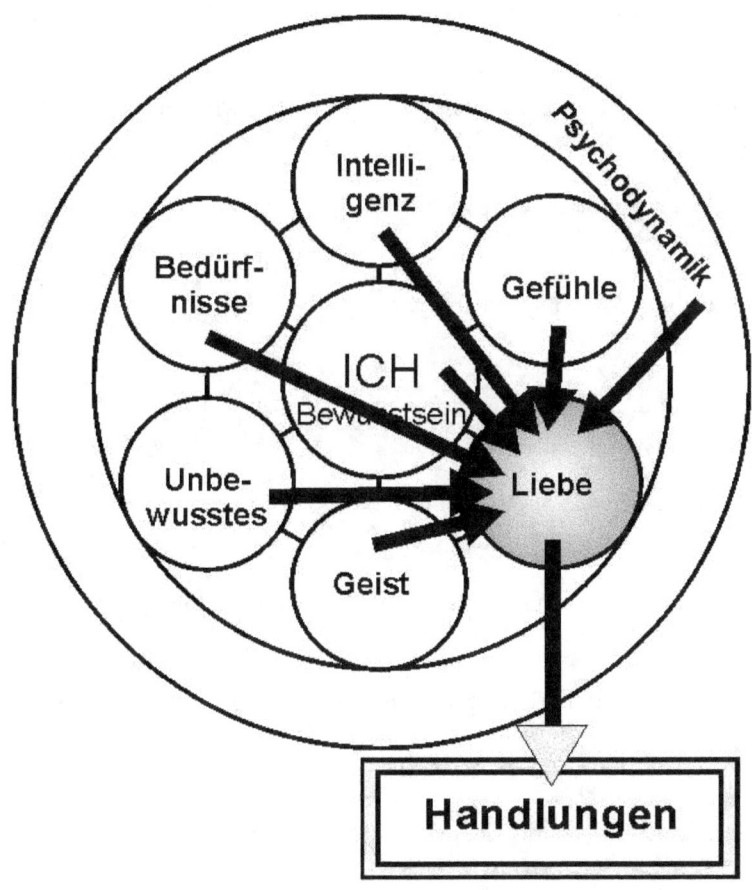

English translation: (From left above to right below)
Psychodynamics & intelligence & needs & emotions & "I"-consciousness & unconscious & spirit affect
Love
affects **activities**

2.2.7. Working unit

2.2.7. Working unit - 1

1. a) How do you love yourself?

1. b) Explain the life forms of self-love with an elementary example:

2. Give each aspect a very concrete example. Man is largely human with his psychical organism. Self-love reaches the psychical wholeness and, in this context, means:

a) Being interested in one's own psychical reality
Example:

b) Attention to one's own psychical powers
Example:

c) Affirming and taking seriously one's own psychical reality
Example:

d) Living consciously with one's own psychical wholeness
Example:

e) Discovering and protecting the values of this psychical life
Example:

f) Nurturing, protecting, developing and promoting one's own psychical powers
Example:

g) Systematically acquiring knowledge and thereby becoming alive
Example:

h) Taking responsibility for one's own psychical reality
Example:

3. Formulate an educational goal for you for self-love in general:

4. a) Imagine the expression of your self-love:

b) Your conclusion in one sentence:

2.2.7. Working unit - 2

1. a) Explain the meaning and value of self-love for life:

1. b) Explain with one example the thesis that self-love is / must be the basis for any other form of love:

2. Formulate with 10 concrete forms of self-love that self-love also has a concrete positive effect on other forms of love.

1)	
2)	
3)	
4)	
5)	
6)	
7)	
8)	
9)	
10)	

3. Formulate an educational goal for the understanding of self-love:

4. a) Imagine the effects of your self-love on life:

b) Your conclusion in one sentence:

2.2.7. Working unit - 3

1. a) How do you experience the power of love as a "transcending activity"?

1. b) Extend the "joy of life" aspect in the context of the transcending power of love:

2. Give 10 short examples of what in society could move people to learn and live the transcending power of love:

1)
2)
3)
4)
5)
6)
7)
8)
9)
10)

3. Formulate an educational goal to use the transcendental power of love:

4. a) Imagine the transcending effects of your power of love:

4. b) Your conclusion in one sentence:

2.2.7. Working unit - 4

1. a) How do you experience the consequences of missing love?

1. b) What is a life without meaning of a "value"? (Watch out, trap!!!)

2. Create a list of values that make sense for life:

a) in personal life (for yourself): ....

b) in social life (relationships, encounters): ....

c) in the design of the habitat: ....

d) in the production and use of goods: ....

e) in political, national and international life: ....

f) another example: ....

3. Formulate an educational goal to promote love in life:

4. a) Imagine the need for love that is still due in your everyday life:

4. b) Your conclusion in one sentence:

2.2.7. Working unit - 5

1. a) How do you experience the variety of possibilities of the power of love?

1. b) Give an example of the power of love in everyday life:

2. Give each aspect a concrete example from everyday life. The characteristics of the power of love are:

a) Urge for life

b) Living with the entire psychical life

c) Living with spirit (feedback in dream and meditation)

d) Life in individuation and for individuation

e) Expressing inner life out of individuation

f) Create external living conditions and opportunities for individuation

g) Life out of joy in experiencing the inner wholeness

h) Living in the anchorage in the inner mind

i) To shape life outside in the "governmental principle" of the spirit

k) To shape more and more creatively from the inner potential

l) Life for growth, i.e. for the collective psycho-spiritual evolution

m) The regulatory force for the collective well-balanced life

n) Life of inner freedom and autonomy

3. Formulate an educational goal to promote the aspects of love:

4. a) Imagine an aspect of the list from a) to n):

4. b) Your conclusion in one sentence:

2.2.7. Working unit - 6

1. a) How do you experience the complexity of love as an active expression of life?

1. b) Expand the consequences of human education with a core idea:

2. Give some concrete capabilities coupled with the power of love to:

a) Love relationship / marriage: ....

b) Leisure: ....

c) Economic life: ....

d) Workplace design: ....

e) Political life: ....

3. Formulate an educational goal for you to "love as a life expression":

4. a) Imagine how people can be made more capable of love:

4. b) Your conclusion in one sentence:

2.2.7. Work unit - 7

The European Council in Brussels has decided that, collectively, love should be of political and practical importance to society in society (in front of the economy). You decide on the following specific programs:

Multiple Choice Test 4

Choose the four correct answers:

4.1. Self-love includes:
☐ a) Interest in one's own life
☐ b) Appreciation of psychical life
☐ c) Consideration for recognition
☐ d) Need for development
☐ e) Conscious self-control
☐ f) No responsibility to others

4.2. The love for life means, among others:
☐ a) Act competently   ☐ b) Act with foresight
☐ c) Making the environment human   ☐ d) Commerce has top priority
☐ e) Living without having   ☐ f) Living with spirit

4.3. "Transcending" means:
☐ a) One should (must) dissolve oneself (the "I").
☐ b) The goal is to rise completely to God.
☐ c) Can overcome something by processing.
☐ d) Living beyond ego values for life values.
☐ e) Anchoring real values in values of individuation.
☐ f) Embedding particular interests in holistic concepts.

4.4. Meaning and value of love include:
☐ a) Truthfulness   ☐ b) Internal growth
☐ c) Spirit principle   ☐ d) Self-abasement
☐ e) Authenticity   ☐ f) be free from solidarity to love

4.5. Characteristics of love include:
☐ a) Joy of life   ☐ b) Individuation living
☐ c) Sexual experience   ☐ d) Realizing the main archetype
☐ e) Renunciation of lust   ☐ f) Spirit order

4.6. The unfolding of love requires:
☐ a) Thorough thinking   ☐ b) God directs everything
☐ c) Clarifying unconscious   ☐ d) Not taking needs too seriously
☐ e) Willpower   ☐ f) Clear view

3. The Unconscious

Essential theses

Everything that we experience pictorially with a certain meaning is stored as an image unit from the time of conception.

All images in the unconscious can activate psychical energy and affect the entire system of the psyche.

Even in the first years of life, the images condense into "prototypes", which then contribute to life as inner patterns of life such as code programs.

The picture variety can be divided into function types:

☐ Life experiences   ☐ Superego (conscience)
☐ Attitudes   ☐ Ideas of man

The images are not directly accessible with thinking and not rationally processing. Only dreams and inner image viewing give access and only with pictures (and symbols) can the pictures be changed.

The more balanced these inner images interact with each other, the more constructive is their energy and thus the thinking, feeling, willing and acting.

3.1. The unconscious psyche

3.1.1. The unconscious as a vessel

You can take a step-by-step journey into your past. Imagine, you can relive your entire lived life, from the present moment to the prenatal time, like in a movie again.

The first steps are simple: One sees with closed eyes some experienced moments from the previous day. Anyone who has some practice with inner image viewing will easily have clear and colourful pictures.

You can see other people with all the concrete frame. You can hear spoken things again. Odours and noise can be perceived. Own thoughts and feelings from the experienced moment appear. From the day before you can go back step by step for more days and see many moments inwardly again and relive in all the essential components.

In this way you can go back month by month, year by year in your own past. All experiences, which at that time had an emotional meaning, reappear pictorially concretely. Long forgotten events are suddenly back, in form, colours and sound.

All childhood can be so rolled up and considered. Even the birth can be relived in this picture-viewing. Then the steps can be ventured into prenatal time.

Images and moods emerge: The spaces where the mother was staying; the father reading the newspaper; a quarrel between father and mother; siblings and neighbours; furniture and clothing of people in the vicinity. Even thoughts, words and feelings of the mother show themselves. For this one experiences one's own feelings once again.

It is an easily detectable fact: A fetus "thinks", feels and experiences in a variety of ways what happens in the environment. Until the day of conception, the entire book of life opens for the one who opens the pages. This forgotten and repressed material is the unconscious.

Everyone carries a huge number of pictures. Anyone who reface his own life will learn that many memories are still as active as the real experiences of that time.

As soon as the events, thoughts and occupations of the past are relived, some of them receive the same psycho-energetic charge as before.

It clearly shows that the past, which was markedly stressful or positively experienced, causes the same feelings in the recall. Suffering, embarrassing situations, emotionally intense thoughts, threatening moments, emotionally overwhelming circumstances, moods of the environment and the like are obviously present in the unconscious.

Herein lies the "code program" of the current life. For this world of images influences man throughout his life.

Reflections and discussion

The unconscious is something like a vessel: From the prenatal time onwards, the human being absorbs experiences that can be sustained throughout his life. Experiences always refer to situations and therefore are pictorial, no matter whether the situation is real or imaginative. Experiences always contain a sense and value experience in existence. The unconscious is generally the reservoir of experience.

Inventory in the unconscious are images with meaning value. Different incriminating meaning entities can be grouped into categories:

Pain	embarrassment	offense	failure
Mortification	punishment	unpleasant	mourning
Suffering	threat	uncertainty	effort

In the unconscious are also stored positive experiences and ideas:

Joy	happiness	success
Pleasant	peace	security
Trust	liberation	beauty

Compensatory to experiences of sadness and frustration (deficits), man with his fantasy also forms ideals and ideals that have not become real. Even such images are imprinted in the unconscious.

Man does not want to see some experiences and ideas again and above all, never to experience them again. He pushes them out of consciousness so that they do not come back into consciousness.

The more stressful and painful an experience or an idea was / is, the harder it will be warded off.

Unexplained images activate psycho-energetically through preconscious perception and similar new experiences.

The images in the unconscious have a certain psycho-energetic charge, depending on the meaning the thing had for the person in the moment of experiencing.

The more an image cannot come back into consciousness, because it contains particularly intense feelings, the stronger is its psychical energy.

An image in itself can be "forgotten". The energy, however, remains an active reality. The "I" cannot control this energy. Therefore, the unconscious seems irrational, unpredictable and incorrigible.

Diagram 3.1.1: Inventory of the unconscious

Diagramm OS8-1: Das Inventar im Unbewussten

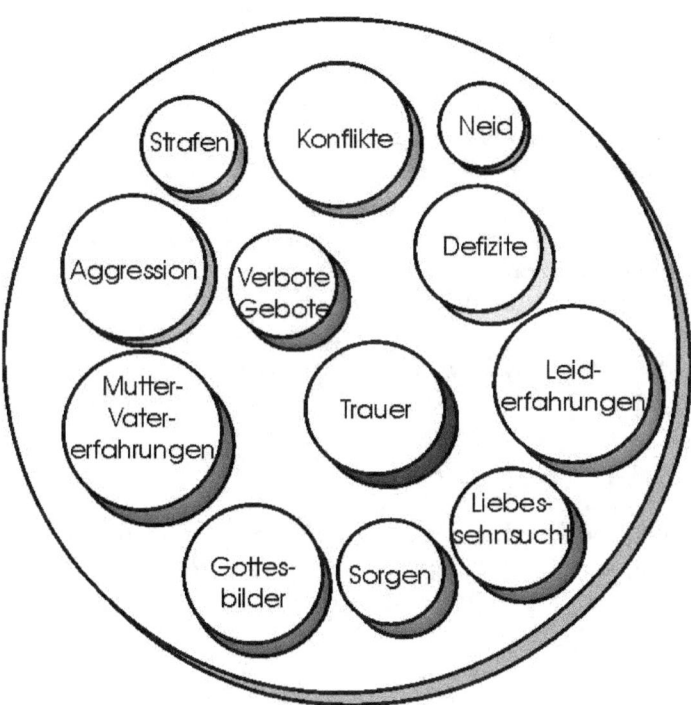

English translation: (From left above to right below)

Punishments	Conflicts	Envy
Aggression	Prohibitions, Order	Deficits
Mother-father experience	Grief	Suffering-
experiences		
Images of God	Sorrows	Longing for love

The unconscious in psychoanalytic view

The "unconscious" receives in the literature various aspects, apart from those psychological schools that simply deny the existence of the unconscious. The core aspects are psychological and philosophical:

1. The psychical real being in general (i.e. a transcendental dimension)
2. In the brain stored, not in the consciousness avaible material
3. The material is repressed, suppressed, pushed away, ignored ...
4. The not-remembered, but rememberable
5. The unrecognized and the unintentional.
6. A power within, source of creativity
7. The never before entered the consciousness, e.g. instinctual, libidinous
8. Especially infantile wishes and fantasies
9. A part of the "I" and the superego
10. A reality that encompasses more than the sum of external experiences

From the tradition of psychoanalysis, we present two views:

Psychoanalysis:

The distinction of the mental in the consciousness and the unconscious is the basic requirement of psychoanalysis. We have learned that there are very strong psychical processes or ideas that can all have consequences for the psychical life, only they are not aware of themselves, because a certain force opposes that they can otherwise become aware.

Thus, we derive our concept of the unconscious from the doctrine of repression. The extrusion is the model of the unconscious. But we see that we have two different unconscious things, the latent, yet able to consciousness, and the repressed, in itself and without further not able to consciousness.

From the "I" go also extrusions out by which certain psychical strivings are to be excluded not only from consciousness, but also from other forms of validity and activity. This resistance comes from the "I" and belongs to it. In the "I" itself is something that behaves just as the repressed, i.e. expresses strong effects without becoming aware of itself.

Analytical psychology:

The personal unconscious contents lost memories, repressed and deliberately forgotten, embarrassing ideas, so-called below threshold (subliminal) perceptions, i.e. sense perceptions, which were not strong enough to reach the consciousness and contents, which were not conscious mature enough.

The unconscious corresponds to polymorphic figures of the shadows in the dreams.

Certainly, the unconscious is not dangerous under all circumstances; but as soon as a neurosis appears, it is a sign, that the unconscious has a special accumulation of energy, namely a kind of charge, that can explode.

In all common cases is the unconscious only unfavourable or dangerous, because we are in opposition to it. To be unconnected with the unconscious means loss of instinct. and roots.

The unconscious is always active and creates new combinations of its materials which serve the determination of the future.

Considering aspects of the unconscious

If we collect in the psychoanalytical literature the modules to the issue of the unconscious, we find outstanding parts, depending the specific theory. We can describe these "parts", "issues" and "forces" as considering aspects of the unconscious. We list the most important ones:

- ☐ The unconscious inventory, so all kinds of "normal" life experiences
- ☐ The so-called complexes, i.e. the painful, "unsaved" experiences
- ☐ Specific life experiences, which dealing with the sexual drive
- ☐ Especially difficult child-parent-relations, with denial-bonding-ambivalence
- ☐ Deficit experience of generally basic needs
- ☐ The underlying conscience (super-ego), first by the father-relationship
- ☐ The internalization of religious images and practices as truth
- ☐ Inferiority feelings that tend to turn into power needs
- ☐ Overemphasized affective constricting attachment of a parent to the child
- ☐ Voluptuous interest in oneself, in others and in the world of life
- ☐ Cramped unilateral pleasure bonds
- ☐ "I"-ideal images of all kinds; in addition: one-sided positive misperceptions
- ☐ Wishes in all conceivable directions (allowed, unauthorized, fulfilled, unfulfilled).
- ☐ Emotional bonds through fear of punishment and fear of life.

- Bindings through primary relationships of trust and love
- Unredeemed guilt, subjective and objective
- General unwanted but pleasant (interesting) sensory experiences
- A "secret" defence mechanism that keeps content out of the unconscious
- "I" aspects that are unrecognized or averted (shadows, masks, etc.)
- Injured, offended self-esteem aspects
- Shifts / transformations (of a complex) into other topics
- Indirect, difficult to recognize utterances: e.g. somatization, constraints
- A psychical energy that acts according to the inventory element
- A (often very) strong imbalance between the unconscious and the consciousness.
- The distortion of the 'truth' into the opposite.

Our thesis:

The most peculiar characteristic of the unconscious is that the "I" undertakes everything to deny its contents, its current modes of action and the defence mechanisms belonging to the "I", whatever the cost!

Causes of the acting of the defence mechanisms are:

Fear: Not having brought one's own existence to the full and mature development to which we are called.

Guilt: From the failure resp. non-fulfilment of the request for existence; i.e. an existential guiltiness (not law / moral guilt!).

General narcissism: Excessive pleasure in one's ego (or parts of it) combined with the inability or unwillingness to perceive resp. wants to perceive the reality in its fullness (lack of interest).

Principal rebellion against the vital demand for mental-spiritual education.

The refusal of the "I" to fit into a 'higher' cosmic order.

The intuitive suspecting of the powerfully active forces from the unconscious of all.

Phylogenetically conditioned archaic stage: Lack of trained instincts, a chaotic, unrestrained greed for having, experiencing pleasure, exploiting, taking possession, being dominated, let off steam.

Notes and perspectives

How does man (on average) experience his unconscious?

Write down the key words in this subchapter:

What causes the neglect or ignoring the unconscious?

Reflecting on one's own unconscious is essential because: ...

What did you learn about the unconscious in your parents' home, school and church?

What meaning in living together has the conversation about the unconscious?

What are the unconsciously held (repressed) topics in politics and economics?

How does advertising deal with the modes of action of the unconscious of people?

Formulate an important question for the unconscious:

3.1.2. The inventory in the unconscious

The enormous richness and quantity of images from the lived life urges the question of an order. We can arrange the material how we can divide the habitat into systems, or how we can classify the different contents of consciousness. Different category systems are possible.

We choose a simple model that has proven to be practicable from hundreds of "journey to the past" with numerous people from our own practice.

Remarkable are at first the scarcely countable life experiences of all kinds. These are situations in one's own living space, in the environment of school and workplace, in churches and rooms, where an eventful life takes place. Here we place our own actions and the actions of other people.

The wealth is still enormous: Punishments, learning situations, recreational situations, food rituals, religious celebrations, festivals, political events in one's own place and on television, moments of being in love, sexual experiences, efforts and omissions, etc. Some of these pictures are painful, many are joyful.

We call a second group of images the superego. These are those internalized situations where it was said, "Thou shalt not do that ... obey this commandment ... obey this rule ... obey or you will be punished ... that is good ... who that is, is evil ... ".

This is how the conscience forms from early childhood. There are usually also conflicting images available. Childhood demands are like a foundation for later norms and "laws of life". Later self-imposed norms overlay this diversity.

A third category of images represent people as they all experience: The father in many situations, other fathers too; the mother and other mothers; the grandparents and other old people; the teachers, the pastors, the doctors, the dentists, the officials and many typical professionals such as the farmer, the baker, the garagist and so on.

These pictures are grouped into "prototypes", emotionally partly positive and partly negatively charged.

The fourth group of pictures we call "attitudes". The images contain an attitude of man to all the elements that belong to life: "So is life ... man ... everyday life ... religion ...".

At the same time, complementary images are formed in each person. These are such ideas that contain another desirable state: "So I want it to be". Many of these attitudes are not thought out, but adopted from the environment: the parents ... the teachers ... the pastors ... the friends said that's the way it should be, so it's good and right.

Reflections and discussion

The internalized and internal created images (fantasies) can be divided into different groups. We focus on the following main categories:

☐ The life experiences   ☐ The people pictures
☐ The superego (conscience)   ☐ The attitudes

Each category has specific functions that distinguish the category from the other. In all categories, "prototypes" of experience and compensatory ideals are formed. The images push for realization or repetition.

The life patterns net the space of general life experiences via:

Family life	relationship life	work	leisure
Politics	economy	state	culture
Sexuality	society	school	church

The human images form "prototypes" and roles:

Man	woman	mother	father	child

The super-ego is the place, where norms, commands, prohibitions, judiciary behaviour and sanctions are grouped. The images have obligatory claim. They differ in "good" and "evil" resp. "Bad" and "right" and "wrong in the normative sense.

The attitudes are the valuing patterns over the life:

So should be life	That's the life
That is how man should be	That's the man
So should be the transcendence	That's the transcendence

Images that are especially emotionally charged and therefore repelled by consciousness are called "complexes". They affect destructive throughout.

All images in the unconscious have a tendency to repeat themselves or unconsciously act as an inner orientation. Each new life experience is built into the existing imagery and determined with the already formed patterns.

A checklist for the inventory in the unconscious

We lean on the so-called "association experiment" of analytical psychology and construct an exercise:

Part 1 of the exercise: Write a spontaneous word for each word that comes to your mind, as quickly as possible and without 'censorship'!

Emotive words list:

head		mountain		part	
green		to die		old	
water		salt		flower	
to sing		new		to beat	
death		custom		box	
long		to pray		wild	
ship		money		family	
To pay		stupid		to wash	
window		notebook		cow	
friendly		to despise		strange	
table		finger		luck	
to ask		expensive		to lie	
village		bird		decency	
cold		to fall		closely	
stem		book		brother	
to dance		unfairly		to fear	
lake		frog		stork	
sick		to divorce		false	
proud		hunger		fear	
to cook		white		to kiss	
ink		child		bride	
nasty		to look out		purely	
needle		pencil		door	
to swim		sad		to choose	
travel		plum		hay	
blue		to marry		satisfied	
lamp		house		mockery	

to sin		dear		to sleep	
bread		glass		month	
rich		to fight		pretty	
tree		fur		woman	
to sting		large		to rant	
pity		turnip			
yellow		to paint			

Part 2 of the Exercise: Write a small imaginative story using all the words you have entered in this list. The order of words used is unimportant. Delete the word in the list as soon as you have written it in a sentence. Several of these words may be used in one sentence.

Part 3 of the exercise: What does your fantasized story tell about your life story? (This part can also be worked out together in a group).

Diagram 3.1.2: The balance of the unconscious

Abbildung OS8-25: Das Gleichgewicht des Unbewussten

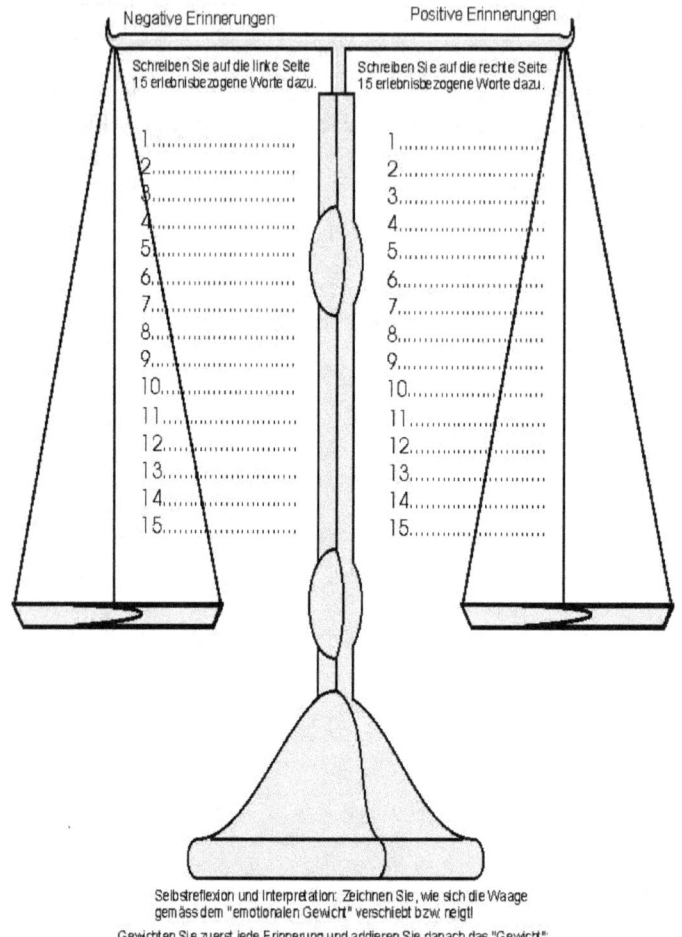

Negative Erinnerungen   Positive Erinnerungen

Schreiben Sie auf die linke Seite 15 erlebnisbezogene Worte dazu.

Schreiben Sie auf die rechte Seite 15 erlebnisbezogene Worte dazu.

1.......................   1.......................
2.......................   2.......................
3.......................   3.......................
4.......................   4.......................
5.......................   5.......................
6.......................   6.......................
7.......................   7.......................
8.......................   8.......................
9.......................   9.......................
10.......................   10.......................
11.......................   11.......................
12.......................   12.......................
13.......................   13.......................
14.......................   14.......................
15.......................   15.......................

Selbstreflexion und Interpretation: Zeichnen Sie, wie sich die Waage gemäss dem "emotionalen Gewicht" verschiebt bzw. neigt!

Gewichten Sie zuerst jede Erinnerung und addieren Sie danach das "Gewicht": Punkte: 5= sehr; 4= übermässig; 3= mittel; 2= nicht sonderlich; 1= wenig gewichtig

English translation:
Negative memories
Note to this on the left side
15 words of lived experiences
Self-Reflection and Interpretation:

Positive memories
Note to this on the right side
15 words of lived experiences

Draw the displacement resp. dip of the scale corresponding to the "emotional weight"!

Weight first each memory and add then the "Weight": Points:
5 = very much, 4 = excessive, 3 = medium, 2 = not odd, 1 = few graw

Notes and perspectives

What are the predominant life experiences of humans?

Write down the key words in this subchapter:

What causes an imbalance of the positive and negative inventory in the unconscious?

Reflecting on attitudes and beliefs is essential because: ...

What did you learn in the home, school and church about the effects of images in the unconscious?

What significance does the conversation about life patterns have in living together?

Which life ideals predominate in politics and economy?

What does advertising convey about positive and negative life patterns?

Formulate an important question for you to re-create the content in the subconscious:

3.1.3. The modes of action of the unconscious

Past events, which emotionally move in the inner experience of pictures, can be energetically neutralized by meditative processing. This is done by understanding, clarifying, reconciling, accepting and saying goodbye.

After that, the images can be visualized internally, without affecting emotive.

Another way of experiencing to the "discharge" of such images is to start from a current problem situation (a feeling, a psychosomatic reaction, a disorder) and look for the cause within the inner image. Thus, those moments of experience which have bound psychical energy become pictorial.

You can also call keywords as triggers: Father, mother, being child, love, punishment and so on. If a word moves a feeling, one can fetch in the picture-seeing the earlier situations, which are accordingly "loaded".

From this one recognizes a fact: Many past and forgotten life circumstances activate themselves psycho-energetically, as soon as they are addressed by an external influence.

From these experiences with the energy charge of past life circumstances we can conclude that the inventory in the unconscious lives like fishes in the sea. Large fishes dominate the small ones, aggressive ones eat the peaceful ones and many fishes swim in many directions.

In other words, many images create opposing forces inside, causing tension and "surface" problems.

The active images press hard the "I". They force repetition, the realization of what was inside an image and earlier an inner or outer reality.

The inventory is thus not merely "ballast" or "memory", but the "motor" of thinking, of feeling, of actions and also of the energetic cause of psycho-somatic suffering.

Who wants willingly and voluntarily to look at his entire life lived again and feel again emotional? Only a few dos that.

The norm is that the lived past is "forgotten". Every day almost everyone tries to keep the cover of this vessel tightly closed.

Since the inventory "lives" to a certain extent, these "ghosts" work in a roundabout way: They create fears, depressions, moods, constraints, behavioural problems, relationship disorders, projections and repetitions in acting.

What man has experienced from others; he lets others feel.

What he has absorbed and not consciously changed is the reality that must be reproduced: In thought systems, in rules, in laws, in the way of life. What one does not want to see in oneself, because it may not be, can be seen in others.

Reflections and discussion

If the images are psycho-energetically charged in the unconscious, they act in different ways:

- ☐ on the other psychic forces or subsystems
- ☐ on the actions
- ☐ on the body and organ functions
- ☐ on the people in the living environment
- ☐ on the psycho-energetic space in the environment

If an energy charge cannot express itself according to the image, then this energy shifts and manifests itself disfigured.

All images that are not clarified, reconciled, purged, and balanced have the tendency to be disturbing without the "I" is able to influence it with an act of will. The inner lack of freedom of man is based essentially on the inner connection to this irrationally active world of images. Projections are a phenomenon of this internal disturbing effect.

Experience without burdensome value, positive images and adjusted life experiences become entities in the unconscious that can be taken into consciousness. They serve as "preconscious" orientation patterns, in a sense as valuable "life treasures". Much of this can be called "wisdom," i.e. "evaluated life knowledge".

Cleaned images affect not irrational or disruptive, but constructive and progressive. Life competence is not only a question of behavioural skills but also of life knowledge.

The unconscious therefore has a positive vital function. It is also a source of inspiration and intuition.

Man cannot live independently outside this inner world of images, just as he cannot communicate without a learned language.

In consciousness are more images than linguistic signs. These images are part of the internalized reality in consciousness.

The pictures act like a code program on the psychical system.

Therefore, one can say: "The past determines the present".
Or: "Everyone takes his past with him from prenatal time, wherever he goes".

Diagram 3.1.3: Directions of effects of the unconscious

Diagramm OS8-3: Wirkungsrichtungen des Unbewussten

Merke:
Ist das Inventar im Unbewussten "kritisch",
so hat dies immer belastende Folgen.

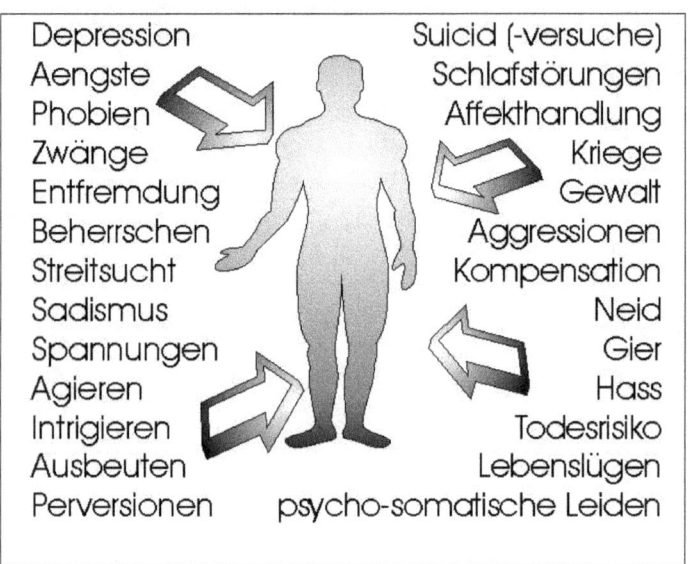

Depression	Suicid (-versuche)
Aengste	Schlafstörungen
Phobien	Affekthandlung
Zwänge	Kriege
Entfremdung	Gewalt
Beherrschen	Aggressionen
Streitsucht	Kompensation
Sadismus	Neid
Spannungen	Gier
Agieren	Hass
Intrigieren	Todesrisiko
Ausbeuten	Lebenslügen
Perversionen	psycho-somatische Leiden

English translation: Notice:
Is the inventory in the unconscious "critically",
than the consequences are always stressing:

Depression	Suicide (attempt)
Fears	Sleep disorder
Phobia	Emotional act
Compulsions	Wars
Alienation	Violence
Dominating	Aggressions
Quarrelsomeness	Compensation
Sadism	Envy
Tensions	Greed
Acting	Hate
Plotting	Risk of death

Exploiting
Perversions

Lies of life
Psycho-somatic sufferings

The agitating of the unconscious

The unconscious, i.e. the inventory in the unconscious, according to the definition has "charged" psychical energy, in the mode of action depending on the meaning of the content.

In the following, we will present a list of "disturbances" that often, but certainly not always and rarely alone, has to do with this force.

The defence mechanisms themselves act, a fact that is almost always rejected by the "I". Then certainly missing or wrongly shaped competences are also involved in disturbances, e.g. in (through) the communication.

Even life itself daily provides many disruptive factors. The list should be thought-provoking where it seems important to the student.

List of errors, conflicts and difficulties:

• lack of concentration	• constipation
• fundamentalist thinking	• general inability to be loyal
• memory weakness	• shortness of breath
• revenge behaviour	• strong emotional lability
• fear of life	• pressure on chest / in the abdomen
• sudden violent palpitations	• excessive experience hunger
• phobias	• mourning
• excessive sweating	• theatrical behaviour
• work inhibitions	• exhaustion reaction
• communication inhibitions	• tics
• unlust	• self-insecurity
• authority conflicts	• greed
• envy	• inhibitions
• nervousness	• authority faith
• hate	• excessive introversion
• violence behaviour	• fascist thinking
• infantile behaviour	• excessive extraversion
• rape	• cheat
• insomnia	• weakness of will
• compulsion to asceticism	• inability to order
• eat too much	• greed for consumption
• life negation	• increased risk behaviour
• smoke excessively	• narcissism
• aggression of all kinds	• exploitation of other people

• excessive alcohol consumes	• overcontrolled lifestyle
• humble others, humiliate	• disability of relations
• tensions	• impotence
• compulsive jealousy	• repeated adultery
• migraine	• being down
• suicides / attempts	• inability to take responsibility
• depression	• excessive need for validity
• torture others mentally	• value indifference
• explosive reactions	• can nothing 'pull through'
• paternalistic behaviour	• reject strong people
• constraints	• erratic chaotic life
• maternalistic dominance	• compulsion to be brave
• intrigue	• lust hostility
• indifference to humanity	• constant rigid criticizing
• lie	• chronic guilt feelings
• gross pollution	• principles "rider"
• political abuse of power	• red light milieu addiction
• power / dominance	• fanaticism
• talkativeness	• self-righteousness
• feeling of inferiority	• mythological-dogma belief

Oedipus and Elektra in the game

One of the first basic life experiences is the parent relationship. Every human being forms his first (also sexual) identity, his role patterns in the I-You relationship and its dynamics in the small group behaviour.

Boys and girls each build up their own relationship with mother and father, sometimes emotionally stronger to the father, sometimes stronger to the mother. It depends on the relationship between the parents, including the masculinity and femininity that the parents live.

The mother is the first source of food and oral pleasure. The father brings the money home; that is the beginning of sexism in patriarchal society. This is the first source of erotic pleasure for the boy and for the girl.

The father likes to dominate his wife; the mother may terrorize her husband with suffering. Even the toddler experiences the tensions between the parents, especially the suppression of sexual desire.

It may be that the parents live their sexuality 'neurotically' and behave according to fixed rigid values or norms. The child receives many signals in this regard, speechless and incomprehensible.

From this different relation variants of the child to the parents develop. The boy wants to protect (or comfort) the mother, loving her more than the father; the girl the other way around with the father.

"I am better / more affectionate than the father / mother", so a first attitude develops. The respective parent takes this well and occupies this affection with "libido", with life and energy of Lust.

At the same time, the child experiences a threat from the other parent: Punishment is in the air. Fear is the result. From one parent attitudes or suffering are internalized, from the other the threat (fear), which at the same time forms the superego (prohibitions, commandments).

But as with the mother's milk, superego parts are also taken from the mother (not only from the father!).

In neurotic development, the basic patterns of attitudes and behaviour deepen. The child wants to take the place of the rejected parent in order to make the libidinally bound other part happy.

Binding need and autonomy attempt alternate, identification with the mother or with the father, perhaps alternately in the struggle for rivalry, creates early childhood tragic suffering.

When the child grows up later, then on the one hand the behavioural repertoire is imprinted, on the other hand the early childhood story is present in the unconscious.

The conflict, all early childhood stages, is repeated in a new form with the current relationship partner.

The mate choice itself cannot take place outside this pattern. Usually, foreign relations limitations are not respected, indeed the unconscious has an urge to influence in foreign difficult relationships according to this pattern.

The unconscious dynamics do not distinguish between past and present; the dynamics contain:

Pleasure and unpleasure, punishment and fear, hunger and emptiness, "I"-ideals and "ego-bad", prohibitions and desires, identification and object occupation, hostile tints to sadistic impulses, open surrender or covert refusal, longing for attachment and release from attachment.

The man wants to find his manhood and his strength; the woman her femininity and attractiveness.

Thus, the same dynamics of power are repeated in same-sex leisure and business relationships: One cannot let oneself and / or the other one become strong / stronger, least of all promote others in their position and development.

The man practices wars in politics / business / industry to take revenge at his mother and his father, kills other "fathers" and competitors to be "the big father" himself.

The woman from inner emptiness becomes mother and housekeeper of her husband.

She wants to be desired and attractive. The continuation of the Oedipus / Elektra drama! Sometimes with war.

The daughter may get the feeling from the father and the son from the mother to be somebody special.

It should never be revealed what the parents really are in their mental and spiritual development. The father is right; the mother is the best. That's how it should be.

If religion comes into play early on, this relation constellation is transferred to the incumbents and to God.

High esteem, peculiarity through being chosen, task and duty, renunciation of instinct and care, need of protection with fear of life, feelings of guilt and longing for redemption ensure the maintenance of the early childhood relation pattern.

Notes and perspectives

What do we see in the daily collective life about the action of the unconscious?

Write down the key words in this subchapter:

What are the general images (patterns) in the unconscious of the people (the majority) that are not clarified and unedited?

Searching and working with introspection life experiences of early childhood is essential because: ...

What have you learned in the home, school and church about the causes of disturbances, conflicts and difficulties?

What meaning in living together has the conversation about the acting of the unconscious?

How does the unconscious of actors in politics and economy act?

What does advertising convey about the parent-child relationship?

Formulate an important question for the early childhood:

3.1.4. Exercises

1. Which memories from your former time appear now and then spontaneously?

2. What times in your life do you no longer want to look at?

3. You see your whole lived life in a movie. What touches this idea off?

4. Are there topics from your lived life that you did not meditate on?

5. You see all the people you have ever met. What touches this off?

6. How do you experience your conscience emotionally?

7. What were the decisive attitudes of your parents, teachers, pastors etc.?

8. How do all your pictures affect the "good life", "God", the "good man"?

9. A look into the unconscious: mark what is probably meaningful to you.

☐ Strong mother bonding through duty, deficit, longing, dedication, feelings etc.
☐ Painful, intense experiences (mentally and / or physically painful)
☐ Concise embarrassing life experiences related to sexuality
☐ Difficult child-parent relationships, with denial-binding ambivalence
☐ Deficit experiences of general basic psychic needs
☐ Strict, controlling and severe punitive conscience
☐ Religious images that easily activate feelings such as longing and guilt
☐ Feelings of inferiority, always experiencing oneself in comparison to others
☐ Overemphasized (or under-emphasized) affective bonding on the part of a parent
☐ Absence of interest in oneself, in others and in the world of life
☐ Lots of experience of dishonesty, lies, cheating, exploiting etc.
☐ Unreachable "I"-ideal (I want to be like ...)
☐ Intolerance, xenophobia and self-righteousness in the living environment
☐ One-sided, overpowering positive or negative self-perceptions
☐ Unauthorized and therefore unfulfilled desires from education
☐ Emotional attachments through fear of punishment and / or fear of life
☐ Strong inner attachment to externally long separated love relationships
☐ Unsaved guilt (fast diffuse feelings of guilt), subjective and objective
☐ Strong ambivalent aversion to the opposite sex
☐ Lack of interest in intuition, feelings, dreams, imagination
☐ "Shadows" occasionally breaking through (anger, grumbling, glee, defiance etc.)
☐ Injured, offended self-esteem (i.e., slightly offended, irritable, vulnerable)
☐ Strongly focused on consumption, sports, hobbies, materialism, religious practices, work
☐ Indifference to the fundamental values of human dignity and integrity
☐ Little active (or flooded) awareness of the lived life
☐ Paternalistic and / or maternalistic dominance

What do you feel about the overview of these topics?

What does your emotional response to this list of topics mean?

10. Indications for internal stress. Take the list of errors, conflicts and difficulties. Find out what applies to you:

10.a) Regular:
How do you explain that?

10.b) Sometimes:
How do you explain that?

10.c) Rarely:

Interpret your overall situation:

Outline solutions where something should be done:

11. Balance of the unconscious.

11.a) Spontaneously write down five important negative memories:

11.b) Spontaneously write down five positive memories:

11.c) What is the balance between negative and positive memories?

11.d) How can you create the missing balance? Give five suggestions:

Multiple Choice Test 5

Choose the four correct answers:

5.1. The unconscious as a vessel. The following statements are considered to be fundamental to the topic:

☐ a) The inventory in the subconscious are images and pictorial realities.
☐ b) In the unconscious store only painful life experiences.
☐ c) The unconscious can be neglected in the way of life.
☐ d) Even from prenatal time the unconscious absorbs experiences.
☐ e) Unprocessed images in the unconscious bind shaped psychical energy.
☐ f) The unconscious works without its own moral and rational control.

5.2. The inventory in the subconscious. The following subsystems belong to the subsystem "the unconscious":

☐ a) The non-perceived
☐ b) Superego
☐ c) Attitudes
☐ d) Human images
☐ e) Life experiences
☐ f) Thinking operations

5.3. The effectiveness of the unconscious. The burdened unconscious acts:

☐ a) Not on the body
☐ b) On all actions
☐ c) On the psychodynamics
☐ d) To other people
☐ e) Through its energy
☐ f) On the whole psyche

3.2. The dominant unconscious

3.2.1. Picture pattern and effect dynamics

The unconscious - as the pictorial reservoir of experiences - is the sum of all life experiences from prenatal time. This includes all forms of pictorial, situational, imaginative, emotional and judgmental experience.

That is, the unconscious is the part of the memory that contains this kind of inventory. There is nothing in this unconscious that was not previously conscious or sensually absorbed, or perhaps was absorbed vaguely and undifferentiated. The quality of this awareness is different. It depends on the concentration, the language and the cognitive abilities to "grasp" the corresponding reality.

Basically, the reverse process is possible: What was once in the consciousness, then embedded in the unconscious, can be brought back into consciousness, so it is "able to awareness". However, there are considerable differences: A part of this inventory is easy to recall, a part only with voluntary effort, and a part only with systematically used methods (dream interpretation, transference).

Each image material contains different elements: The image, the meaning, the value, the subjective meaning, the feeling. This means that such elements always activate and shape psychical energy. With the storage in this memory (picture reservoir) and the "forgetting" the energy remains.

The greater the valence of an image, the greater the energy charge. In addition, the characteristic of the formed energy corresponds to the meaning of the picture: Loving experiences have a pleasant (just "loving") energy, aggressive or highly unpleasant pictures (e.g. anger, embarrassment) have a correspondingly negatively shaped energy.

The energy itself tends to decompose, to some extent dissolve. But if the picture is neither processed nor clarified and reconciled, then it has a high ability to reactivate. Each new, equal and distant similarity of a new situation (of a new image) reactivates the energy charge of the original image.

The stronger the negative experience, the stronger the defence acts and prevents a return to consciousness. What remains active is the formed psychical energy. Images are as necessary and meaningful to life as language.

Reflections and discussion

The graphical material in the "reservoir" is grouped into four main areas, which in turn are subdivided into subgroups. All new pictorial realities are stored according to the meaning of the same and similar content:

☐ Life experiences   ☐ human images
☐ Superego   ☐ attitudes
☐ Ideals

☐ The characteristics of the inventory in the subconscious are:

☐ Pictorially   ☐ life reference
☐ Experience   ☐ sense
☐ Subjective meaning   ☐ value
☐ Sense

Basically, all inventory is able to awareness. This depends on the meaning of the image, the defence forces, the methods and also personality characteristics (e.g. from the psychodynamics).

Each image activates and forms psychical energy that discharges itself in different forms:

☐ Automatic solution   ☐ repetition
☐ Suspended activity   ☐ conversion to symptoms
☐ Irritated activity   ☐ eruptive activity

The mode of action is independent of:

☐ Will and desire   ☐ rationality
☐ "I" control   ☐ positive / negative value
☐ Real or imagined reality

Emotionally extra significant images form "complexes." A single painful or intense experience can form a complex.

In many cases, complexes are formed by frequent repetition of the same experience (in ever new variations). This starts in the earliest childhood.

Complexes can often only be retrieved to consciousness through special effort.

Group: Collect the negative effects of the subconscious in the areas:

a) Body / organs:

b) Psychical forces:

c) Actions:

Group: Collect the positive effects of the subconscious in the areas of:

a) Body / organs:

b) Psychical forces:

c) Actions:

Diagram 3.2.1: Cleared and uncleared unconscious

Diagramm OS8-4: Geklärtes und ungeklärtes Unbewusstes

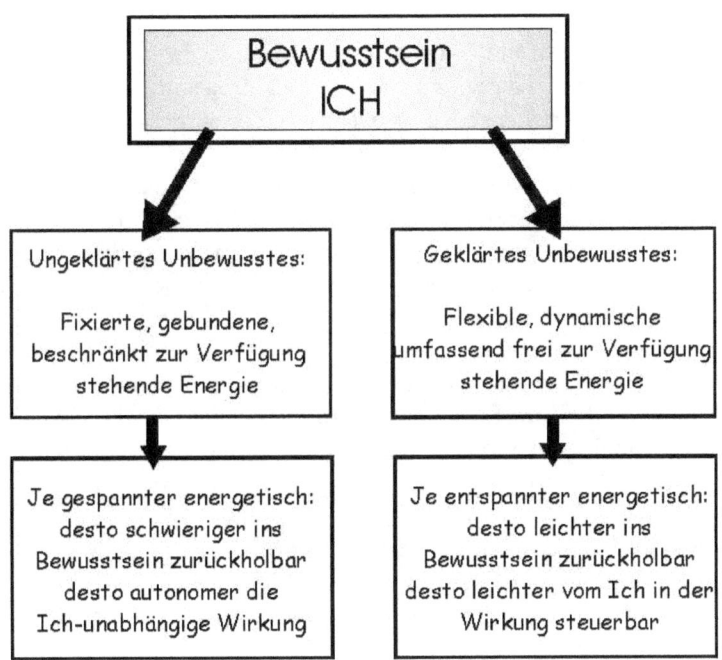

English translation:
Consciousness / "I" affects:

Uncleared unconscious:	**Cleared unconscious:**
Fixed, bond	Flexible, dynamic,
limited available energy	free comprehensive energy
➢ affecting	
The more tensed energetically:	The more relaxed energetically:
the more difficult to bring	the easier to bring
back to the consciousness,	back to the consciousness,
the more autonomic the	the easier to regulate
"I"-independent Impact	the impact by the "I"

3.2.2 The life experiences

The first experiences of man begin prenatally: this is the mother, the father, the environment; that is how the mother feels; that is the atmosphere and there are other people. Even before birth man has an identity experience, is aware of his wholeness, independent of the mother.

Through birth the experience of life changes: From being in the womb of the mother to being in the world. Every day the baby absorbs impressions and moods, hears words and experiences love or hate, peace or aggression.

The first experiences of the environment form the first images in the unconscious: A hundred, a thousand, a ten thousand and always more. With physical and psychical growth, the child experiences and interprets this reality in its subjective meaning, depending on his status. This process is called education, socialization and enculturation.

The reality of life becomes more and more extensive with age, first the school, then the expanded leisure field, then the professional life, the church and later the increasingly autonomously designed own habitat: Living, working, relationships and so on.

Many life experiences are associated with irksome feelings. There are moments of sadness, anger, embarrassment, failure and so on. But there are also positive experiences: Satisfaction, warmth, happiness, success, pleasure and much more.

In addition, each child has fantasies, experiences thoughts pictorially and interprets the recorded reality child appropriated linguistically and pictorially.

These pictures form "prototypes" about life. What life is (existence) has its own interpretation and experience for every human being.

The variety of images becomes confusing, heterogeneous and contradictory. Right from the beginning, the psycho-energetic "space" forms in the human being. The one pictures become complexes. Other images have a balanced content. Some pictures are disturbing, irritating, de-structuring.

Many images can be constructive as orientation. Thus, inside is formed a reality about the being and this inner pictorial reality urges the human to repetition, to constructive continuation and often also to conflictive new developments. Being is "experiencing realities". Thus, everybody has his own inner pictorial reality.

Reflections and discussion

Every human being absorbs pictures about the realities from prenatal time on. Central topics are:

- ☐ Parents, siblings, relatives, neighbours, acquaintances
- ☐ Habitat, environment, world
- ☐ Goods, things, utensils, clothes, money
- ☐ Acting of the people
- ☐ Lifestyle, daily design,
- ☐ Cultural goods: conventions, customs, pictures, music

The life experiences contain different aspects:

- ☐ Feelings
- ☐ Values
- ☐ Sense
- ☐ Subjective meaning
- ☐ Interpretations
- ☐ Effects

The images can be distressing in various aspects:

woebegone	painful	sad
embarrassing	frustrating	threatening
Failure experience	humiliating	hurtful

Many pictures also have a very positive experience:

- ☐ Joy
- ☐ Satisfaction
- ☐ love
- ☐ success experience
- ☐ lust
- ☐ interest

The pictures of life experiences look like a "code program":

- ☐ through its psycho-energetic charge
- ☐ through its "responsiveness"
- ☐ by its familiarity as orientation (known-unknown)
- ☐ attractive or repellent to action and experience through its meaning
- ☐ through its information as an interpretation scheme

The images can be processed consciously and targeted. This can change this inner "programming". The paths are eidetic (pictorial), since the inventory has pictorial character:

☐ Meditation (Imagination)

☐ Processing with dreams

Discuss the future-oriented effects of:

a) Life experiences in childhood and adolescence

b) Life experiences as a young adult (about 18-35 years)

c) Life experiences until mid-life (about 35-55 years)

Diagram 3.2.2: Elements of life experiences

Diagramm OS8-5: Elemente der Lebenserfahrungen

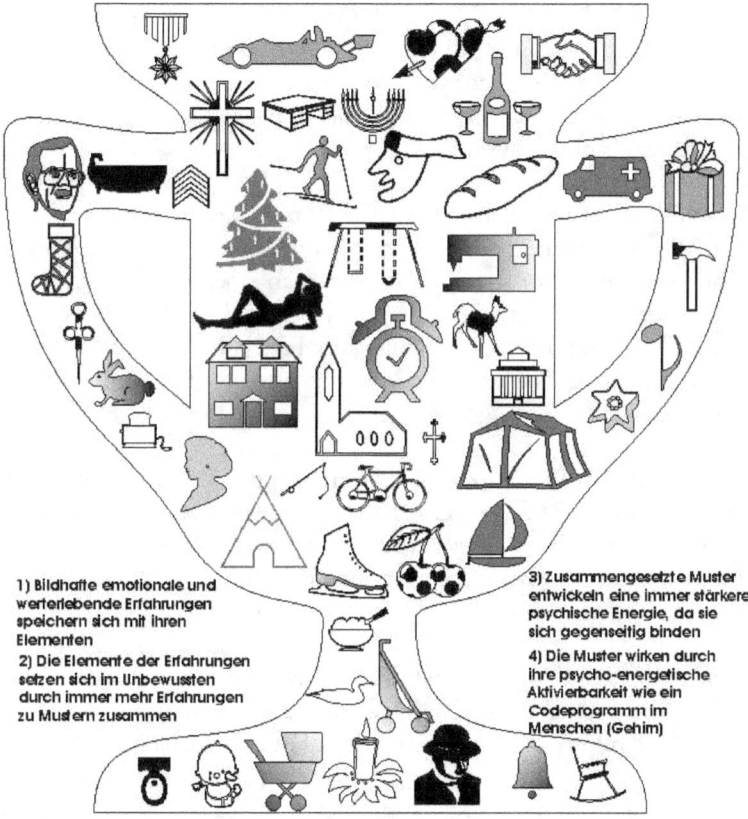

1) Bildhafte emotionale und werterlebende Erfahrungen speichern sich mit ihren Elementen

2) Die Elemente der Erfahrungen setzen sich im Unbewussten durch immer mehr Erfahrungen zu Mustern zusammen

3) Zusammengesetzte Muster entwickeln eine immer stärkere psychische Energie, da sie sich gegenseitig binden

4) Die Muster wirken durch ihre psycho-energetische Aktivierbarkeit wie ein Codeprogramm im Menschen (Gehirn)

English translation:
1) Pictorial emotional and valuing experiences are memorized with its elements
2) In the unconscious the elements of experiences consist of more and more experiences to patterns
3) Composite patterns develop more and more intensive psychical energy by reciprocal bonds
4) The patterns act with its psycho-energetic possibility to activate them as a code-program in humans (brain)

3.2.3. Superego and the conscience

What man experiences as a "conscience" may perhaps be regarded as an inescapable duty for him, as the "voice of God" or as an experience of "absolute values". That is not the case in fact. Duty experience and conscience are not the same. The conscience is to be understood first of all from the point of view of the learning processes, whereby a certain kind of image units are addressed in the unconscious.

Early on, every child takes up norms, laws, laws and rules of conduct from the environment. The one pictures say: "That's good"; others include: "This is evil / bad". This includes taboos, i.e. parts that man does not look at, not thinking and not acting may enter. The one norm is socially valid, others refer more to the family frame or the closer habitat in which the individual moves. These pictures are called the "superego". Conscience is first the sum of these internalized, learned normative images.

Internalized images urge to be realized. These normative images imperiously demand, order and request. These forces may be constructive or destructive. Whether they prove themselves or not, they always want to enforce: Strict, rigid, uncompromising; unless the internalization contains directly conciliatory and compromise-worthy aspects of value.

The non-fulfilment of norms or commandments usually implicates penalties too. Who deviates, depending on the habitat will be in many ways punished by love deprivation, by punitive measures, by denial demonstration, etc.

If man does not enter into this urge and does not realize these internal measures of value, he experiences an inner tension. This is experienced as the "bad" or "good" conscience, varied between tension and restlessness as well as relaxation and calm.

The power of this conscience is usually stronger than the "I", it works urgently from the "unknown ambush," as much as man counteracts with his thinking.

People have different conscience contents depending on their life history, cultural space, social and religious environment. What they experience is not the "Absolute" or the "Divine Voice" or "the law of God", but what they have internalized.

Reflections and discussion

The superego = the conscience contains various characteristics:

- ☐ Contents: Norms, values, laws, prohibitions
- ☐ Judgmental force: Valuing and measuring
- ☐ Claim: Challenging, imperious
- ☐ Enforcement: Strict, uncompromising, rigid
- ☐ Punishment: According to the experience
- ☐ Guilt experiencing: Positive-negative
- ☐ Momentum: Independent of thought, will

The experience of conscience is:

- ☐ "Good": Calming, light, relaxing, relieving, "pure"
- ☐ "Bad": Tense, boring, heavy, depressing, plaguing, "unclean"

The content of the superego is dependent on:

- ☐ Education: Parents, family, environment, school
- ☐ Socialization: Extended environment, relationships and living space
- ☐ Zeitgeist: Social requirements
- ☐ Religious environment: Church activities

A change in the contents of the superego cannot be accomplished by thinking alone; necessary are:

- ☐ Extended experience space
- ☐ Imagination
- ☐ Dreams

The conscience receives supra-individual value by:

- ☐ Experience in dealing with the inner spirit in dreams
- ☐ Experiences of the transcendental reality about "Archetypes"
- ☐ The experience of the power of love or the effects of love
- ☐ The experiences of the transformation processes of individuation
- ☐ In-depth systematic reflections on transcendental experiences

Make a list of known positive and negative values and norms for individual areas of life and discuss in the group:

Communities of all kinds	
Strangers	
Sexuality, tenderness, physical lust	
Nature and wildlife, general environment	
Politics and economy	
Psychical life	
Communication (talking in everyday life)	
Acting in the everyday	

Diagram 3.2.3: Superego – conscience

Diagramm OS8-6: Das Ueber-Ich - Das Gewissen

"Kritische" Inhalte sind:

☹ alles sinnliche ist zu unterdrücken
☹ nur geistiges ist als wert zu pflegen
☹ sei nie schwach und hilfebedürftig
☹ der teller wird immer ausgegessen
☹ eine mutter liebt ihre kinder immer
☹ sei anständig, freundlich und brav
☹ arbeite immer fleissig und perfekt
☹ sexuelle befriedigung ist schlecht
☹ man hat keine probleme und konflikte
☹ nur wer erfolg hat, ist ein guter mensch
☹ gehorche der kirche und ihren vertretern
☹ der staat vertritt die gerechtigkeit
☹ rede immer wahrhaftig und transparent

English translation:
Critical" contents are:

- Suppressing all sensuality
- Caring only intellectuality as value
- Never being weak and needy
- Always eating everything from the plat
- A mother loves her children always
- Be proper, friendly and good
- Work always busy and perfect
- Satisfaction of sexual needs is evil
- One doesn't have problems and conflicts
- Only with success one is a good human
- Obey to the church and its representants
- The state represents the justice

- Speak always truthfully and transparent

3.2.4. Attitudes and ideals

A specific group of images in the subconscious is called "attitudes". The "weakest" attitudes are prejudices.

The strongest are pictures that are considered as conviction. Ideals are strong positive images with a corresponding attitude tone. The word "attitude" means the basic characteristic of such images:

"Being triggered" according to a certain positive or negative value, partly with a fugitive theory, partly with a sophisticated differentiated theory, partly with a fundamentalist starting position in the sense of "thus it is written".

Beliefs are very differentiated emotional images about a value in life. These are opinions with thoughts, arguments and a strong experiential situation.

Ideals represent a value that is so positively experienced that the image as a guiding idea and goal direct people in this direction.

Basically, there are all kinds of prejudices, attitudes, ideals and beliefs in the unconscious. They are conditioned by the life history of the person and the mental-spiritual development.

The less the human being uses his psychical powers, for example thinking and the spirit, the more accessible he is to blanket, absolute and unrealistic attitudes.

The dealing with one's own feelings, the needs and the power of love, along with education and socialization, determine decisively how someone shapes and lives this inner world of images.

Man can gain new attitudes in the course of his life through experiences and thinking achievements.

If the original images are not processed, then conflicting forces or in hidden form result in a further development of the previously internalized image patterns.

With increasing age, the first images become stronger again, where previously external bonds and life possibilities have created a distance.

As is known, around the globe billions of people have established innumerable different attitudes, partly religious, partly ideological, partly materialistic and egocentric or psycho-humanistic or emotionally influenced to all circumstances of the outer and inner life.

Reflections and discussion

Attitudes are pictorial, emotional judgmental patterns about all aspects of life, people and the world.

The following gradations are possible:

- ☐ Prejudices: little reflective, strong emotional, superficial
- ☐ Opinions: An argued preview, revisable
- ☐ Attitudes: Reflected, justified, variable
- ☐ Ideals: Far removed from reality, perfect target image
- ☐ Beliefs: Strongly religious or ideologically argued or networked

Characteristic of these judgmental patterns are:

- ☐ Learned in life, i.e. in situations and thus coupled with pictures
- ☐ Regulating affection and avoidance
- ☐ Activating motivations for actions
- ☐ Justifying intentions and action goals
- ☐ Determine specify the acceptance area
- ☐ Having a strong controlling power especially in the social
- ☐ Can be drawn from life or illusionary
- ☐ Can be useful or harmful
- ☐ Are linked with positive and negative amplifiers (praise / punishment)
- ☐ Estimating the perceptual content quickly and directly, without thinking
- ☐ Being in abeyance also means being "bedded in" i.e. a kind of insertion
- ☐ Flexible or rigid, depending on the roots of the argument and feelings
- ☐ Are culturally learned in life history

The history and the social reality show that the differences and the rigidity of the attitudes cause many problems and partly dramatic circumstances:

- ☐ In the relationship with oneself: Inner conflicts, life inhibitions
- ☐ In man-woman relationships: In all areas of coexistence
- ☐ In dealing with other people: Conflicts of interest, exploitation, violence
- ☐ In political life: Party struggles, devaluations, power struggles, wars

☐ In religious life: Incommunicability, condemnations, wars

Group: Discuss some "tricky" attitudes and their changeability:

Diagram 3.2.4: Attitudes and behaviour

Diagramm OS8-7: Einstellungen und Verhalten

Allgemeine Einstellungsdispositionen
regulieren das Handeln:

Beziehung-Beziehungslosigkeit
Ernsthaftigkeit-Gleichgültigkeit
Mass-Masslosigkeit
Interesse-Interesselosigkeit
Verantwortung-Verantwortungslosigkeit
Zuwendung-Abwendung
Billigung-Missbilligung

Erklärung: Informationen aller Art,
die der Mensch über den Lebensraum,
über andere Menschen und sich selbst ins Bewusstsein
aufnimmt, formen ein unspezifisches "Eingestelltsein".
Solche Einstellungsdispositionen
wirken auf alle Handlungen in allen Lebensbereichen.

English translation:
General dispositions of attitudes regulate the behaviour:
Related – unrelated & seriously – indifferent & modest – exorbitant &
interested – uninterested & responsible – irresponsible & attention –
avoidance & acceptance – reprobation

Legend: All kind of information a human take in his conscious about the habitat, other men and himself shape an unspecific "adjustment". Such dispositions of attitudes affect all acts in all areas of life.

3.2.5. The human images

Part of the life experiences are the people. The picture of the mother is formed since the prenatal time. Manifold aspects come together: The loving, caring, listening, reprimanding, active, and angry mother. Thus, the image of the father is also a complex wholeness with the most diverse aspects together.

Accordingly, the child experiences the interaction: Being a child is beautiful, terrible, sad, exciting, funny, a permanent experience of powerlessness and anxiety, and so on.

The next family members extend these pictures: The siblings, the neighbours' children, the father and the mother next door, the grandparents and relatives. With the school time new human experiences are added.

The child internalizes pictures about teachers, pastors, work colleagues of the father, about different people in the most different areas of life, e.g. policeman, salesman, garagist, etc.

At an early stage, the doctor and dentist, the father's / mother's employer and others can supplement this diversity. "These are the people," the child learns.

Later, new experiences are added. The first friend, the first girlfriend, the colleagues in sports and leisure, work colleagues and more and more people from other circles of life become figures in this image book on the people.

If you travel a lot, live different relationships, run in the most diverse social classes, you will internalize and build up a correspondingly diverse world of images.

Negative experiences or the absence of positive possibilities enliven the imagination: Ideal human images are built; ideals are formed; Enemy pictures as well.

All these pictures contain a value aspect, a feeling and a subjective meaning.

The stronger the psychical energy is charged, as a result of irksome experiences, positive experiences or unreal fantasies, the stronger they affect humans.

Some pictures attract while others reject. They also form a diverse contrasting network of images. The result is then simple and complex "prototypes", each coordinated: Man-woman, father-mother-child, child-adult man.

The man allows outside what his pictures pretend inside; the woman allows to be a woman, as it lives in the inner pictures.

Reflections and discussion

The pictures about the people are grouped by type:

Mother	father	man	woman	child
Old people	life partner	friends acquaintances	teacher	pastor

The images of man contain some basic components:

☐ Value   ☐ Sense
☐ Psycho-energetic "charge"   ☐ Subjective meaning

Just as these groups of people "play together" in life, so too do they form inside complementary and opposing figures:

☐ Husband-wife   ☐ Man-man
☐ Father-daughter   ☐ Mother-son
☐ Adult-Child   ☐ "Adults" / children-old people
☐ Women-woman   ☐ Teacher-student
☐ Employer-employee

There is not simply an ideal image about man or woman, father or mother. The male and the female can still be drawn one-dimensionally as "anima" or "animus". Each picture consists of many variations.

The man and the woman have inside pictures about the opposite sex and about the own sex, which determine the development and shaping scope.

☐ The woman outside is what her inner pictures about "man" allows.
☐ The man outside is what his inner images about "woman" allows.
☐ The adult deals with children as he has inner pictures.
☐ The adults deal with old people the way their pictures are about them.

Handling:

- ☐ The politician with the people:
- ☐ The believer with the pastor:
- ☐ The employer with the employee:
- ☐ The strong with the weak:
- ☐ Everyone with strangers:
- ☐ The catholic with the Muslim:
- ☐ The party member "right" with the "left":

Discuss in the group the possible variations, how human images mutually determine each other.

Write down further examples below:

Diagram 3.2.5: The prototypes of the idea of man

Diagramm OS8-8: Die Prototypen der Menschenbilder

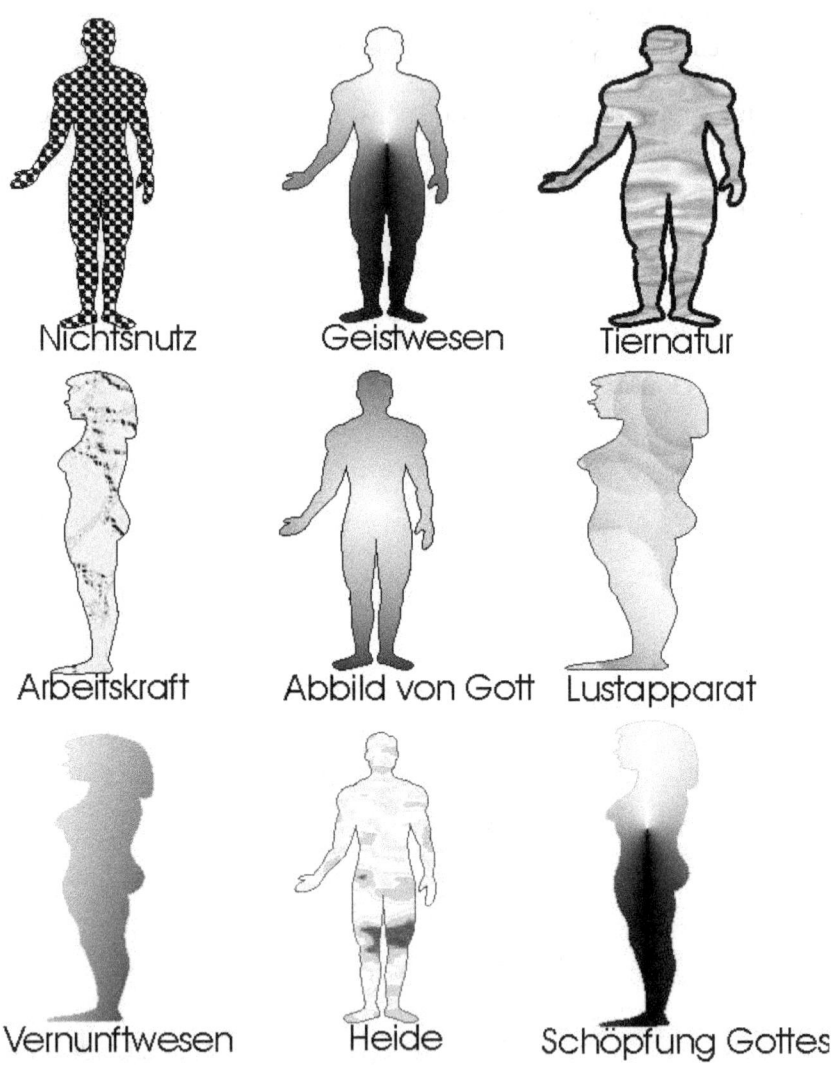

Nichtsnutz	Geistwesen	Tiernatur
Arbeitskraft	Abbild von Gott	Lustapparat
Vernunftwesen	Heide	Schöpfung Gottes

English translation: (From left above to right below)

Waster	Spiritual being	Animality
Worker	Image of God	Generator of lust
Rational Being	Pagan	Creation of God

3.2.6. The collective unconscious

Telepathy and clairvoyance are proven facts. Regardless of all the aberrations in the market and the open scientific questions, we basically hold: A pictorial idea (a thought) can "flow" from one place A to another person in place B and be perceived by that person.

We also speak of the "radiance" of a human being, the joy written in the face, or directly: an energetic aura. This fact is experimentally easy to prove.

Even if the majority of so-called magneto paths do more dubious work, it is clear that magnetopathy also works at longer distances, i.e. no body contact is required. Anyone who is sensitive to psychical energy also experiences it in rooms and in areas where people previously existed. The people leave a psycho-energetic "ejection". We call this "psycho-smog".

Based on these conditions as well as numerous research results, we assume an energetic space around man and around the earth that contains psychical energy and can guide shaped psychic energy (thought, imagination).

Let's keep that in mind: Just as people let exhaust gases of all kinds into the air, they also release psychical energy. As the air is poisoned more and more, so people poison more and more of this cosmic psycho-energetic space. Billions of people's thoughts are stored in this room. Everything that corresponds to the intensity of complexes also acquires an energetic reality in this space. Thus, this energetic space is forming and filling more and more, since time immemorial and into the future.

Psychologically, we 'breathe' the ancestral psycho-osmosis, along with all the stored meaning: Suffering and joy, wars and dramas, hatred and love.

Let's go one step further in the hypothesis: In the universe is a psycho-energetic sun, like the real sun. The psychical system of human lives from this source, "inhales" this "air". The people are connected in this energetic network. This is the collective unconscious.

Reflections and discussion

We venture here into an augmented reality. Much is still unexplored here. Many defend here what has been scientifically proven. Many clearly demonstrated experiments and phenomena investigated by many researchers are the starting point:

☐ Telepathy
☐ Dream predictions
☐ Psychokinesis
☐ Telepathy in animals
☐ Clairvoyance
☐ Alternative therapies
☐ Psycho-energetic radiation
☐ Phenomena of spook

The collective unconscious is based on the following aspects:

☐ There is also a psychic energy outside the psyche that acts as a "leader".
☐ Shaped psychical energy can be sent over long distances.
☐ Psychical energy fields affect the body and the organs.
☐ Things are also "impregnated" by the psychical energy.
☐ Limited, the behaviour of humans can be telepathically influenced.
☐ Where many people with strong emotions are together, they are afflicted psycho-energetic mutually.

It is possible to work systematically with the psychical energy in humans and in space. We refer to it with keywords:

☐ Magnetopathy
☐ For health and well-being (relaxation)
☐ Psycho-energetic rituals
☐ Meditation and contemplation
☐ Experiments with "room impregnation"
☐ Experiments and rituals with "space catharsis"

The lived lives of the past and present, and above all the actual daily life, activates and shapes cosmic energy according to what people think, feel and do.

So, all people are bound in this collective "psycho-energetic net".

Discuss in a group the possible consequences if these theses apply. What significance does the collective psychical energy have in the following topics?

a) Individual responsibility:

b) Collective solidarity:

c) Solutions for hatred, violence, riots and wars:

d) Transcendence as a real psychic and physical experience:

e) Qualities of a next possible evolutionary stage:

Diagram 3.2.6: The "psycho-smog" of the collective unconscious

Diagramm OS8-9: Der "Psychosmog" des kollektiven Unbewussten

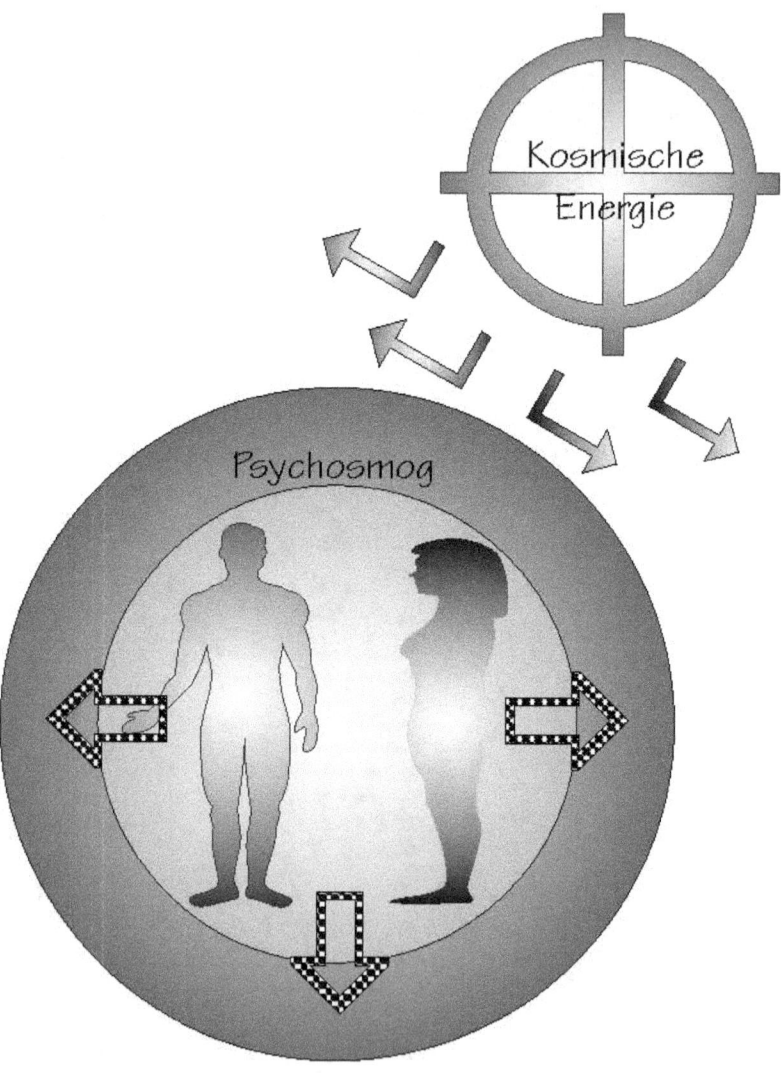

English translation:
Cosmic energy is warded off by
Psycho-smog

3.2.7. Working unit

3.2.7. Working unit - 1

1. a) How do you experience your visual memory?

1. b) Reflect the defence of the meaning of a picture with an example:

2. a) Name the negative effects of the unconscious in the areas:
a) Body / organs:

b) Psychic powers:

c) Actions:

2. b) Name the positive effects of the unconscious in the areas:
a) Body / organs:

b) Psychic powers:

c) Actions:

3. Formulate an educational goal to the negative effects of the unconscious:

4. a) Imagine the work of your unconscious:

4. b) Your conclusion in one sentence:

3.2.7. Working unit - 2

1. a) How do you experience the diversity of your life experiences?

1. b) Extend the "prototype" aspect with your experience:

2. Describe the future-oriented effects (on an example) of:
a) Life experience in childhood

b) Life experience in the youth period:

c) life experience as a young adult (about 18-25 years)

d) Life experience as an adult (around 30-40 years):

e) Life experience around the middle of life (about 42-47 years)

3. Formulate an educational goal in the context of your life experiences:

4. a) Imagine a still lasting life experience:

4. b) Your conclusion in one sentence:

3.2.7. Working unit - 3

1. a) How do you experience the tension dynamics of your conscience?

1. b) Extend the contents of the conscience with 3 concrete examples:

2. a) Create some of the positive and negative values and norms you know about individual areas of life:

Communities of all kinds

Strangers

Sexuality, tenderness, physical pleasure

Nature and wildlife, general environment

Politic and economy

Psychical life

Communication (speeches in everyday life)

Acting in the everyday

3. Formulate an educational goal for your conscience education:

4. a) Imagine the tension of your conscience content:

4. b) Your conclusion in one sentence:

3.2.7. Working unit - 4

1. a) How do you experience the diversity of people's attitudes?

1. b) Expand the diversity of effects of attitudes in society:

2. History and social reality show that the differences and the rigidity of attitudes are the cause of many problems and many dramatic realities. Give an example about negative conflict-promoting attitudes and a constructive (positive) alternative:
a) In the relationship with oneself: Inner conflicts, life inhibitions

b) In man-woman relationships: in all areas of coexistence

c) In dealing with other people: Conflicts of interest, exploitation, violence

d) In political life: party struggles, devaluations, power struggles, wars

e) In religious life: incommunicability, condemnations, wars

3. Formulate an educational goal for your attitude formation:

4. a) Imagine the basic characteristics of your settings:

b) Your conclusion in one sentence:

3.2.7. Working unit - 5

1. a) How do you experience your imagery about people?

1. b) Expand the variations of the possible pictures:

2. Man has inner pictures about (almost) everything that defines the scope for development and shaping. These pictures also influence the action. Edit:

a) The woman outside is what her inner images about "man" allows.
Example:
b) The man outside is what his inner pictures about "woman" allows.
Example:
c) The adult deals with children as he deals with his inner child.
Example:
d) The adults deal with old people as their pictures are.
Example:
e) The politician with the people:
Example:
f) The believer with the pastor:
Example:
g) The employer with the employee:
Example:
h) The strong with the weak:
Example:
i) Everyone with strangers:
Example:
k) The catholic with the Muslim
Example:

3. Formulate an educational goal to design your pictures about people:

4. a) Imagine the relationship between your actions and your inner pictures:

4. b) Your conclusion in one sentence:

3.2.7. Working unit - 6

1. a) What experiences do you have with telepathy and clairvoyance?

1. b) How can one still experience 'cosmic energy'?

2. Reflect the possible consequences if our theses about the "collective unconscious" apply. What significance does the collective psychic energy have in the following topics?

a) Individual responsibility:

b) Collective solidarity:

c) Solutions for hatred, violence, riots and wars:

d) Transcendence as a real psychic and physical experience:

e) Qualities of a next possible evolutionary stage:

3. Formulate an educational goal for collective psychic energy:

4. a) Imagine the collective psychic energy:

b) Your conclusion in one sentence:

3.2.7. Working unit - 7

Take a newspaper. Find 10 short pieces of information that can be interpreted as an expression of the individual unconscious:

Multiple Choice Test

Choose the four correct answers:

6.1. Characteristic of the impact dynamics is:
- ☐ a) Controllable by others
- ☐ b) tendency of recurrence
- ☐ c) Energy charge
- ☐ d) reasonableness
- ☐ e) Momentum
- ☐ f) independent of reality

6.2. The following statements about the unconscious apply:
- ☐ a) Life experiences influence action more than thinking.
- ☐ b) Life experiences always have a subjective meaning dimension.
- ☐ c) The past life experiences have no effect on the present.
- ☐ d) Positive experiences do not shape the unconscious decisively.
- ☐ e) The pictures of life experiences look like a "code program".
- ☐ f) Even before birth, humans take pictorial experiences.

6.3. The superego contains i.e. following components / characteristics:
- ☐ a) Content such as norms, values
- ☐ b) Valuable judgment
- ☐ c) School life
- ☐ d) Momentum towards thinking
- ☐ e) Subjectivity, therefore superfluous
- ☐ f) The "true" value / norm experience

6.4. Characteristic of attitudes, beliefs and ideals:
- ☐ a) All learned / accepted in life
- ☐ b) thought through analytically
- ☐ c) Lifelike or illusionary
- ☐ d) regulate avoidance / avoidance
- ☐ e) Universally given as "true"
- ☐ f) Cause of many ailments / conflicts

6.5. The images of the human unconscious act through:
- ☐ a) Shaping into prototypes
- ☐ b) complementary figures
- ☐ c) Emotional "charge"
- ☐ d) its value aspect
- ☐ e) Authenticity
- ☐ f) external appearance

6.6. Point to the collective unconscious:
- ☐ a) Telepathy
- ☐ b) psychic energy
- ☐ c) clairvoyance
- ☐ d) Experiments
- ☐ e) genetic structure
- ☐ f) psychical inheritance

4. The Functions of the Dreams

Essential theses

The dreams contain meaningful messages about the dreaming and his life.

Dreams inform about other people and institutions, even if the dreaming has had no conscious perception of it and perhaps also can not perceive any information.

The dreams are created by an intelligent spiritual force that wants to advise and guide the people. This power also has extra sensory abilities.

The language of the dreams is as manifold as the language of man in everyday life, literature and art.

Through dreams, the human being can experience everything about the human being, also about the transcendent reality and the divine.

Inner picture viewing (= Imagination and contemplation) is conscious dreaming; Here the spiritual power can be purposefully used for knowledge and changes over all psychic powers.

Imagination = targeted viewing of psychical realities.

Contemplation = viewing images of common symbols and archetypes.

4.1. The dream and the imagination

4.1.1. The dream reality

If we ask others if they are dreaming, many say first, "No, I cannot remember a dream ...", or "I never dream ..." After some pause, memories suddenly pop up.

Other people can remember their dreams on a regular basis. Some remain alive for decades. Many can remember a dream almost every day.

So much we know: People dream and people have always considered dreams to be important. Just as there are people who think that thinking is unimportant and never think about it, there are many who consider their dreams irrelevant and never reflect on them.

Rarely does anyone in the home learn that dreams are important. We never learn anything about dreams at school. Neither at work nor in the Christian faith living do dreams take up a space.

Many dream books inform about the rich world of the dream life. Although some dream theories may be quite wrong or one-sided, it is common to all that different typical dream images and symbols in human or animal form, in circumstances or actions, report on the day-to-day reality of the dreaming.

All dream interpretations assume that the dreams and dream elements are not mere coincidences.

Anyone who claims that dreams are the "wastepaper basket" of everyday life, and curiously researches it, still assumes that this research can lead to a meaningful result: What is found there is material about the dreaming person and his life. From this material conclusions can be drawn on the person.

Since some people dream a lot, others few and many rarely, it becomes difficult to deduce from these dreams the daily activities of the person. But everyone can learn to dream as well as thinking and dealing with the emotions.

So, you can dream about certain life themes.

It is generally known that even in antiquity "big dreams" were considered to be messages of God. It is not just popular opinion from archaic times, when many assume that a message is hidden in dreams.

Some dream theories contain a systematic concept to be able to recognize these messages from the dream images. They all start from the self-evident that the messages are useful: They inform, they advise, they warn and they develop further, where thinking has no access.

This means that an intelligent force organizes the dream elements into a meaningful entity, a "message to the "I"".

We refer to this intelligent psychical power as "the inner spirit".

Reflections and discussion

It is a fact that all people dream several times during their sleep. However, many people can only remember little or nothing at all. Dreaming is a psychical function as well as thinking, for example.

The dreams contain, with rare exceptions, inventory from the life of the dreaming person, from the near past to the earliest childhood:

☐ Elements of the habitat   ☐ Other people   ☐ Actions
☐ Experience   ☐ Perceptions of events

Dreaming also shows mental functions like:

Thoughts	needs	unconscious	assessments
Feelings	will	love	"I" control

The dreams can also contain visual material that does not come from the personal experience of the dreaming.

These include above all the so-called archetypes, i.e. symbols and symbolic acts that are not space / time bound.

The dreams can also contain facts about other people and institutions, about events and developments that the dreaming cannot know.

It must be concluded from an extrasensory perception that can function independently of the day's awareness.

The dreams contain meaningful messages about the dreaming, about other people, about realities in the world and also about the transcendence. Therefore, dreams can be used in a practical way; the dreams:

inform	warn	advice	support	promote	help
heal	free	unfold	rate	analyse	forecast

Dreams are created by an intelligent force called "the inner spirit".

This power is part of the psychic system, but differs significantly from all others in its specific performance.

The mind can neither be formed nor directed. He is completely autonomous of the ego and life. This power is "divine".

Diagram 4.1.1: Dream material and dream message

Diagramm OS10-1: Traummaterial und Traumbotschaft

English translation: (From left above to right below)
Dream: Material, content: consists of:
The external world & The social life & The own external life & The own psychical organism & The psychical life of others & The transcendence and God & The collective unconscious & The life of other humans

Dream interpretation by S. Freud to C.G. Jung

Interpretation of dreams is the "Via regia" (the king's way) to the knowledge of the unconscious in the psychical life, so the psychoanalysis teaches since approximately 100 years. Probably this dream theory is no longer acceptable today. Many discoveries about psychical life have broadened the horizons of dream content.

Our core thesis:

Dreams are the language of the spirit and thus the via regia from the first stage of individuation to the goal. Dreams are the silver bullet to the entire psycho-spiritual personhood.

In the following, we focus on some basic ideas of well-known dream concepts in order to emphasize the importance of dreams for psycho-spiritual development. Whoever deals with the dream practically, comes to the idea of superior the dream building and leading authority.

The dream apparently has the most comprehensive knowledge of all psychical events and possibilities. It is as if it lives in a centre from which the gaze goes beyond the nearest to the darkest humanity, and it seems as if it is always asking one question: How do I form the whole soul situation of my human in the material of a person? and over personal experience.

In the dreams are the reports of all the events of our present life. All that was once ours, in any way related to us, forms the content of the personal unconscious. In the magazines and pantries of the soul and in storerooms near to the awareness, what we have experienced awaits us, whether the dream needs its contents, its figures again.

The primal wisdom of life reveals itself in the dream, and an answer comes up that says where one stands; the ways indicate which one has best to go now.

Certainly, there are also dreams that manifest fulfilled wishes or fears. But what else is not there?

Dreams can include inexorable truths, philosophical sentences, illusions, wild fantasies, memories, plans, anticipations, even telepathic visions, irrational experiences, and God knows what else.

A phenomenon that is hidden in the individual dream behind the respective compensation, is a kind of development process in the personality. At first, the compensations appear as respective adjustments of one-sidedness and balancing of disturbed equilibrium positions.

With deeper insight and experience, on the other hand, these seemingly unique compensatory acts arrange themselves into a kind of plan. They seem to be interdependent and subordinated to a common goal in a deeper sense, so that a long dream series does not appear to be a futile juxtaposition of incoherent and unique events, but a process of development and order as if at a planned stage.

The healing truth of dreams

If it is true that the crisis of the 'environment' in fact represents a crisis of Western humanity, then one cannot ignore the fact that the problems that are actually pending are ultimately of a religious nature.

For its very sake, Christianity should regain an interest in grounding and rooting its own teachings and commandments from the depths of the human psyche.

Instead of systematically contradicting the powers of the unconscious in the name of faith, one should recognize that in the fight against the myths of the pagans and thus against the world of the archetypal configurations of the unconscious, the foundations of any religion are shattered and left a human who, as foreign as he is at the mercy of himself, has to try more and more to create a shelter in the midst of a world that had become soulless and homeless with the help of his intellect and his will forgetting the godless world.

Western man will more and more only encounter himself, and the only chance is therefore that he finally takes his own tragic inevitability as an occasion to encounter oneself more truly and more deeply than before.

Depth psychology, in the broad sense of its present doctrine and practice, is neither willing nor able to trace man back to the denied, profoundly religious layers of his soul, and yet it is a first and indispensable step in the right direction.

The religion of Christianity, itself the main cause of the existing one-sided consciousness of the Western people, has been trying desperately to defend against the recognition of the psychical sources of their dogmas and rites.

The way out of the "dead end" is: A Path of integration of the human psyche and in fact a decision question for the salvation and calamity of all people. Dreams are a place where man can encounter the real truth about his life, where a religious experience is more than an unwanted embarrassment.

Dreams are the origin of myths. The destruction of dreams and the destruction of religion are but two sides of the same process; and whoever removes man from his spiritual and religious attachments must, as has been shown, inevitably destroy human relationships with the surrounding nature. As a result, dreams are the most likely to begin.

It can be said with all seriousness and force that the salvation of man and the salvation of life on this planet are intimately connected with the return to the "dream time", with the remembrance of the religious.

The crisis of the "environment" is a crisis of religion and the human psyche, then only a crisis of politics and the economy. Precisely for this reason, dealing with the world of dreams is such an important means of reviving the religious depths of the human psyche.

Dream psychology is the universal key to understanding all important religious phenomena.

Notes and perspectives

What do most people think about dreams?

Write down the key words in this subchapter:

What causes indifference to your own dreams?

Editing dreams is essential, because: ...

What did you learn in the home, school and church about the variety of positive possibilities of dream interpretation?

What meaning in living together has the conversation about your own dreams?

What would be the seriousness of dreams in politics and business?

What does advertising convey about the value of dreams?

Formulate an important question about the healing effects of dreams.

4.1.2. The language of dreams

A spiritual power in man "speaks" to the "I". How can we understand this language? Which dream interpretation is right and which wrong?

Consider this problem in terms of reality: You want to understand another person: What does he mean? Why is he talking like that? What moves him to live that way? The more you know about the psychical life, the more you can recognize and the more differentiated your answers become. The more one-sided the image of man is, the more one-sided are the answers.

Life itself offers many possibilities of existence: Economical, religious, material, spiritual, political, ethical-moral and cultural. The more a person knows these realities, the more material he has to understand another human being.

Dreams are always interpreted from the knowledge of life.

Not some philosophy, not some instinct theory or social theory or religious doctrine should be the basis for the interpretation of dreams. The comprehensive reality of life, the psychical organism and individuation are the basis and orientation framework of dream interpretation.

Or to put it another way: The intelligent power in man that creates dreams can make messages to all inner and outer realities.

Man has many ways of communicating to someone. One can speak loudly or emphatically softly, because the other does not want to hear. Or you make an indication, because you cannot come straight to the point because of the defence of the person. Sometimes we talk in parables, attack comparisons or exaggerate something extremely, so that the other becomes attentive. We can bring something closer to the other objectively or emotionally intensively.

We've all known the difficult thing for a long time: Man wants to know the truth and does not want to see it. With many mechanisms, man averts what is actually important for him.

Then there are messages that report, others warn, others explain or are forward-looking. We evaluate and judge, we inform and interpret according to some aspects.

For the dream interpretation, we can draw parallels to it: The spiritual power also uses this diversity of the design of a message.

The more people live in communication with their dreams, the more they can experience how that inner mind works. Anyone can realize that this intelligent power obviously knows more than the I can know.

The spirit can also report about itself or about the spiritual world (transcendence). It is free.

Reflections and discussion

Man has many ways in which he can communicate the experienced and imagined reality in words and pictorial embellishments, with feelings and loudness.

So, it can be assumed that the messages in the dreams are designed in just such a variety, for example:

- □ real direct
- □ causal-explanatory
- □ experience intense
- □ contrasting
- □ disfiguring
- □ reversing to the opposite
- □ arranging-classing
- □ emotive
- □ superimposed

- □ allegorically
- □ pictorially decorating
- □ balancing through stress / reduction
- □ compensatory: show the missing
- □ suggestive
- □ retrospect
- □ judgmental
- □ proactive / predictive
- □ comparative

Dream elements are:

- □ Pictures with subjective meanings (through your own experience)
- □ Images with general meanings (for example, objects of culture)
- □ Symbols with global universality
- □ Archetypes: Symbols with specific meanings about psychic life
- □ Everyday actions and rituals
- □ Language or words

The dreams are based on an "intelligence" that is not comparable to cognition. Likewise, meaning and value orientation is not culture-specific subjective. The dream-creating power has some peculiarities, which we emphasize here:

☐ The spirit knows how and for what purpose it communicates messages to the "I".
☐ The spirit knows the "code program" of holistic growth.
☐ The spirit organizes the processing of the unconscious.
☐ The spirit knows the ways and gradations to a balanced life.
☐ The spirit is the source of information about God and transcendence.
☐ The spirit sees solutions where the "I" does not see any way with rationality.

The dream language is to be learned like a foreign language. The more one deals with dreams and seeks this inner communication, the more cooperative becomes the inner spirit. The more man knows about the psychical organism and the individuation, the more appropriate is the interpretation.

Diagram 4.1.2: Aspects of the dream-language

Diagramm OS10-2: Aspekte der Traumsprache

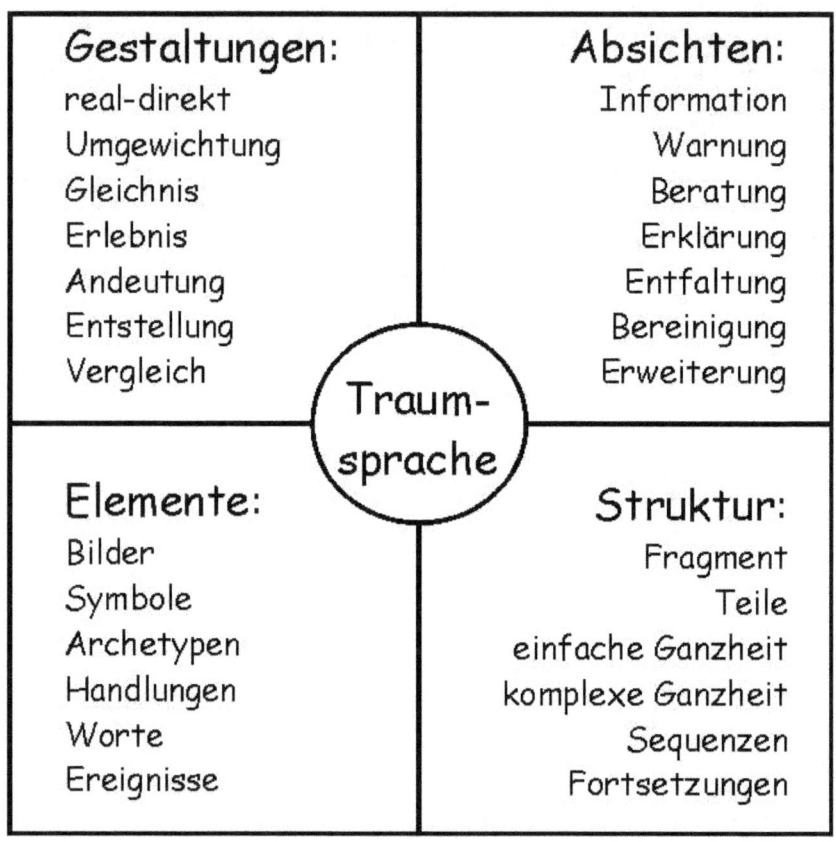

Gestaltungen:	Absichten:
real-direkt	Information
Umgewichtung	Warnung
Gleichnis	Beratung
Erlebnis	Erklärung
Andeutung	Entfaltung
Entstellung	Bereinigung
Vergleich	Erweiterung
Elemente:	**Struktur:**
Bilder	Fragment
Symbole	Teile
Archetypen	einfache Ganzheit
Handlungen	komplexe Ganzheit
Worte	Sequenzen
Ereignisse	Fortsetzungen

(Traumsprache)

English translation: (From left above to right below)
Aspects of the Dream-language:
Arrangement: Real-direct, reassess, parable, adventure, indication, distortion, comparison
Intensions: Information, warning, advice, explanation, development, revision, expansion
Elements: Images, symbols, archetypes, actions, words, events

Structure: Fragment, parts, simply entity, complex entity, sequences, continuations

Theoretical building blocks for dream interpretation:

We focus on getting started on elementary knowledge that everyone needs to dream interpretation. The formulations are partly taken from well-known texts of the analytical dream interpretation, partly with own theses expanded formulated:

Anyone who interprets dreams must know the following:

Dreams have a compensatory function, i.e.:

☐ The consciousness becomes the missing parts of the whole for more comprehensive and better understanding.
☐ The further the awareness of the reality and the optimal attitude is removed, the clearer the compensatory function.

Dreams have a prospective function, i.e.:

☐ Dreams develop solution concepts for conflicts, problems; are with it "final".
☐ Dreams are designed for development, deployment and maturation.
☐ Dreams contain self-healing tendencies.

Dreams respond to conscious and unconscious realities, i.e.:

☐ Dreams illuminate the tension between consciousness and unconscious.
☐ Dreams are a reaction to experiences.
☐ Dreams make aware of unconscious material that needs to be processed.
☐ Dreams are aimed at changing attitudes.

Dreams also contain 'objective' information, i.e.:

☐ Dreams show other people and reality as they are.
☐ Dreams illuminate social facts.
☐ Dreams reveal all lies.
☐ Dreams contain a critical look at ideological and religious practice.
☐ Dreams correct beliefs and philosophical concepts.

Dreams show and execute decisive mental-spiritual processes, i.e.:

☐ Start of self-education and individuation
☐ Turning points of crises
☐ Dissolution of old (thought) patterns and complexes
☐ Liberation processes of persons and attitudes / beliefs
☐ Critical, biographically significant situations

Dreams illuminate archetypal meaning themes of human being, i.e.:

☐ Transcendental originality of man
☐ The reality of God and spirit in man and in the cosmos.
☐ The true, the good and the bad
☐ The meaning question of true religious rituals
☐ Organisation of the spiritual destiny of a person
☐ The innermost goal orientation of human existence

Interpreting dreams contains the following basic elements:

☐ The subjective horizon of meaning in extended reflecting
☐ The semantic space through associations of the dreaming person
☐ The general meanings of general realities and objects
☐ The meaning, function and mode of action of individual psychical forces
☐ The meaning of the primal symbols (archetypes), tangible through contemplation.

Practical interpretation of dreams in elements

We give some examples, fragments of dreams, which reveal the different functions and design forms.

Identify these designs.

Dream example of design and interpretation:

☐ Friend Toni visits me. He looks very hard, rigid, his hearty smile is set. He has a buddy with him, with a very round boyish face, looks like a (somewhat caricatured) dutiful and dutiful officer. After some hesitation and quite surprised, I do not shake his hand. Wonder: What does he want from me?

☐ Otto: I want to become a member of the company X; this is in a modern building, known for modern philosophical questions of the future. In the dream I come to a poor house, everywhere dark, old furniture, old pens and mountains of files.

☐ Beat: I live with my mother. My brother is cooking, seems to live there too. My mother steals money from my pocket; I catch her. She insults me. I defend myself, yell at her and awake with guilt.

☐ Eva: I'm in jail, want to get out, protest violently. The director gives me a package and tells me to open it. In it is a crossword puzzle, the key to freedom.

☐ Annabelle: I first read a book about personality development. Dream after: I learn to drive a car, feel good at the wheel; I like the car, it suits me.

☐ Mrs S., for years without relationship, 28 years old: I stand in a dream naked in front of the mirror, I find myself quite attractive and first feel comfortable with my chubby upper body.

☐ Mr. T. wants to buy a new car to surprise his wife, dreams after visiting the garage: I have a lot of arguments with my wife and do not know why. - Real, there is no reason to do so, he says.

☐ Mr. H. dreams: I'm in the office, talking to the secretary and suddenly teeth start to wobble; some even fall out. The secretary calls the boss, he should take a look at it. I am very embarrassed.

☐ Mrs. Y., 45 years old, children grow up, live separately. Her dream: I am in the mountains, I do not know where, dangerous slope, partly snow, cold; I do not know where to go, have lost my way, lost my way. Further up it seems very dangerous. I cannot go back either. Nobody is there to help me.

Notes and perspectives

How do most people explain their dreams?

Write down the key words in this subchapter:

What is the difference between "life without dream interpretation" and "life with dream interpretation"?

Thoroughly learning the dream language is essential because: ...

What did you learn about the spirit as a dream-creating force in the home, school and church?

What meaning in living together has the conversation about the language of the spirit?

How are the capabilities of the spirit in people used in politics and the economy?

What does advertising convey about the power of the mind?

Formulate an important question for the dialogue with the spirit:

4.1.3. Visualizing as conscious dreaming

Daydreaming is a variant of dreaming. We call this "imagination" or "inner picture viewing". Now man can see images inwardly at will, without a plan, without a goal, without a methodical procedure. Assuming that the same intelligent power works in the imagination as in dreams, we can learn to use this spirit purposefully. Again, there are parallels to communication in everyday life.

If we talk without purpose and without special meaning, or talk to please or enjoy, then that is hardly fruitful. Similarly, the imagination is a communication that works by rules.

If we know what we want and have made a clear agreement in the language, then we get an intelligent communication. In this way, we can purposefully summon and design a world of images that informs and works.

The inner vision contains an unimaginable potential.

The human being can say: "I want to see how my biography puts a strain on me, in concrete reminders about X and Y." Then we get the pictures or we can say: "I want to see how my needs are stands. I agree: My needs show up as animals on a farm." – "Which masks does man sit on and what does he hide behind it?"

In addition, one can look in the imagination in a mirror and ask for the masks, or for the faces behind it. Both can then be shown in animal form, in fairy-tale characters or in real life. You can also go into the "basement" (the unconscious as secret cellar rooms) and find some imprisoned forces: One's own child, unused forces, hidden judges, dusty tables of law, hidden life plans, etc.

Everyone can discover himself with imagination and find his own realities that are still hidden from him.

The pictures come from the own picture inventory. It is possible to see what you want to see. You can easily project something into it. The more resistance someone has to seeing what is real, the more illusions will show up.

Everything that one experiences in the inner picture viewing is to be grasped from the current consciousness, from the current mood and in the context with the own interests. Imagination shows pictures, symbols and archetypes.
The interpretation follows the same rules as in the interpretation of dreams. Imagination, like dreams, opens up the entire psychical organism, other people, foreign institutions, the entire reality of life, and the meaningfulness of archetypes.

The creative force is the spirit. In Imagination, one can enter directly into the dialogue with this spirit, in the form of the sage or mythical animal.

Reflections and discussion

Other words for "inner picture viewing": Imagination, autogenic training upper stage, meditation, daydreaming, conscious dreaming, inner vision etc.
The appropriate definition is: Imagination is systematic, purposeful inner picture viewing according to clear methodical rules.

Contemplation is a special form of imagination. Here symbols and archetypes are experienced internally to understand deeper meaning and to use their energetic power.

Medial viewing is the imagination of foreign psycho-spiritual realities: The psychical life of other people, the meaningfulness of institutions of all kinds.

Imagination can actively work with the pictures. In this way, one can cleanse and reorganize the entire inventory of the unconscious. With inner pictures, psychical energy is activated, shaped and used. With systematic images one can relax and centre the existing psychodynamics.

Concrete imagination means: Seeing in inner pictures the present or a certain past situation, just as it is / was concrete. This kind of picture-watching is called "regression".

Symbolic imagination means: One chooses a certain image (symbol), which should stand for something and inform with the inner expression about this "something"; e.g. The tree is an image of the inner life growth (tree of life).

The following procedure is recommended:

Step 1: Sit down or lie down comfortably.

Step 2: Setting a goal: What do I want to know? What do I want to meditate on? What for?

Step 3: Defining the way images are viewed: Concrete, symbolic or archetypal.

Step 4: Create relaxation.

Step 5: Call images on the topic through targeted concentration.

Step 6: Slowly let the pictures run, sense meaning at the same time.

Step 7: Finish after 3 - 5 minutes (who has a lot of experience: 10 minutes).

Step 8: Write down the picture experience and the feelings about it.

Step 9: Process (interpret) experiences like a dream.

Step 10: Put the knowledges into life context. Formulate conclusions.

Recommendation: only one goal per exercise; at most 1-2x per day; abort at flood of pictures; do not want to force anything; proceed slowly and carefully.

Diagram 4.1.3: Pictures/symbols as image of psychical realities

Diagramm OS10-3: Bilder/Symbole als Abbild psychischer Wirklichkeiten

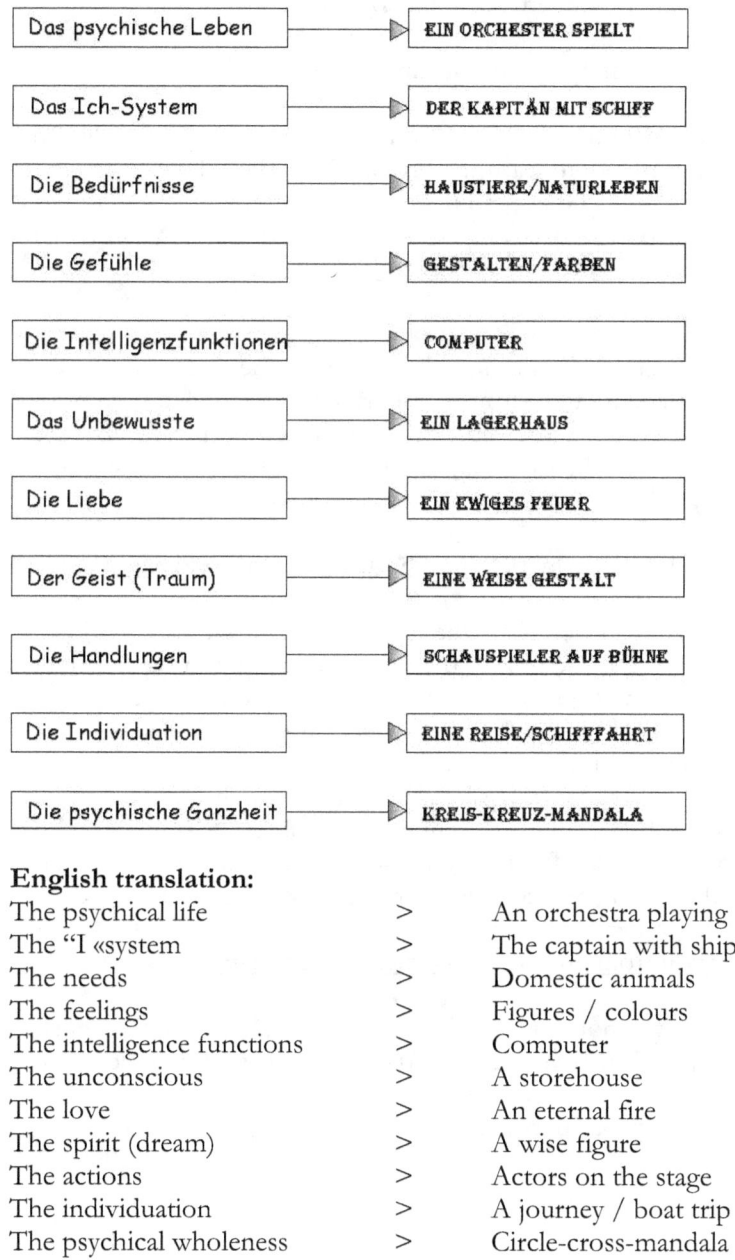

Das psychische Leben	EIN ORCHESTER SPIELT
Das Ich-System	DER KAPITÄN MIT SCHIFF
Die Bedürfnisse	HAUSTIERE/NATURLEBEN
Die Gefühle	GESTALTEN/FARBEN
Die Intelligenzfunktionen	COMPUTER
Das Unbewusste	EIN LAGERHAUS
Die Liebe	EIN EWIGES FEUER
Der Geist (Traum)	EINE WEISE GESTALT
Die Handlungen	SCHAUSPIELER AUF BÜHNE
Die Individuation	EINE REISE/SCHIFFFAHRT
Die psychische Ganzheit	KREIS-KREUZ-MANDALA

English translation:

The psychical life	>	An orchestra playing
The "I «system	>	The captain with ship
The needs	>	Domestic animals
The feelings	>	Figures / colours
The intelligence functions	>	Computer
The unconscious	>	A storehouse
The love	>	An eternal fire
The spirit (dream)	>	A wise figure
The actions	>	Actors on the stage
The individuation	>	A journey / boat trip
The psychical wholeness	>	Circle-cross-mandala

Practical imagination: 10 model examples

Pay attention to three main rules:

1. Decide on the goal of the exercise: What do you want?
2. Choose suitable pictures, symbols and symbolic actions!
3. Be self-critical in the interpretation of experience!

The exercises "imagination" of the individual work units have already given the student the opportunity to learn the imagination. The following examples are very simple structured and expand the range of topics.

1. Scope: Immobilization and general relaxation

"The face is ... soft ... relaxed ... warm ... calm ... easy ... relaxed ..."
And continue with: "... the forehead ..., the mouth ..., the eyes ..., the neck ..., the nape ..., the shoulders ..., the arms ..., the hands ..., the fingers ..., the chest ..., the back ..., the cross ..., the hips ..., the stomach ..., the pelvis ..., the buttocks ..., the thighs ..., the calves ..., the feet ..., the toes ..., all the muscles ..., the whole body ... "

2. Scope of application: General psychical hygiene (= Mental training)

Imagine: All big and small clouds are the thoughts and images that are in your consciousness now (come and go). In the imagination you can see the clouds: Bright, dark, heavy, lighter; just like the thoughts and pictures: heavy, light ... Small thoughts are small clouds, big thoughts are big clouds. Now comes a wind that blows away all the clouds, each one after the other. So, the sky is gradually turning blue, at first only shimmering through, then every now and then more and more bright, blue sky ... until the whole sky is completely blue. - You can talk to the wind: "Bubble here, blow away ... Cloud go away now, dissolve ...". At the end of the exercise, the head is light, free and relaxed.

3. Scope: Exemption from unprocessed experiences of harm

For profound, most serious, regrettable experiences, you should do such exercises with a specialist. If you want to dare to tackle such a topic on your own, then do it step by step, one aspect daily. And write down your experiences and reflections afterwards.

The exercise: Remember the scene. Imagine getting started and let the events take place in your inner eye. Talk to the persons. Defend yourself. Tell them what you want to say. Experience your feelings, do not suppress the pain. Then try to say goodbye by saying "yes" that this is now part of your biography, albeit perhaps with drastic consequences. Search exactly what you can learn about this experience of suffering, about other people, about "destiny" and about yourself.

4. Scope: Reflection on the way of life

Imagine how you lived the past week was filmed. The most important aspects of lifestyle can now be played in slow motion. Watch this movie. The exercise may take up to 20 minutes. If you already have some practice, you can interrupt all minutes and write down a keyword, so that you can later reconstruct the experienced scenes. After that, you evaluate the picture scenes self-critically.

5. Scope: Extension of perception

Now think of a scene that is an hour or a day ago. You are with other people, in a buying situation, at a meeting, in the middle of an argument or during a telephone conversation. Let the scene in all details, meticulously run again in front of the inner eye. Concentrate on details, accents, nuances. Ask questions: What did I not exactly perceive, not exactly hear, not consciously recognize? - You will be surprised how much you have paid inaccurate or not at all. You can also experience meditatively why you have not sufficiently perceived these parts, what you are missing out on and what it is useful to enhance your perception.

6. Scope: Other people understand

Who do you want to understand better? What exactly do you want to understand more clearly? Why? Then imagine in the imagination these humans. Look closely at him. Ask him what you want to know. Try to get into his life situation in order to understand his feelings, thoughts, decisions, actions. Inner picture viewing opens up the psychical reality of this human being. Self-critical, fair and humane attitude is the highest order!

7. Scope: Solution of difficulties

Imagine the difficulty in a (in the corresponding) situation. Focus on your feelings, thoughts and attitudes. Try different solution strategies. Ask to the inside, "What is the appropriate solution? What do I have to do to make the solution real? What do I lack to realize the solution?" That's how completely new doors can open.

8. Scope: Understand psycho-somatic complaints

First, go through your life story and try to recognize the respective life context exactly. Then you feel your discomfort. Go into the feeling with the consciousness. Talk to your body: Why do I have these complaints? Call in the imagination a doctor or consultant. He should show you what these complaints "want to say". Look for the "message" of this suffering. Only in a later step do you work out the possible solutions.

9. Scope: Find and realize the meaning of life

Your lifetime is your capital. Your psychical powers are your tools. Your experiences are your life competences. Imagine a wandering with it. You have your potential with you. Then call scenes where you can use them. Ask a wise figure: What should I do? What should my life be good for? - You will be guided by life challenges that will show you how to make life sense with your life.

10. Scope: Recognize one's own location in individuation

Individuation is a life process. The goal is not the "end", but a beginning for a "life in individuation". There is the "sun," the "life symbol" (a pyramid, a mandala in the light). Ask: Where am I? In the imagination you can experience yourself in different scenes that show what you have done to date, and especially what to expect in a next stage. With a side view, you can look out where others (for example, friends, acquaintances, but also "enlightened" of the esoteric scene, human educators, etc.) stand.

Notes and perspectives

What do most people think about meditation (imagination, contemplation)?

Write down the key words in this subchapter:

What is the (life-practical) difference between "life without meditation" and "life with meditation"?

Meditating (imagining) is essential, because: ...

What did you learn about the methods of meditation (imagination and contemplation) in home, school and church?

What meaning in living together has the conversation about your own meditations?

What would happen if politics and the economy were meditating on their own actions?

Which pictures and main symbols does the advertising convey?

Formulate an important question about the practice of the imagination:

4.1.4. Exercises

1. What do your dreams mean for your daily life?

2. How do you deal with your dreams?

3. Which pictures, symbols, events and actions are current in your dreams?

4. What experiences do you have with imagination and contemplation?

5. Do you experience in you a spiritual power that wants to lead you through life?

6. How do you experience this spiritual power in your everyday life?

7. Dream themes. Describe from your dream diary short dream images and dream scenes that address the following:

Dream areas	Dream images
Biographical:	
Shadows, personality aspects:	
Psychic powers:	
Unconscious, complexes:	
Instinctual nature, sexuality:	
Actions:	
Relational aspects:	
Transformation issues:	
Self-realization:	
Attitudes	
Lifestyle, way of life:	
Health:	
Archetypal:	
Dangers:	
Other people:	
Occupation, work:	
Churchly-religious, spiritual	
Social:	

Amoral, moral:

8. ideas. Take some of your ideas from your dream journal:
8.a) Real ideas (memories, circumstances, a reference etc):

8.b) "Spiritual" ideas (conclusions, thoughts, ideas etc):

8.c) "Aha" experience and special inner experience through the dream:

9. Design forms. Give each of your dream diaries a short example:

Design form	Dream image
Real image:	
Indication:	
Mixing, compaction:	
Displacement, distortion:	
Reversal to the opposite:	
Compensation (equalization):	
Comparison, contrast:	
Experience, mood, energetic loaded:	
Bizarre, illogical, word-, number-games:	
Retrospective perspective:	
Prospective, forward-looking:	
ESP phenomena:	

10. Dream- "I". Give short examples of how you are in various dreams:

Location:
Constitution, expressiveness, mood:
Ability to integrate (accept, affirm, turn, acknowledge, recognize):
Ability to act and manage:
Defence, resistance, refusal, escape, denial:

11. Process a dream according to the following 8-point dream protocol:

☐ Dream:
☐ Dream experience:
☐ Key images:
☐ Dream "I":
☐ Ideas:
☐ Concern, being addressed:
☐ Total interpretation:
☐ Consequences:

Multiple Choice Test

Choose the four correct answers:

7.1. The dream reality. Central statements on the subject are:

☐ a) In dreams all mental functions can be reflected.
☐ b) Dreams inform about the whole life of the dreaming person.
☐ c) Dreams are consistently caused by repressed sexuality.
☐ d) Dreams are an accident product of the central nervous system.
☐ e) Dreams are the result of an intelligent psychical power.
☐ f) Dreams are the source of all truth about life / humanity.

7.2. The language of dreams. The language of dreams is:

☐ a) Not forward-looking
☐ b) Always related to the past
☐ c) Often real
☐ d) Mixed many times
☐ e) Also allegorical
☐ f) Mainly explanatory

7.3. Inner picture viewing as conscious dreaming. With inner picture viewing one can:

☐ a) Process the unconscious
☐ b) Relax
☐ c) Find solutions
☐ d) Foresee sports results
☐ e) Recognize inner values
☐ f) Become rich

4.2. Living with dream and imagination

4.2.1. The dreaming

We all dream every night. Sleep can be divided into four to five phases, alternately in deep sleep and light sleep. Above all, the human being dreams in the phase of light sleep (REM phase), where the eyeballs move markedly ("Rapid Eye Movements").

This has a meaningful function in two regards: Dreaming regulates inner psychical life. At the same time, in the REM phase, physiological processes that are important for the organism take place: Brisk brain activity, activated respiratory rate, increased pulse values.

The dream has an important function in regulating health and psychical life. During sleep, the body regenerates.

The complete retreat from outer reality to sleep is vital.

Sleep and wakefulness are two poles of existence.

In the waking we perceive and we think; in sleep we dream.

Being "asleep" is an actual form of existence. This is not a waste of time; but where dreams are not absorbed by consciousness, one can speak of a loss of experience. Dreaming a lot is a reality and who knows how to use it, extends his life possibilities.

In dreams, psychical processes take place, as in perception, thinking, feeling. The dream interpretation is the "royal road to the unconscious", with which we get a deep insight into the intrapsychic processes. Because dreams always contain sense and meaning.

As you know, there are many theories about dream interpretation. Each is based on a theory about psychical life and personality.

One may say that the dreams are "the secret desires", another "the voice of God resp. his spirit", another "the processing of daily thoughts, feelings and impressions" and yet another "the atonement of the person in his existence ".

All have one thing in common: With dreams, the psychical life is more differentiated and deepened to recognize and to understand. It used to mean "I think, therefore I am", so we can go on an evolutionary step and say: "I dream, so I am".

Dreaming is a non-dispensable form of existence.

Reflections and discussion

Dreaming has important functions:

☐ Physiological, as a being experience, psychically, as an extended self-experience

In waking, we absorb the reality with the senses, process on them with thinking and react operating. In dreaming something similar happens:

☐ We perceive reality differently.
☐ The realities are presented irrationally (illogically).
☐ The logic of dreams is different than thinking operations.
☐ The language of dreams is different than the real language.
☐ The relation to action is different than the conscious acting.

Dealing with dreams depends on various factors:

☐ Interest and knowledge about the psychical life
☐ Theories about the psychical life resp. the "personality"
☐ Openness to the out-of-rational
☐ Willingness to look at the undeveloped own aspects as well
☐ Interest to use extended perspectives of existence
☐ Openness to other "linguistic forms" of message delivery

In the current stage of evolution, man has developed his thinking and made it technically usable, freeing himself with myths about the creation of the world. In the next stage of evolution, man can free himself from the myths of religions:

Dreams convey everything about the psychical life, which man cannot open up with thinking.

Dreams are the expression of a "higher spiritual intelligence", which is nothing other than this "spirit of God"; resp. the "spirit of the universe".

In dreams, the principles of psychical functioning can be recognized in the holistic growth.

This spiritual power is also the power in which love and conscience can be centred.

The dream interpretation is the active work of the individual to find the bridge to the external reality and to implement the knowledges.

Discuss with others what they have learned about dreaming to this day, and what opportunities are given to life by this spiritual power.

Diagram 4.2.1: The dreaming as editing process

Diagramm OS10-4: Das Träumen als Bearbeitungsprozess

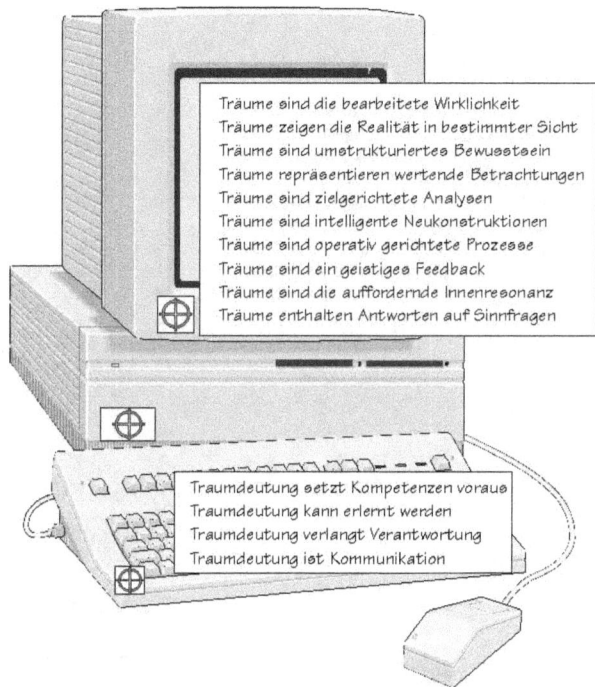

Träume sind die bearbeitete Wirklichkeit
Träume zeigen die Realität in bestimmter Sicht
Träume sind umstrukturiertes Bewusstsein
Träume repräsentieren wertende Betrachtungen
Träume sind zielgerichtete Analysen
Träume sind intelligente Neukonstruktionen
Träume sind operativ gerichtete Prozesse
Träume sind ein geistiges Feedback
Träume sind die auffordernde Innenresonanz
Träume enthalten Antworten auf Sinnfragen

Traumdeutung setzt Kompetenzen voraus
Traumdeutung kann erlernt werden
Traumdeutung verlangt Verantwortung
Traumdeutung ist Kommunikation

English translation:
Dreams are the processed reality
Dreams show the reality in a certain sight
Dreams are the restructured awareness
Dreams represent valuing considerations
Dreams are purposeful analysis
Dreams are intelligent new constructions
Dreams are operative directed processes
Dreams are a spiritual feedback
Dreams are inviting inner response
Dreams include answers to sense questions

      Dream interpretation presumes competences
      Dream interpretation can be learnt
      Dream interpretation demanded responsibility

Dream interpretation is communication

4.2.2. Pictures, symbols, actions

If we take a few hundred dreams of one person, a few thousand of several persons or even fifty thousand or more of many people, we can see that the actual material consists of all sorts of life themes, of all sorts of people and of actions far more comprehensive than the actions of a single person.

In dreams we find elements from the earliest childhood of a person, from all years of life, from the passed days and from the hours of awakening before dreaming.

There are people with faces and without faces, acquaintances and unknowns.

Dreams also include animals, pets as well as wild and dangerous animals.

A dream event can take place in various personal and impersonal locations, in known and unknown habitats, in churches and castles or military barracks, etc.

The actions contain the diversity of all possibilities of human activity in the awake life. What else is there in dreams that people have not already "tried out"?

There are events of joy and suffering, of death and birth, of all conceivable circumstances during a life course.

Disasters and horror never experienced by the dreaming can occur in dreams.

Thus, it is to be expected that in dreams also all objects and circumstances occur, which exist in the life of humans around the globe: From the own clothes up to money, food, machines, airplanes and so on.

Sometimes strange things come up:

Symbols and actions that are far removed from the "normal" life that actually does not exist in real life. "Flying" may be funny or dangerous.

In contrast, a "white elephant", an owl in the living room, a talking animal, a 'sacred act', an oracular condition, seem mysterious.

Fights and 'mystery actions', as in heroic epics, can occur in dreams.

The fact is undoubtedly clear:

Such images, symbols, real and symbolic actions, events and circumstances have a deeper meaning; they contain a message to the "I".

Dreams are language and reality at the same time, mixed and often confusing, illogical and considered "stupid" by the ego. They open up the deepest form of existence of man.

Reflections and discussion

Dream content can be:

Dream content	Examples
People:	
Animals:	
Places:	
Objects:	
Events:	
Factual issues:	
Actions:	
Conversations:	

The elements of a dream can contain three qualities:

Pictures from the life of the person: The entire personal inventory of life, which has a subjective meaning for the dreaming.

Symbols: These are those images that belong to the area of experience, but which have no personal meaning, but are seen as general good from the inventory of the world.

The archetypes: These are symbols that transcend generality beyond a transcendental, i.e. are not of worldly importance and do not appear in form as a common cultural object or as a normal reality.

These include: Abstract symbols such as circle-cross-mandala, pyramid, a spiritual light, a burning spiritual fire, a wise figure, an animal with special characteristics, a temple, a mandala, and so on.

Dreams can be designed very differently:

- ☐ direct, real and concrete
- ☐ strangely disfigured and "illogical" acting
- ☐ mixing past, present and future
- ☐ mixing of people and places

Group work: Take some of your dreams and sort them all elements by their kinds, for example:

a) People:

b) Actions:

c) Places:

d) Subjects:

Diagram 4.2.2: Dreams as new constructed reality

Diagramm OS10-5: Träume als neu konstruierte Realität

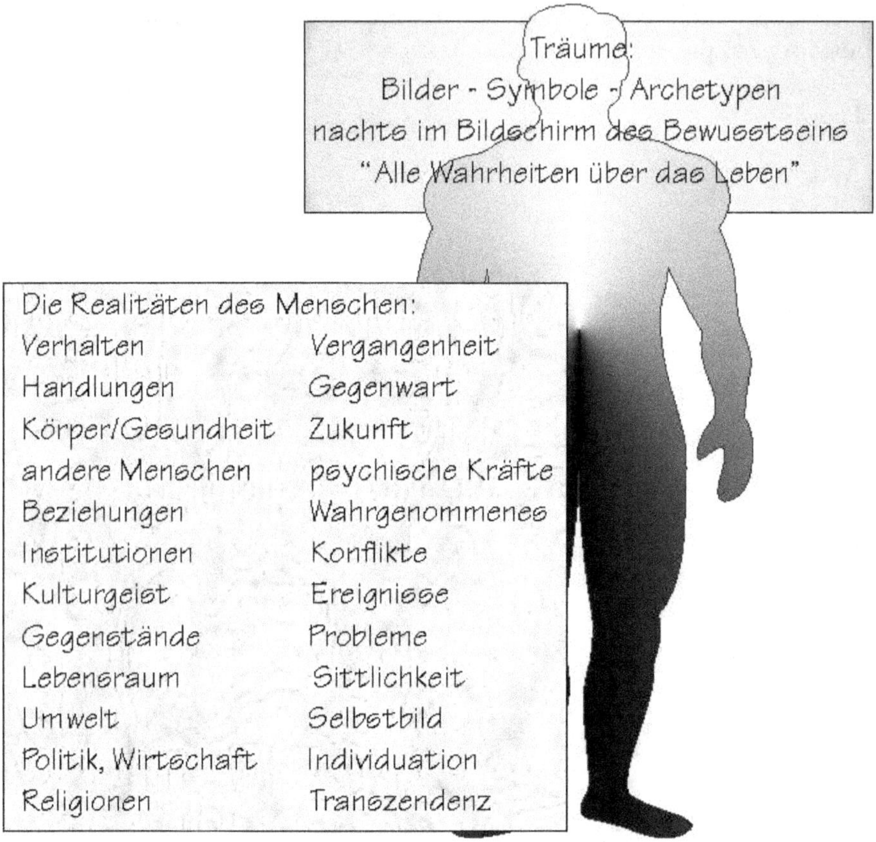

Träume:
Bilder - Symbole - Archetypen
nachts im Bildschirm des Bewusstseins
"Alle Wahrheiten über das Leben"

Die Realitäten des Menschen:

Verhalten	Vergangenheit
Handlungen	Gegenwart
Körper/Gesundheit	Zukunft
andere Menschen	psychische Kräfte
Beziehungen	Wahrgenommenes
Institutionen	Konflikte
Kulturgeist	Ereignisse
Gegenstände	Probleme
Lebensraum	Sittlichkeit
Umwelt	Selbstbild
Politik, Wirtschaft	Individuation
Religionen	Transzendenz

English translation:
Dreams:
Images – symbols – archetypes; at night in the screen of the consciousness; "All truth over the life"
The realities of the human:
Behaviour, actions, body/health, other people, relations, institutions, culture spirit, objects, habitat, environment, politics, economy, relations, past, present, future, psychical forces, perceptions, conflicts, events, problems, morals, self-image, individuation, transcendence

4.2.3. The dream creating intelligence

Man has a "second intelligent power" - along with the intelligence functions - that he can use. However, this works a little differently, is organized like a "second "I"" (also called the "higher self").

This is what we assume: The inner spirit speaks to the "I" through dreams and meditative experiences. For this purpose, this power uses the entire possible personal and general image inventory of the dreaming person.

The spirit can expand these "language elements" optionally, partly through combinations (a talking animal), partly through archetypes whose meaning is barely captured by a concrete image.

However, the human interprets the dreams, he accepts, and also experiences, that the images designs in the dream are intelligent, resp. not coincidentally and senselessly (groundless) put together.

Since the practice of interpretation may be drive oriented or oriented toward a need for power, the parts composed with "intelligence" accept all those who interpret dreams.

Often the dreams have a processing effect. Life inventory is restructured and dissolved; e.g. quiet crying in the dream can liberate a not-mourned grief.

It may be assumed that the more consciously the person integrates the dream, the greater the effect of processing. The processing often consists of the dream showing connections between past events and present thinking or feeling.

Sometimes dreams show pretty drastically what to think of a particular behaviour or complex.

What appears in the dream as a criminal or "completely wrong", sometimes means: "So you have been yesterday in your actions".

Some dreams warn or give some advice: "Further development is possible in this direction". Such dreams prepare the future.

Possibilities are opened that cannot be grasped by thinking.

Other people are often portrayed as they really are, not as "own shadows," but to reflect on the relationship with them.

There are also dreams that can only be explained as the result of an extrasensory perception.

Those who systematically process the process of individuation experience dreams as the actual management authority.

The spirit knows how the "tree of life" can and should grow. Those who work with archetypes, be it in contemplation or with psycho-energetic rituals, learn that this spirit is a force that also organizes the succession of the changing energy in an energetically intelligent way.

Reflections and discussion

The inner spirit has eight characteristics:

1) He speaks through dreams and inner pictures (meditation) to the "I".
2) The language consists of pictures, symbols and archetypes (actions).
3) He has access to inner, outer, foreign and spiritual realities.
4) The succession works in the direction of processing.
5) The main function is human guiding (better: human education).
6) The spirit is based on its own system of values and norms.
7) The spiritual "intelligence" is centred goal-oriented on the individuation process.
8) The spiritual "intelligence" also works in dealing with the psychical energy.

The more man turns to his dreams, the more he can experience this power as a spiritual guiding authority and he experiences:

☐ Information about his unconscious and everything he does not look at.
☐ Growth forces that escape the "I".
☐ Values and judgments that are over individual and over cultural.
☐ Judgements about religion and religious practice.
☐ Advice in conflicts, crises, difficulties, suffering situations.
☐ The view behind political and economic scenes.
☐ A critical look at all psychic-spiritual teachings / organizations.
☐ Correction to his values and attitudes.
☐ The formation of life building images in the unconscious.
☐ The realities that hinder life / growth inside and outside.
☐ Paths that do not correspond to the "Zeitgeist" but lead to people.
☐ A clear challenge to unfold and live the power of love.

If there is a "God," whatever that may be, or a "Spirit of God," how should he speak to man, if not through dreams and meditations?

Discuss in the group the possibilities that exist in this intelligent spiritual power in relation to:

a) Relationships:	
b) Life processing:	
c) Habitat design:	
d) Politics:	
e) Intercultural understanding:	
f) Interreligious contact:	

Diagram 4.2.3: The inner spirit and its functions

Diagramm OS10-6: Der innere Geist und seine Funktionen

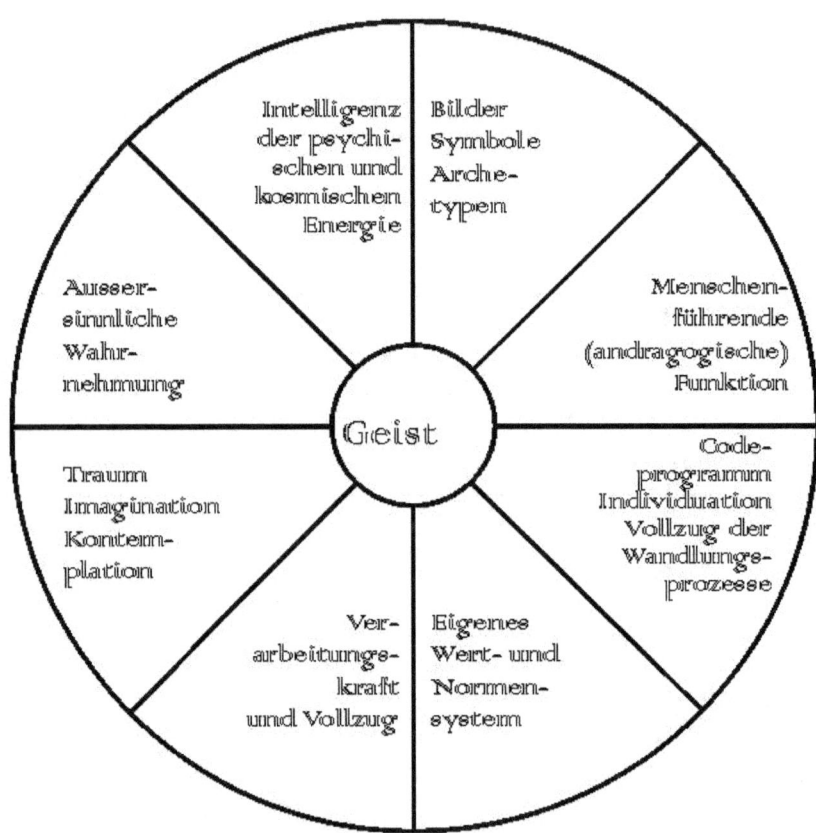

English translation: (From left above to right below)
Spirit:
Intelligence of the psychical and cosmic energy
Images, symbols, archetypes
Extrasensory perception (ESP)
Human guiding (andragogical) function
Dream, imagination, contemplation
Code program individuation, implementation of the transforming processes

Processing force and implementation
Own value and norm system

4.2.4. The scheme of dream interpretation

The dream interpretation must be learned like a foreign language. The spirit invites: "Do you want to communicate with me, then learn to understand me." One becomes competent by engaging oneself in the dreams and thus also in one's own psychical life. He who does not understand and unfold his whole psychical life does not become competent.

The one who sets the "I" higher than this spirit must first learn where it leads to. Anyone who sticks in his one-sided theory and does not accept the spirit as a conversation partner, never looks beyond the self-built wall.

Let's go one step further: Anyone who wants to talk to God, but does not strive for self-knowledge and individuation, must live with a replacement. The relationship between the "I" and the spirit is clear:

Man is free to say yes or deny what he is and is in himself. Either way, that has consequences.

Three aspects are always to be considered in the interpretation of dreams:

First, the dream elements are to be disassembled. The single parts are to be placed in the context of experience. This can be traced back to early childhood. The core question relates to the subjective meaning of one's own experiences (associations). Then the general elements can be sensed interpretatively.

Second, every language has a variety of expressions. Also, in everyday life we talk in parables, make only indications, exaggerate or understate, shift certain elements to emphasize something, speak loudly or very quietly, make jokes, bring comparisons, let someone feel something to let a message experience up close etc. Each dream is to explore what kind of "talking" with pictures and actions could be up to date here,

Third, consider the various functions of the mind, i.e. it is to be sought in which direction the leadership tendency pushes:

Will the dream inform?

Is this an explanation or an opening of a new topic?

Should forward-looking perspectives be reflected?

Is a delicate or even dangerous thing current?

Reflections and discussion

There are four main rules for dream interpretation:

1. The inventory refers to the entire psychical system of man and his life, including all elements of all life systems.

The key question is: "What are the personal associations?"

2. Certain elements refer to general meanings which presuppose non-specific own experiences.

Reflection is needed. Amplifications can help.

3. Archetypes and archetypical acts are transcendental experiences.

They reflect the main transformations of individuation. Experiences about transcendence go hand in hand with determination by individuation.

4. In a dream, all three variants can occur simultaneously. The "spiritual gold" shines even in dreams only very reserved and always in the context of the inner psychic reality of the person.

Practical interpretation of dreams involves a few elementary steps:

Step 1: Write a dream.

Step 2: Divide the dream into parts and sequences.

Step 3: List main elements separately.

Step 4: Determine your own location in a dream.

Step 5: Associations (life experiences, links).

Step 6: Which psychical powers are addressed?

Step 7: Which life topics are addressed?

Step 8: Which other persons and circumstances are addressed?

Step 9: Are archetypes up to date?

Step 10: Link existing work results to a new whole.

Step 11: Compare with previous similar dreams or dream themes.

Step 12: Expand your dream experience with imagination.

The most valuable source of all truths about man and life is the inner spirit.

No path leads so deeply and comprehensively to the inner and outer human, such as dreams and meditations.

A path without dreams can never lead to God and transcendence.

Discuss a dream in the group according to the given scheme. Check different interpretations for its causes.

Diagram 4.2.4: The legs of dream interpretation

Diagramm OS10-7: Die Etappen der Traumdeutung

Assoziationen zum Traum (Ganzes, Elemente):
Spontane Einfälle, Gedanken, Gefühle
Erinnerungen, Erfahrungen
Angesprochene psychische Kräfte und Subsysteme
1. Etappe — Ideen in Verknüpfung mit Assoziationen
Ideen in Verknüpfung mit angesprochenen Themen

Zerlegen des Traumes:

2. Etappe		
Kontraste	Mass	
Komplementäres	Werte/Sinnelemente	
Gegensätze	Ursache-Wirkung	
Polaritäten	Ausgleichelemente	
Prospektiven	RichtigstellungeN	

Neukonstruktionen:
Zusammensetzen mit den erarbeiteten Elementen
Vom Aufbau des Traumes zur Botschaft
3. Etappe — Verschiedene Träume (derselben Nacht) verbinden
Traumaussage im Ueberblick "Mensch-Umwelt"
Vernetzungen mit Psyche und Transzendenz

Folgerungen für's Leben:
Konzequenzen für die Selbstbildung
4. Etappe — Folgerungen für das tägliche Handeln
Evaluation der Selbstbildung und Handlungen

English translation:

1. **Leg: Associations to the dream (Whole, parts):** Spontaneous ideas, thoughts, feelings, memories, experiences & addressed psychical forces and subsystems & ideas linked with associations & ideas linked with addressed issue.

2. **Leg: Disassembling of the dream:** Contrasts, mass, complementary, values, meaning elements, contrasts, cause-effect, polarities, balance elements, prospective, rectifications.

3. **Leg: New construction:** Compounding with the processed elements, from the structure of the dream to the message, linking different dreams (of the same night), dream expression at a glance "human-environment".

4. **Leg: Conclusions for the life:** Consequences for the self-formation, conclusions for the daily handling, evaluation of self-formation and handlings.

4.2.5. The extrasensory perception

Extrasensory perception is actually nothing more than an imagination about strange spiritual and factual circumstances to which one has no direct access to experience.

Instead of asking with inner pictures "How am I?", one can also ask: "What is Mr. X or Mrs. Y?" The own inner perception is able to capture all foreign psychical-spiritual realities. For example, one can take an advertisement where "best-kept secrets" are promised.

Suffice it to hold the ad in your hand and inwardly ask, "What can I find out?"

Or another example: If a politician speaks, you can close your eyes while listening and see with inner pictures what he is covering and how he is dealing with his listeners.

Similarly, one can ask inwardly what astrology, spiritual healing (as commonly offered), and esoteric teachings and practices are all about.

The spirit gives a clear answer in medial vision. Any institution can be developed psychically-spiritually through medial vision.

Especially helpful is the media vision, if you want to understand other people better. For example, one might ask: Why is this person ill? Whereby does this person suffer in his soul? What is his deepest inner conflict? Why is this person in such a difficult situation? What is the solution? What does this person hide from me? What (secret) intentions does this person have? How does this person relate to me? Where does it lead to when I engage in a relationship (or business) with that person? Am I really welcome to these people? What can I do for this person?

Nothing is hidden from the "third eye". Distances are insignificant.

Sometimes it is enough to know a person's name, to hold a photograph, a garment or a letter from that person in hands, and to access the psycho-spiritual reality of that person on ESP channels.

Such objects, which produce the access to a foreign person parapsychically, are called "conductor".

The time is relative too. For example, one can see into the childhood of another person with medial vision, or in a strange house with medial vision, see what (how) lived in this house (place) earlier.

Reflections and discussion

The main difficulty with medial vision lies in the interpretation of the image material. The same problems arise here as in dream interpretation and imagination. You see foreign realities with your own pictures. You can run the risk of confusing your own with something foreign, of projecting something that is not there. Or one simply has to accept resistance that what one sees is really a symbolic expression of the above-mentioned reality.

Interpretation requires the inclusion of consciousness about oneself and, above all, exact knowledge of one's own psychic-spiritual location. The rule applies: The further one has progressed in one's own individuation, the clearer one sees in medial vision and the more precise is the interpretation.

Clairvoyants, astrologers, fortune tellers, media, card and palm readers are all nothing but better or worse medial seers. Their "object field" (astrology, coffee grounds, crystal balls, cards, etc.) is simply an activated conductor.

The medial vision has not yet been fully explored. The lower the psycho-spiritual state of the meditating person, the more there is a risk of misinterpretation and "contagion".

Therefore, first of all, practice imagination in a versatile way!

In the following table, evaluate your experience with meditations in general:

I experience:	mostly	frequently	rarely
no noticeable pictures			
only vague silhouettes			
blurry pictures			
only vague ideas			
clear spoken sentences			
excessive image flow			
not durable picture flow			
flowing confusion			
real very concrete pictures			
fabulous, fairy-tale pictures			
without emotional experience			
emotionally very intense			
very strange pictures			
pictures yes, but without understanding anything			
with a clear sense of meaning			

Discuss with others how you (and the others) have meditated to this day and what deviations from the procedure outlined here are.

Diagram 4.2.5: Practice possibilities of the imagination

Diagramm OS10-8: Anwendungsmöglichkeiten der Imagination

Checkliste zur Selbstanalyse:

☐ Entspannung, Harmonisierung der Energie
☐ Selbststärkung, Kräfteerneuerung
☐ Veränderung der psychischen Energiesituation
☐ Erfassen der Alltagsgestaltung/Lebensweise
☐ Verstehen der Beziehungen zu andern
☐ Lösungsentwicklung von Herausforderungen
☐ Klärung von Schwierigkeiten und Konflikten
☐ Verstehen von psycho-somatischen Leiden
☐ Befreiung von vergangenen Leiderfahrungen
☐ Verstehen von Träumen durch Wiedererleben
☐ Kommunikation mit dem inneren Geist
☐ Klärung aller inneren Gewissenskräfte
☐ Befreiung aller unangenehmen Erfahrungen
☐ Erfassen und Handhaben aller Gefühle
☐ Umgang mit den eigenen Bedürfnissen
☐ Wille und Selbststeuerung bewusst stärken
☐ Erkennen von Projektionen und Identifikationen
☐ Erleben von Widerständen/Abwehrmechanismen
☐ Klärung der Vielfalt des täglichen Handelns
☐ Selbststeuerung der Integrationsdynamik
☐ Das eigene Schicksal gestalten und managen
☐ Alle intelligenten Kräfte bewusst nutzen
☐ Erweiterung der Wahrnehmungsfähigkeiten
☐ Erkennen von lebendiger Weisheit
☐ Erschliessen der Mysterien des Lebens
☐ Stand der psychischen Bildung erkennen
☐ Geist als Wert und Sinn in sich erleben
☐ Wahrnehmung von fremden Menschen und Orten
☐ Weltlage in geistiger Sicht erfassen
☐ Den Weg der Individuation planen und gehen

English translation: Checklist of self-analysis:

Relaxing, harmonizing of the energy & self-enforcement, renewal of forces & changing of the psychical energy situation & capturing of the daily design, lifestyle & understanding of the relations to others & solution development of challenges & clearing of difficulties and conflicts & understanding of psycho-somatic sufferings & freeing of past harmful experiences & understanding of dreams through reliving & communication with the inner spirit & clearing all inner conscience forces & freeing of all unpleasant experiences & realizing and managing all feelings & handling with the own needs & will and "I «control consciously strengthen & recognizing of projections and identifications & clearing of the manifoldness of the daily acting & self-control of the integration dynamic & designing and managing the own destiny & using consciously all intelligent forces & amplifying the perception abilities & recognizing of living wisdom & developing the mysteries of life & recognizing the state of the psychical formation & perception of foreign man and places & world situation seeing in spiritual sight & planning and going the path of the individuation.

4.2.6. The contemplation

Contemplation is a special form of imagination with well-defined goals.

The contemplation deals exclusively with symbols and archetypes, i.e. not with single psychical forces, not with the life of other people and not with the collective unconscious.

Symbols grasp the general of human existence, the general of cultural creation and the general of human activities.

Archetypes always refer to general patterns of shaped psychical forces, to the processes of change of psychical life, to the stages of individuation, to the general life-themes of man, to the general characteristics of meaning and value, and to transcendental reality.

Whether the goal of relaxation, for example by means of the image of the sun, should be referred to as contemplation or mental training, is a decision question.

Imagination with the goal of harmonizing the psychical powers and "emptying" the consciousness is not really contemplation.

Whoever seeks meaning and value in life, wants to understand and accomplish psychical-spiritual evolution, who wants to see "behind" the material external world, and who tries to open up the transcendence, needs the path of contemplation.

Here, too, precise goals have to be defined: "What do I want to see?" and "How do I want to see this (that is, with what symbol motif)?".

In contemplation, a meaningful fact must be taken into account: Even the contemplation happens in the context of one's own psychical and real life.

The pictures usually show with personal experience material, with the state of their own development.

The rule is that the further someone has progressed in the process of individuation, the clearer and more directly he sees and experiences the transcendental realities and what archetypes represent.

This means, for example, that to see God without advanced individuation is not possible or only in the perspective that the intrapsychic state allows.

Every experience is bound to the internalized images of these realities: You see what you have learned about as long as the internalized images are not processed.

Reflections and discussion

Contemplation means looking and experiencing:

☐ Transformation processes of individuation
☐ Defined milestones in individuation
☐ Typical patterns of shaped psychical forces
☐ Meaning and value of general activities
☐ Meaning and value of existence, of human life
☐ The realities that the archetypes represent
☐ The actual transcendental realities

The result, and especially the experiencing of contemplation, is related to:

☐ State of general psychodynamics
☐ State of dynamics of emotions
☐ Condition of unconscious inventory
☐ Activities and abilities of thought operations
☐ Inner freedom from dogmas, ideals, ideologies
☐ Urge of unfulfilled needs
☐ Differentiation and strength of the power of love
☐ Ability of dream interpretation
☐ Ability (sensitivity) to experience and grasp meaning and values
☐ Dynamics of defence mechanisms and ability of integration
☐ Total inventory available to consciousness
☐ State of own individuation

The procedure in contemplation:

1. The same steps and rules apply as in the imagination.

2. The goal decision is particularly important, because also difficult: You can only formulate goals that you know.

3. It does not make much sense to want to storm high "summits" at first "walking attempts".

4. The performance levels should begin with lifelike topics.

5. It is not possible and barely sensible to seek "God" (whatever that means) if one does not want to search and process on one's own psychical life comprehensively, or if one has barely taken steps forward.

Formulate some goals of contemplation. Compare with others.

Diagram 4.2.6: Model of a contemplation (circle-cross-mandala)

Diagramm OS10-9: Muster einer Kontemplation (Kreis-Kreuz-Mandala)

English translation: Contemplation circle-cross-mandala:

Close your eyes. You relax now. Your thoughts dissolve. You breathe deeply and slowly, more and more deeply and quietly. Deep quiet is covering you more and more …

Imagine: You look in the deep blue starry sky. From far away a small light is coming closer and closer to you. The light becomes bigger and bigger, it looks like a little sun. You feel increasingly the warmth of the light rays, fist in the face, then more and more in the body …

Now the sun is in front of you, looks like a circle-cross-mandala and radiates a pleasant warmth …

Speak to this source of light: What are you? Where do you come from? What can I do with you? Experience inside the answers …

Now the light is coming nearer and nearer until you are completely in this sun. The light is flowing through your entire body. You feel pleasant well and secure in it. The light carries you. The light protects you. The light strengthens your whole psychical energy. The centred of this sun is in the middle of you. You can feel this inner centre. Rest a moment in this state …

Gradually this image of this sun is leaving.

Now you see nothing. But the energy of this mandala is in you. Feel now the strengthen and centred energy …

Breathe deeply. Then open your eyes.

4.2.7. Working unit

4.2.7. Working unit - 1

1. a) How do you experience your dreams?

1. b) What do your acquaintances say about dreams and dream interpretation? And your conclusion:

2. Describe in 7 points, what you have drawn from your dreams or the interpretation of dreams for a benefit:

1)
2)
3)
4)
5)
6)
7)

3. Formulate an educational goal for you to dream interpretation:

4. a) Imagine the "success" of your dream work until today:

4. b) Your conclusion in one sentence:

4.2.7. Work unit - 2

1. a) How do you experience the richness of dreams?

1. b) Extend the list of possible dream content from personal experience:

2. Briefly describe what you have already learned about dream content:

a) People:	
b) Animals:	
c) Places:	
d) Objects:	
e) Events:	
f) Subjects:	
g) Actions:	
h) Conversations:	
i) Mysterious:	

3. Formulate an educational goal about dealing with the diversity of dream content:

4. a) Imagine your way of dealing with the dream content:

4. b) Your conclusion in one sentence:

4.2.7. Working unit - 3

1. a) How do you recognize an intelligent dream structure?

1. b) Comment on the "human leading function" of dreams:

2. Reflect, with an example, the possibilities that exist in this intelligent spiritual power with regard to:

a) Relationships:	
b) Life processing:	
c) Habitat design:	
d) Politics:	
e) Intercultural understanding:	
f) Interreligious compound:	

3. Formulate an educational goal for using the power of the inner spirit:

4. a) Imagine the "use" of the power of the spirit:

4. b) Your conclusion in one sentence:

4.2.7. Working unit - 4

1. a) How do you experience the 'spirit' as interlocutor and manager?

1. b) What about the "I"'s freedom from this 'spirit'?

2. What problems/difficulties do you experience for practical dream interpretation?

Step 1: Write down a dream

Step 2: Divide the dream into parts and sequences

Step 3: List main elements separately

Step 4: Capture your own location in a dream

Step 5: Associations (life experiences, links)

Step 6: Which psychical forces are addressed?

Step 7: Which life topics are addressed?

Step 8: Which other persons and circumstances are addressed?

Step 9: Are archetypes up to date?

Step 10: Link existing work results to a new whole

Step 11: Compare with previous similar dreams or dream themes

Step 12: Expand your dream experience with imagination

3. Formulate an educational goal about the relationship "I and spirit":

4. a) Imagine your freedom towards your inner spirit:

4. b) Your conclusion in one sentence:

4.2.7. Working unit - 5

a) How do you experience the "play" of images when imagining?

1. b) Formulate 3 questions that can ever qualify as an introduction to an imagination for general self-knowledge:

How many times have you meditated (imagined) about the following topics?
5 = very common; 4 = frequently; 3 = sometimes; 2 = rather little; 1 = rare; 0 = never

Issue	Frequency	Comment/explanation
Self-knowledge in general		
Way of living, lifestyle		
Acts of all kinds		
Conflicts, difficulties		
Health, illness, suffering		
Relationships, people		
Biography, unconscious		
Sexuality, lust		
Attitudes, beliefs		
Meaning of life, questions of existence		
Love, love for life		
Feelings, moods		
Institutions of all kinds		
Politics, environment, world situation, etc.		
Religion, God, church, etc.		

3. Formulate an educational goal for self-knowledge with imagination:

4. a) Imagine your responsibility towards your own imagination practice:

4. b) Your conclusion in one sentence:

4.2.7. Working unit - 6

1.a) What exactly is 'subjective' in the experience of a contemplation?

1. b) What kind of contemplation (symbols, archetypes) do you find difficult? In what way?

2. Explain with an example. The result, and especially the experience of contemplation, is related to:

a) Condition of general psychodynamics
b) Condition of the dynamics of feelings
c) Condition of the unconscious inventory
d) Activities and abilities of thought operations
e) Inner freedom from dogmas, ideals, ideologies
f) Urge for unfulfilled needs
g) Differentiation and strength of the power of love
h) Ability of dream interpretation
i) Ability (sensitivity) to experience and grasp meaning and values
k) Dynamics of defence mechanisms and ability of integration
l) Total inventory available to consciousness
m) State of own individuation

3. Formulate an educational goal for the practice of contemplation:

4. a) Imagine the meaning and value of your contemplation:

4. b) Your conclusion in one sentence:

4.2.7. Working unit - 7

Write an open letter to the politicians that they should integrate their dreams into their political work. And justify:

Multiple Choice Test

Choose the four correct answers:

8.1. The dreams are:
- ☐ a) A spiritually processed reality
- ☐ b) expression of an inner view
- ☐ c) Purposeful mental analyses
- ☐ d) free of value judgments
- ☐ e) Unstructured content of consciousness
- ☐ f) Operational directed processes

8.2. Elements in the dream reality are:
- ☐ a) Always objectively real
- ☐ b) Fragments from everyday life
- ☐ c) Everyday symbols
- ☐ d) Actions
- ☐ e) Life topics of all kinds
- ☐ f) Driving forces

8.3. Characteristic of the inner mind is:
- ☐ a) Communication to the "I" through dreams
- ☐ b) Andragogic purpose
- ☐ c) Purposes the dissolution of the "I"
- ☐ d) Organizes individuation
- ☐ e) Access to all realities
- ☐ f) Non-binding structural dynamics

8.4. The following statements are correct:
- ☐ a) Interpretation of dreams is based on pure art and intuition.
- ☐ b) Interpretation of dreams always remains subjective and arbitrary.
- ☐ c) Dream interpretation can be learned like a foreign language.
- ☐ d) The dream elements are always or mostly to disassemble.
- ☐ e) The dream language has many forms of expression.
- ☐ f) The dream-creating power has different functions.

8.5. Risks in the practical imagination are esp. in the area:
- ☐ a) Superficial consideration
- ☐ b) Own projections
- ☐ c) Extrasensory manipulation
- ☐ d) Interpretation of symbols and images
- ☐ e) Overestimation of an exercise
- ☐ f) Become victims of indoctrination

8.6. Allow contemplations:

☐ a) Conversion processes   ☐ b) Sense experiences
☐ c) Value experience   ☐ d) Archetypes experience
☐ e) Increase in faith   ☐ f) self-dissolution

5. Concept Individuation

Essential theses

The human being as a psychical-spiritual being is in need of education and capable of education. This inner formation is human evolution.

The basis of this education is the affirmation of the inner life, the attention and the awareness of all shape able and usable psychical powers.

The formation and progressive unfolding of all forces in the direction of a holistic, interdependent, intertwined wholeness is called "individuation".

The education process has three stages (phases):

☐ 1st stage: Recognition and understanding of the psychical systems and forces
☐ 2nd stage: Changing, strengthening, unfolding, renewing all psychical forces
☐ 3rd stage: Creating a new wholeness and living it

Through education in this process, man finds all the answers about human and his existence in the experience of the spirit and the processes of change.

5.1. Individuation as a growth process

5.1.1. The psychical-spiritual evolution

The scientific and technical advances of the industrial nations are impressive. The manifold goods, the superstructures, the systems of communication and much more show us: Man has a tremendous creative intellectual potential.

The living conditions in industrialized countries have changed dramatically in quantity and quality since about 1970. The medical care provides services that were previously unimaginable. The quality of living has improved by millions. One hundred technical devices for everyday use make life easier.

Many people have never imagined possibilities to live an original expression, with clothing, car, home decor. As never before, man today is informed about events in the world.

Women can shape their own lives today, in their jobs and relationships. The "being a mother" is no longer considered a condition for the fully accepted woman in society.

More and more people are also free of ideological and dogmatic control. They can no longer be seduced by totalitarian and archaic-mythical images of man.

There is, however, a counter-reality: In mental life, people have not formed quality. Most still reject the mental life.

Most have no idea about the unconscious and the inner spirit. Their individual psychical subsystems and forces affect unknowingly chaotic. Love, measured by the individuation, is poorly formed.

The quantitative expansion dominates: More and more experiences with simultaneous increasing distance from the inner reality. This creates new illusionary, religious, esoteric and political ideas.

Increasingly, people tend to attach themselves to objects and appearance rather than to real life. There has been no comprehensive psycho-spiritual evolution for 2000 years.

Therefore, there is also the reverse side of technical progress: Nuclear bombs, enormous harmonies, environmental destruction, crime, poverty and so on.

There have always been single individuals and groups of people who have found and lived the inner reality. They have turned to their comprehensive psychical life. They sought and lived the love and the spirit. They have researched the consciousness about themselves and about existence.

This is psycho-spiritual evolution: Forming the comprehensive self-love and living the love out of it. Human life with the psychical organism is the highest good and the highest value in this progressive unfolding. This causes expansion in the internal quality. The technical progress can be built on it.

Reflections and discussion

History shows us the possibilities and realities of man:

☐ Man can reject the inner psychical reality.
☐ Man can negate the power of love or live it only outwardly.
☐ Man can live without communication with the inner spirit.
☐ Man can suppress inner development.
☐ Man can destroy and hate what human and life are.
☐ Man can refuse any expression of life built up inside.
☐ Man can bind himself to external circumstances as a substitute; e.g.: goods, power, ideology, dogmas, laws.

In human affairs, "progress" is evident, not in technology and industrial organizations.

Everything science, research, politics, industry, etc. is created by people and for people. Culture and civilization are products of humans. None of this has value without human.

Much of it is created:

☐ without love
☐ without spirit
☐ without the psychical inner world

Humans also have the other possibility, which we call the psychic-spiritual evolution:

- ☐ Integration of psychical life
- ☐ Consciousness about the inner life, especially about the unconscious
- ☐ Order and structure in the psychical system (between all parts)
- ☐ Spirit as a superordinate "governmental principle": Inside as well as outside
- ☐ Unfolding and growth of all life open internal possibilities
- ☐ Attention to life out of self-love
- ☐ Utilization of all possibilities to give life an equal order in connection with all psychical powers

Humanity is still at the beginning of this evolutionary process.

Most people hardly know what is alive and shape able in psychical realities in them.

Where should man find answers to the fundamental questions of existence, if not in his psychical organism and in the experience of psycho-spiritual evolution?

- ☐ Where does the human come from?
- ☐ Where does man go after his death?
- ☐ What is life for?
- ☐ What is "God"?

Diagram 5.1.1: Evolution of human being

Diagramm OS1-1: Evolution des Menschseins

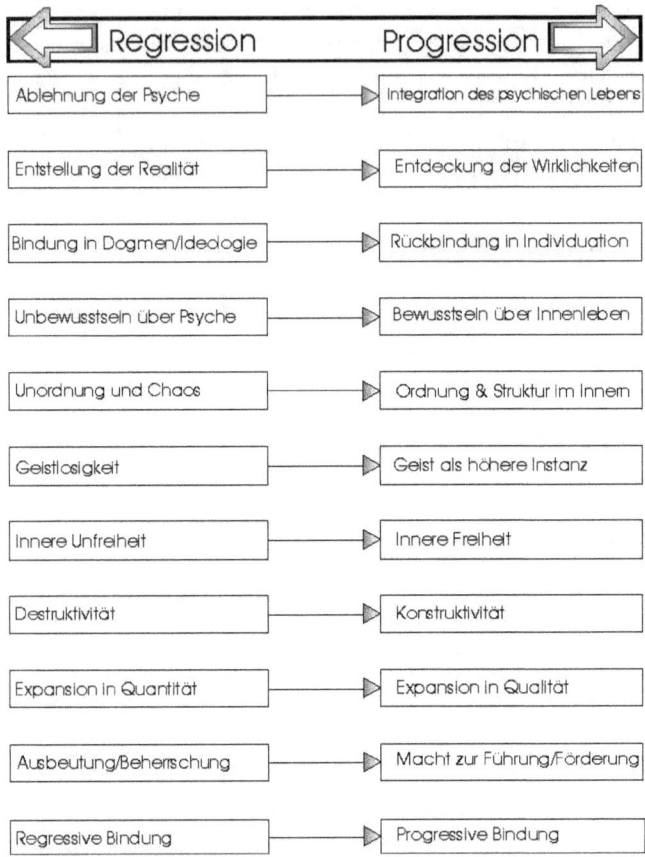

Regression	Progression
Ablehnung der Psyche	Integration des psychischen Lebens
Entstellung der Realität	Entdeckung der Wirklichkeiten
Bindung in Dogmen/Ideologie	Rückbindung in Individuation
Unbewusstsein über Psyche	Bewusstsein über Innenleben
Unordnung und Chaos	Ordnung & Struktur im Innern
Geistlosigkeit	Geist als höhere Instanz
Innere Unfreiheit	Innere Freiheit
Destruktivität	Konstruktivität
Expansion in Quantität	Expansion in Qualität
Ausbeutung/Beherrschung	Macht zur Führung/Förderung
Regressive Bindung	Progressive Bindung

English translation:

< Regression
Denial of the psyche
Distortion of the reality
Formation in dogmas/ideology
Unconscious about the psyche
Mess and chaos
Spiritlessness
Inner bondage
Destructivity
Expansion to quantity

Progression >
> Integration of the psychical life
> Discovery of the realities
> Bonding back in individuation
> Consciousness about inner life
> Order & structure in the inside
> Spirit as highest authority
> Inner freedom
> Constructively
> Expansion to quality

Exploitation/domination   > Power to guidance/assistance
Regressive fixation   > Progressive linking

First tasks of individuation

The standard concepts of human education are now known: Development, deployment, growth, maturity, processiveness, self-development, expansion of consciousness, self-discovery, selfhood, self-realization, spiritual development, personal history, growing up, and the like. These terms all in some way, probably always with certain theories about the personality and with their own philosophies (about the person and the life) the individuation. The student will have realized by now: We constructed a lot of building blocks from a very wide range of knowledge about humans. Our variety of methods has certainly become transparent. With clear concepts and concrete steps, we can grasp the process of development and growth; to this an overview.

The concrete work in the

1st stage of individuation:

☐ Gain an overview of the different psychical power systems
☐ Get to know the central psychical powers and discover its by oneself
☐ Understand the meaning of your own biography and find access to it
☐ Recognize the complexity and interconnectedness of one's own actions
☐ Being able to constructively deal with one's own psychical (life) energy
☐ Find clarity about "awareness" so that this reality becomes manageable
☐ Build concrete ideas about the "I" and its control mechanisms
☐ Discover expertise about the intelligent functions in yourself
☐ Recognize the world of emotions as manageable and find access to it
☐ Acquire precise knowledges of the variety of needs through self-reflection
☐ Understand the unconscious as a reality that can be systematically reshaped
☐ Capture the meaning (functioning) of the dreams and get started
☐ Understanding love as the crucial life force; with a view to the opposite
☐ Concretely grasp the meaning of psychical life for the human being
☐ Recognize the connection between life themes and psychical inner world
☐ Discover the basic values of being human from the psychical life viewpoint
☐ Recognize the difference between conscious and unconscious life
☐ Look at the relationship life from the perspective of psychical interactions
☐ Value the importance of senses and body in the context of the psychical
☐ See the meaning of sexuality and its creative possibilities
☐ Evaluate private life from from practical point of view of self-management
☐ Make learning, especially in self-education, 'intelligent' and interesting
☐ Be able to formulate for oneself bigger and smaller goals of self-education
☐ Understand how people's images come about, how they can be judged
☐ Interpret and nurture health from a holistic view of life
☐ Understand partnership relationship from psychical life

☐ Rediscover maleness and femininity as roles and as experience of being
☐ Understand and apply the methods of self-knowledge
☐ Find clear ideas about intuition, introspection, imagination, contemplation
☐ Understand and practice the first steps of dream interpretation
☐ Be able to use techniques of relaxation in basic stages in a meaningful way
☐ Formulate and realize positive life values for oneself
☐ Discover and take seriously the mode of action of what we call "spirit"
☐ Taking responsibility for one's own actions, life, and lifetime
☐ Experience one's own being in the real and transcendental networking
☐ Competently handle meditative and thought-based handling of life issues
☐ Build life lust, love of life, hope and trust in life
☐ Reflect, ask, discuss, argue about psychical life
☐ Locate the philosophical and religious dimensions in the inner reality
☐ Have a clear critical view of today's psycho-spiritual offerings
☐ Differentiate and understand the present life forms with objective distance
☐ Recognize the inner experience of growth, development, expansion of consciousness

Development and growth

There are many paraphrases and aspects of the development and growth of the personality. The following examples provide suggestions for reflection.

☐ Development causes: False facades and masks letting drop; recognizing more basics behind the masks
☐ Decision to be yourself; fully experience your own attitudes; recognizing dependencies; to turn to: Pain, anger, desire, grief, pride etc.
☐ Recognizing the inner wealth; find the inner pattern; be open to living experience
☐ Reducing defensive posture and rigidity; enduring uncertainties
☐ Experiencing the whole own organism and find confidence in it; recognizing your own source of decisions and value judgments
☐ Accepting yourself as a unique being, experiencing development and assuming responsibility for growth

Process phases of personality change are:

Phase: Self-experience of the reluctance, to communicate, the barriers to internal communication, the black and white categories

Phase: First slight loosening; still strong distancing to one's own feelings and experiences; differentiations still very limited and flat rate

Phase: Relatively distanced, but more fluid communication about feelings, self-experiences; still strongly negative assessment of feelings; gradually more differentiated

Phase: Increasing opening and differentiation of the emotional world, but still little acceptance; experiences become more relaxed; concern about contradictions

Phase: Emotions 'emanate,' are expressed; the personal connection to the feelings is recognized; accuracy and differentiation are sought; more open to contradictions / inconsistencies; assumption of individual responsibility

Phase: Feelings are no longer fought and denied; full acceptance; the experience of feeling becomes part of the self; physical loosening; free and unblocked communication; incongruence between experience and consciousness is experienced and diminished; self-living as 'subject' of experiences (of problems)

Phase: Feeling experience becomes the reference, i.e. to experience / want more clearly to know who you are, what you want, your own attitudes and attitudes, etc.; increasing basic trust in one's own process; situations are experienced and interpreted in novelty; being confident in the process; clear internal communication; experience that one has the choice to live in new ways

Our thesis: In all topics and work areas of the 1st phase of the individuation, these processes run in principles.

But individuation is decisive 'more': Individuation is self-development, that is:

☐ Free the self from the wrong person's covers (masks, shadows)
☐ Dissolution of the contradictions between unconscious and consciousness
☐ Find relation with your own unconscious (also Anima / Animus)
☐ Create unity and centre in (centre inside)

Finding the self - One thesis: Psychically, the self means: The psychical wholeness of the human being. Since man knows himself only as an "I", and the self as a totality is indescribable and indistinguishable from an image of God, self-realization in a religious-metaphysical language means the incarnation of God.

Notes and perspectives

What do most people think about psycho-spiritual evolution?

Write down the key words in this subchapter:

What causes the preponderance of regression in the long term in the collective?

Unfolding and growth is essential because: ...

What did you learn about individuation in your parents' home, school and church?

What significance in living together has the conversation about the individual steps of individuation (per stage or phase)?

What would it do if the actors in politics and economics lived the process of individuation?

What does advertising convey about progression in mental-spiritual evolution?

Formulate an important question about development and growth:

5.1.2. The process of Individuation

The process of psycho-spiritual evolution is called "Individuation". This process can be divided into clear phases and individual stages. Every step is scientifically prepared. All experiences are verifiable. The elements and their meaning are arguable. There is no speculation here or faith is needed.

Individuation does not happen outside of daily life and is not based on mastery. Neither "brainwashing" nor indoctrination are its methods. All steps of this evolution are based on the psychical organism embedded in the habitat. Self-knowledge is the beginning. This leads to a complex growth process in all psychical subsystems. Insofar, individuation is the holistic education process. There are no "shortcuts" and no illusions in this process.

The inner formation of the whole person means work and experience: The journey of discovery begins with the affirmation of the psychical life. All inner spaces, including their "furniture", are to be discovered, analysed and understood.

What is known can also be formed, i.e. changed, differentiated and let grow. This creates a kind of "inner rebirth". The entire lived life is cleaned up step by step.

All inappropriate images in the unconscious can be corrected. Man can find and satisfy his real needs. The feelings can be understood and integrated into everyday life in a balanced way. Perception and thinking are gaining in quality. Instead of defence man finds a creative dynamic of the integration of the entire inner and outer life.

Thus, the consciousness of oneself, of others, of the world and of transcendence is gradually and factually and truly extended. The dreams or the inner spirit lead those on this path who accepts this "governmental principle".

Through these employments, the inner forces change and find a harmonious new unity. Nothing is split off by oppression. On the outside, life receives a clear imprint of these formations. What is lived inside and cared in the personal, also in the human community has a meaning: Love and the spirit become leading forces in the shaping of the world.

The process lasts until man has found his new wholeness. From this he lives for himself and for the others. The circle-cross-mandala is an archetype of this goal. At the goal of individuation man is a living image of this mandala.

Many people can go through this inner process and reach the goal. individuation is the life requirement of love and the spirit.

Reflections and discussion

How does this psychic-spiritual evolution take place? We know the psychical organism and its interrelations with the living space.

We know a lot about the functioning of the individual psychical forces.

If you have a plan, you can organize a process flow.

Whoever maintains communication with the inner spirit has the "governing and guiding principle" for evolution.

The practical process is called "INDIVIDUATION".
(not "individualization)

We divide this process into three stages (phases):

1. Step:

Affirm the psychical reality
Discover, disassemble, understand this psychical reality
Understand the functioning of the individual forces
Learn the methods to understand and form the forces
Elaboration of these steps until the "birth of the new human"

2. Step:

Recognition of the spirit as a principle of order and leadership
Transformation of the individual forces ("die and become")
Strengthening and unfolding of all psychical subsystems
Dissolution of internal contradictions
Development of an internal unit with the subsystems

3. Step:

Dissolution of the old principles of government in favour of the spirit
Creating harmony between inside and outside
Rooting the way of life in love and in the spirit
The inner wholeness living outside (giving an expression)
Completion of wholeness (as an internal process)

There is no "wholeness" without the comprehensive psychical organism and without this psychical-spiritual process.

Those who want to achieve holistic educational goals live in the process of individuation.

Without integration of all psychical forces, especially the spirit, the goal is not achievable.

Those who go through this process not only form "psychical forces" but their entire psycho-energetic structure. Experience and education become energetic being.

Through this process, man becomes more and more what he is inside: That is much more than most people can imagine.

Man has not yet discovered his possibilities (with a few exceptions). Individuation is the realization of being human.

☐ Individuation is the "evolutionary leap" for all people today.

Diagram 5.1.2: The individuation process- main transformation

Diagramm OS1-2: Der Individuationsprozess - Hauptwandlungen

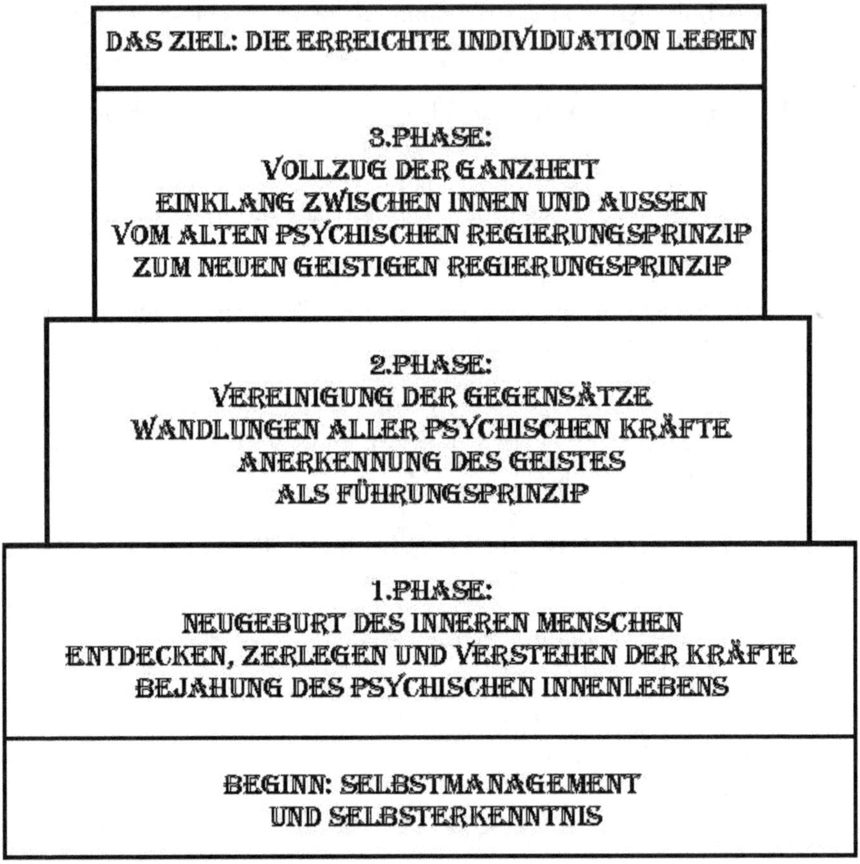

DAS ZIEL: DIE ERREICHTE INDIVIDUATION LEBEN

3.PHASE:
VOLLZUG DER GANZHEIT
EINKLANG ZWISCHEN INNEN UND AUSSEN
VOM ALTEN PSYCHISCHEN REGIERUNGSPRINZIP
ZUM NEUEN GEISTIGEN REGIERUNGSPRINZIP

2.PHASE:
VEREINIGUNG DER GEGENSÄTZE
WANDLUNGEN ALLER PSYCHISCHEN KRÄFTE
ANERKENNUNG DES GEISTES
ALS FÜHRUNGSPRINZIP

1.PHASE:
NEUGEBURT DES INNEREN MENSCHEN
ENTDECKEN, ZERLEGEN UND VERSTEHEN DER KRÄFTE
BEJAHUNG DES PSYCHISCHEN INNENLEBENS

BEGINN: SELBSTMANAGEMENT
UND SELBSTERKENNTNIS

English translation:
The goal: Living the reached individuation
3rd phase: Implementation of the wholeness, unison between inside and outside, from the old psychical regime to the new spiritual regime
2nd phase: Union of the contradictions, transformation of all psychical forces, recognizing of the spirit as guidance principle
1st phase: Rebirth of the inner human, discovering, disassembling and understanding of the forces, affirmation of the psychical inner life.

Start: Self-management and self-knowledge

Forces against Individuation

Mark:

1 = I am relatively free from that
2 = is valid for me
3 = is correct for me

- ☐ Afraid of one's own feelings.
- ☐ I want to, but at the moment I have other things to do.
- ☐ I want, but there is another will, it is even stronger.
- ☐ I'm convinced of the thing already, but ... is that really for me?
- ☐ I am determined, but ... doubt ... questions ... I'm still waiting.
- ☐ I know myself well enough now; that's enough for my life.
- ☐ So, I do not want to become religious!
- ☐ There is no firm knowledge. How should the individuation be 'true'?
- ☐ The truth is in the Bible; everything else leads away from God.
- ☐ I have family, job, career ... I do not have time for so much work!
- ☐ I have no problems; I solve my conflicts efficiently. So why?
- ☐ I basically only read very few books.
- ☐ I have found God, have peace in me; he will already redeem me.
- ☐ We have no difficulties in our marriage; and I always enjoy sex.
- ☐ I know for sure how I think and look through pretty much in everything in the world.
- ☐ My attitudes and beliefs are nothing to shake.
- ☐ I lack the strength to catch myself daily for self-education.
- ☐ Now I have a new friend and he does not want that. Maybe later!
- ☐ I do not need that all; I am an adult and I know how I live.
- ☐ Scientifically, neither the unconscious nor the archetypes are proven.
- ☐ My husband is strict against that. Well, I do not want a martial quarrel because of it.
- ☐ Buying two or three books a month is far too expensive for me.
- ☐ Reading is so exhausting; I cannot do much with it anyway.
- ☐ There are many ways that lead to self-realization ...
- ☐ Make an environmental contribution with self-education? That does not help!
- ☐ I am a simple person; what should I study about psychical life?
- ☐ Wisdom is what silent people; I like to live and think critically-rationally.
- ☐ It would have just been missing if I had to do without something in life!
- ☐ Today you can trust nobody and nothing more - all lies and deception!
- ☐ Only the church leads to the 'truth'; certainly not the individuation.
- ☐ I certainly cannot use individuation in the workplace.
- ☐ Something is true, but that's the case almost everywhere.

- I am happy; I'm fine. Why should I still practice self-knowledge?
- Psychology is difficult for people and just makes life more complicated.
- Why me? That's what others should do that can do it better!
- Certainly, now I have learned a lot. But now I want to live. Later again.
- Scientifically, dream interpretation is not a safe method.
- I cannot handle symbols. I am a realistic person.
- I do not believe that love of life and love of life are so important.
- I am free, I can do what I want; individuation, or not.
- Well, astrology helped me a lot - I do not know what I'm missing.
- Love is important, only private; and I do not really need love.
- It does not matter to anyone, whether I'm neurotic or not - impudence!
- I performed excellently- what else is individuation for?
- I have neither grief, nor worry, nor desperation, nor uncertainty.
- Money determines the future and happiness of people, not individuation.
- Social problems are none of my business at all.
- I have no problems with my unconscious ... Where is that anyway?
- There is no objective truth. There is only utility.
- "Psychotrip for me?" This is only for enthusiasts and disturbed.
- I have become older now; I know how life goes. I do not like anymore.
- The great "enlightened ones" and prophets all just had problems.

The inner experience of archetypes

In general, this particular kind of symbol in the literature on individuation occupies a much too wide space. In general, at most one-thousandth of all dreams of a person who works systematically on individuation should contain an archetypal symbol or an archetypal act.

Decisive turning points of the essential internal procedures are archetypically represented, not every single knowledge, insight and new formation! If one takes some symbolic lexicons and seeks an orientation, confusion is more likely to result in most cases.

It seems that knowledge of the true content of archetypes has been lost through commercialization. Too much is speculation, meaning due to historical-cultural habits or simply 'nice poem'. Perhaps it is even the case that the true meanings have to be worked out again through the individuation of many people.

Contemplation provides ways for clarification, an aid to orientation on what archetypes represent. If it is true that the most important processes in individuation can only be represented and executed by archetypes, archetypes from the collective unconscious, then these must first be worked out anew. Because alchemy and mythology are also historical phenomena with special time and reality experiences.

How can the nine most central processes of individuation be represented in dreams, experienced in pictures and symbolic actions? This is the core question about the archetypes, because they are supposed to make such processes tangible, as informative feedback to the "I" ("that's it"), as a catalyst for initiating such a procedure, or as a confirmation of the internal implementation.

We give some examples, complement archetypal images with general symbolic experiences that highlight aspects:

1. Affirmation of the psychical inner world: Going on a journey, going to school

2. Discovering the psychical powers: Treasure hunt, house inspection, caving, shadowy figures, falling out of teeth, going into dark depths

3. Rebirth: Birth of a child, a new baby, Christmas, opening of a new "thing"

4. Recognition of the spirit: Initiation, inauguration, presentation of insignia, getting a new dress

5. Transformations: Dying / surgery procedures, funeral, bath, washing ritual, farewell, bridge demolition, coming to a new country, new teeth

6. Union: Wedding, embrace with a fairy figure, entering into the sun, light experience

7. New governmental principle: Royal insignia, new 'boss', new land, new laws, new tasks

8. Unison inside-out: Harmony, transparency, music, clothes fit or vehicle 'fits'

9. Wholeness: circle, mandala, sun, eternal fire as the source of all life.

Our theses on archetypes:

- ☐ Archetypes are orientation aids in individuation.
- ☐ Archetypes enliven forces that promote growth and development.
- ☐ Archetypes organize psychical forces into new structures / networks.
- ☐ Archetypes open up / brighten new inner realities.
- ☐ Archetypes represent 'eternal' valid psychical processes and realities.
- ☐ Archetypes enable intercultural communication about inner realities.
- ☐ Archetypes lead to the experience of God.
- ☐ Archetypes are prototypes of a transcendental reality.

Notes and perspectives

What are the essential forces against individuation in society (among men)?

Write down the keywords in this subchapter:

What is a "life without the main transformations" of individuation and a "life after the main transformations"?

The main transformations of individuation are essential for the human being, because: ...

What did you learn in the home, school and church about the main transformations of individuation?

What significance does the conversation about archetypes have in living together?

What would affect the seriousness of the archetypes of the soul in politics and economy?

To what extent does advertising promote ignorance and rejection of individuation?

Formulate an important question about the archetypical processes:

5.1.3. The human in spiritual anchorage

The formation of all psychical forces, including the "purification" of the unconscious ("catharsis"), changes the psycho-energetic body and its charisma. The "wavelengths" are aligned to each "channel".

We can also say that all instruments are tuned, coordinated with others and used in a coordinated way. This leads to a balance of all forces with love and spirit. This is something quite different than generally taught as a whole.

The "glasses" of perception become clear. The spiritual processing becomes optimal.

Through individuation, man sees more and more clearly the comprehensive psychical reality of humans. At the same time, he receives in daily dreams "feedback" from his spiritual power. Through such changes man forms himself internally. He is learning more and more about this inner spirit.

The entry into this educational process is the condition, so that the valuable and mysterious of humans can be experienced. The more man performs the transformations in himself, the more he changes his psychical organism and the closer he comes to the transcendental reality.

If this mind is an aspect of what is meant by "God," then the process of individuation means "experience of God."

The circle-cross-mandala is an image of the person who has reached the goal of this process. On the other hand, this archetype is also an image of what "God" is.

This means that the more man approaches the goal, the closer he comes to God of reality through his inner transformations. We cannot nearly express God in words and pictures - and we do not want to try it.

The experience of this mandala and the transformation processes of individuation bring us to this reality.

Everyone in his own culture and language can communicate this in his own way, visually and linguistically. If one embarks on this journey of discovery and finds this new country, then people do not want to consider this discovery as possible.

If millions discover this land, then the earth in the "heads" can become the image that it really is. This is the case with individuation: Whoever does not go the way can never experience the goal.

Imagine: Many people go this educational path. With all these people, the way of life and the world becomes more and more an expression of what they become through this process.

More and more human is rooted in his transcendental originality and origin. Life becomes so an expression of this rootedness.

The chances to live this are given.

Reflections and discussion

A symbol is a sign (an image) that stands for something else, or at least conveys meaning through pictorial expression. Many symbols can be conceived with the inner experience.

A specific kind of symbol refers to psychical life, to the processes of transformation in individuation and to the different states of the psychical organism, from the beginning of the process to the end.

The archetype "circle-cross-mandala" is an image of the mental-spiritual wholeness. This wholeness is resp. characterized by:

☐ Unity of elements
☐ Openness to the outside
☐ Centeredness
☐ Inner subdivision

We can, as with all images and symbols, with inner visuals approach us more closely to what this archetype portrays. Several main experiences are characteristic:

☐ Strong harmonizing and centring psycho-energetic power
☐ A reality, like the sun, in the universe
☐ A hidden reality that wants to become reality

☐ An inherent intelligent force communicating with the "I"
☐ Man can become a living image of this archetype

Through inner experience, this mandala opens up a new reality:

The more man grows in the individuation, the more he becomes a living image of this mandala, the closer he comes through his inner becoming and being to what the mandala of the universe portrays.

When people increasingly live in the direction of this process, they are increasingly shaping the reality of life and their relations from this inner order.

In this way, the life of the people in the habitat becomes an expression of what the mandala portrays about reality in the universe.

What this "main archetype" from the universe depicts - probably "God" - cannot be adequately described.

People from all cultures may use many words and pictures to describe their experiences of this mandala.

Reality itself, in man and in the universe, remains the same.

Diagram 5.1.3: The human in cosmic anchorage

Diagramm OS1-3: Der Mensch in kosmischer Verankerung

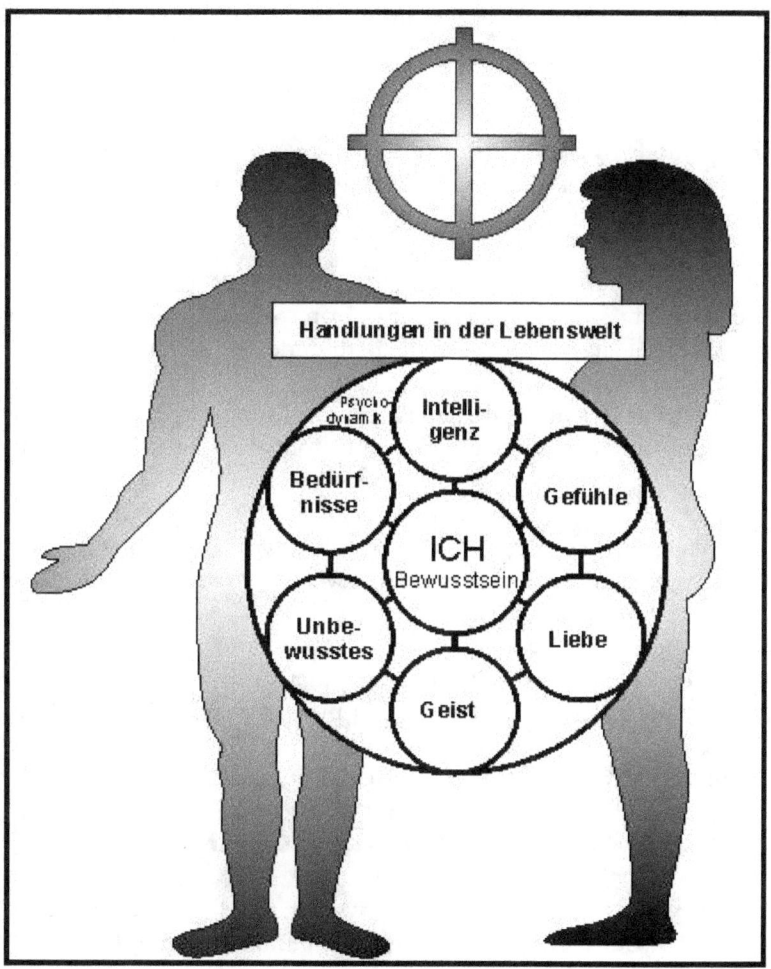

English translation: (From left above to right below)
Activity in the living space
"I" – consciousness with intelligence, needs, emotions, unconscious, love, spirit and psychodynamics.

Contemplations - 12 examples

Contemplations allow the inner experience of central processes of transformation in individuation, of meaningful changes in knowledge and shaping of forces as well as of meaning and value elements from life and individuation.

The procedure is as in the general imagination. Recommendation: Practice step by step! We give some practical examples of the 1st stage of individuation:

1. Contemplation: Imagine you want to go on a world tour, discovering the lives of people who seek the "secrets" of life. A ship is ready. You pack your things. The journey starts.

2. Contemplation: You come to a country that you do not know until today. Ask for entry at the border. Talk to the customs officer. Tell him you want to discover this "soul land". Then take the path under your feet.

3. Contemplation: Imagine a castle. They have heard that therein are kept all the secrets about being human and about God. Ask for access, ask for the "price".

4. Contemplation: Imagine a wise person (man, woman). Tell this figure, you now want to get to know the soul life. Ask what you need to do.

5. Contemplation: Imagine a simple mandala (square with circle, maybe with cross and rosettes), you know: That represents the 'wholeness'. To this image, say that it should transform itself into your present psychical spiritual state.

6. Contemplation: You are sitting in a large pyramid-like room, all alone in complete calm and soft light. Allow this rest to take effect for about 10-15 minutes. "Now I want to feel closer and closer to my inner being ..."

7. Contemplation: You will receive a newly born child (or a small 1-2-year-old child). This is your new life, the new beginning of your being and life. Experience this child. Try to sense what it wants and needs; that it is in you, a part of you.

8. Contemplation: You are in a jail with others. These represent forces of yours, aspects of your character. Ask them what they expect from you. Look for the way to liberation.

9. Contemplation: An owl appears. It represents the spirit and the source of wisdom. Let yourself be guided by this figure.

10. Contemplation: You get a glowing ball, like a little sun, as big as a tennis ball. This is your "source of life". What are you doing with it?

11. Contemplation: Imagine, you have to say goodbye now, you are going into a process of 'metamorphosis' (transformation, cleansing, becoming new). Tell this to all your friends and acquaintances. You are allowed to take only the most important things with you.

12. Contemplation: Say meditating "I want to insert my "I", my willing and my acting into the cosmic order, into the original source of my life ..."

Ególius' point of view

Ególius sees the cause of life and humanity a little differently: "I know what is good for people. After all, I am experienced in life. I have everything under control. I am objective, not like those who always swim in an emotional bath. I control myself. Nothing escapes me. I think it's stupid what those do with digging in the past. That's no use. It's over!

There are people who conjure up their god with meditation from the dark nothing. Nothing is in there! In any case, I did not find anything. Just read the Bible! There is the truth! I believe. Of course, I think. I always analyse the situation exactly. Recently I sold a shack to a stranger. I am good! He will not get what he paid for the next hundred years.

For that I can now buy my son what he wants. I am a good father. And I care for my mother too. Only recently I have bought her new dishes, the finest, of course. I love my mother. She does the housework much better than my wife. Anyway, there are quite ridiculous tones of the emancipated: I should also wash the dishes at home? That's just what was missing. After all, I work the whole day.

I finally buy the whole cellar full of supplies. And I have a great car too. Every Sunday I drive my family out, at least about 500 km every time. And there I have my fun! So, with 170 km/h I feel really free. Sometimes there are idiots on the highway, which hinder the fluid driving. Yes, I am strong. Only immature men and of course women have weaknesses. They can go to the therapist.

Who speaks of "self-knowledge"? That's 'gibberish' for dreamers. I master well. Of course, I enjoy life: I like to eat ... ah and a lot! That feels good! I am a life artist; I am my own king. I have no guilt. I fulfil the laws, sometimes go to church and trust in God that he will receive me after death. He forgives me for sure all my little humanities. Everyone has them. With love, it is something.

You have to take life as it is. I cannot do business with love, I have to feed my family, pay for the children's school ... but I love myself! Because I always buy the very best, After all I am quality-conscious. I also love my wife. But sometimes the flesh is stronger than the will. It's not quite without it; and my wife does not like to participate. Well, then I'll pay a hundred and I'll have some rest for a few weeks. I have no problems. I sleep like a bear, deep and firm. Nothing can wake me up.

My wife is a bit damaged; weird women! She has a lot of trouble falling asleep. The doctor recently gave her sleeping pills. Everything is fine now. It may have something to it with the psyche and such.

But I am a businessman. Only with the strongest of wits and cunning do you still manage to produce capital swiftly. Nothing works without money. You have to talk softly with customers to stimulate needs. I'm good at this. I am also a happy person. That's what people feel. So, why should I meditate?

I drink two glasses of wine at noon, a bottle of wine in the evening, my two cognac to fall asleep. I know how to live well! So, stop the chatter about self-reflection. They are just lying.

They should first learn to work hard; and practice breeding instead of criticizing everything about politics and society. They do not do anything! They have nothing. They are nothing. They exaggerate, just to make themselves important.

I have a clear position on 'artists', good-for-nothings and parasites. After all, I work 14 hours a day. I engage myself. I look to what is right where I can.

The cross belongs in the schoolroom, that's how it has always been! These atheists! They undermine the culture and the spirit. Life will teach them what is proper and what leads to success! With most people you can see how they will not achieve anything. Many are sick and weak anyway, but cover it up.

Technology and the economy are the future, not these dull black paintings. They are demagogues. You have to be careful because everywhere lurks evil.

I advise you - Ególius - on your way: Watch out! Everywhere they lie, twisting everything, blowing their imagination to the truth, acting, intriguing, feigning, and vastly overestimating their ego. "

Notes and perspectives

What about the mental-spiritual evolution of humans?

Write down the key words in this subchapter:

What causes indifference to the cosmic anchorage?

Contemplation is essential, because: ...

What did you learn about the cosmic anchorage in your parents' home, school and church?

What meaning in living together has the conversation about contemplative experiences?

What would be the seriousness of contemplation in politics and business?

How does the advertisement respond to Ególiu's point of view?

Formulate an important question for contemplation:

5.1.4. Exercises

1. What do you know about your inner psychical reality?

2. How do you practice recognizing and understanding your psychical forces?

3. Which psychical forces do you recognize and / or understand little?

4. How do you experience your mental-spiritual growth?

5. What do you want to change, strengthen, unfold and become new?

6. What is the impact of life in your life when you live individuation?

Take the list "1. Phase of individuation very concrete".

7.1. What concrete work did you do to a large extent?

7.2. Which concrete works are particularly difficult for you?

7.3. For which concrete works do you have methodical ambiguities? Describe the ambiguities.

8. Which inner changes (changes) have you already experienced? Describe in comparison "earlier-today":

9. Which external transformations (changes) have you already experienced? Describe in comparison "earlier-today":

It used to be:	Today is:

10. Archetypal processes of individuation. (Collect concrete examples!)

10.1. Affirmation of psychical life
☐ Attention
☐ Interest
☐ Care
☐ Education

10.2. Discover, understand and disassemble
☐ Curiosity
☐ Search
☐ Inform
☐ Interpret

10.3. Rebirth of the inner human
☐ Protect
☐ Form
☐ Seek new life
☐ Grow

10.4. Recognition of the spirit as a guiding principle
☐ Placement in the leadership and order
☐ Experiencing oneself networking on all sides
☐ Affirmation of the spirit
☐ Turning with confidence

10.5. Transformations of all psychical forces
- ☐ Shaping, forming
- ☐ Getting new
- ☐ Detachment of old, not proven
- ☐ Extension

10.6. Union of opposites
- ☐ Masculinity-femininity
- ☐ Chaos-order
- ☐ Unconscious-awareness
- ☐ Reality-request / ideal

10.7. From the old to the new government principle
- ☐ Living a balanced unity
- ☐ Harmony of expertise and wisdom
- ☐ Spirit is across rationality
- ☐ Growth in the spirit instead of "putting on" ideas

10.8. Harmony between inside and outside
- ☐ The external life for the mental life
- ☐ Inner self-expression instead of imitation
- ☐ Physical devotion with the soul life
- ☐ Backbone living on indoor experiences

10.9. Completion of wholeness
- ☐ Individuation as a life expression
- ☐ Life as a realization of individuation
- ☐ Individuation as God-realization
- ☐ Promoting mental-spiritual evolution

Multiple Choice Test

Choose the four correct answers:

9.1. The mental-spiritual evolution. Characteristic aspects of human evolution are:

☐ a) Regressive-progressive bonding
☐ b) Enjoyment - asceticism
☐ c) Unconsciousness - consciousness
☐ d) Mindless - living with spirit
☐ e) Rejection - integration of the inner life
☐ f) Rationality - emotionality

9.2. The process of individuation. Transformations in individuation are:

☐ a) Affirmation of psychical life
☐ b) Understanding the psychical world
☐ c) Ecstatic experiences
☐ d) Recognition of the spirit
☐ e) Exemption from needs
☐ f) Harmony between inside and outside

9.3. Man, in transcendental anchorage. The following statements are core sentences for individuation:

☐ a) Archetypes are "signposts" in the process of individuation.
☐ b) Without individuation, there is no psycho-spiritual evolution.
☐ c) Individuation means detachment from everything worldly.
☐ d) One can go the "inner way" without adjusting the lived life.
☐ e) Without dream guidance, individuation cannot be achieved.
☐ f) Individuation is the challenge of human existence.

5.2. Concept of Individuation

5.2.1. Individuation as mental-spiritual development

Let's sketch a picture of people without individuation and mark the core elements:

This person negates the psychical inner life, experiences this undifferentiated in the area of needs, desires and habits.

Needs revolve around hunger and thirst, sexuality and having goods in the interests of prosperity.

In many situations and times, man experiences certain wishes of a material or social nature.

Man has hardly any access to the unconscious, experiences memories from time to time, but does not find that the past affects the entire richness like a code program.

The result is a steady and increasing burden of more and more chaotic inventory.

Man seeks relaxation externally through entertainment, perhaps through walks or sunbathing. What he pushes from the inside, he fends off, and what is unpleasantly experienced from the outside, he keeps away, no matter how meaningful this may be.

Love for this person is predominantly a feeling, a social action or a renunciation. He has no access to dreams and does not know what meditating properly means. This person lives largely "unconsciously", which affects the entire mental life.

A concerned conscious formation of the psychical organism is unknown to him. All border problems and questions of meaning this man solves in the field of ideologies, dogmas, materialism and power. This is the "archaic man".

From this picture, we deduce the "evolutionary human": This person lives more and more consciously with the entire psychical organism.

He practices different methods, reflects his inner world and integrates unpleasant things.

He creates order in the unconscious, interprets his dreams, mediates regularly and maintains the psychodynamics with relaxation techniques and mental training.

The evolutionary human lives in constant growth and unfolding. He forms the power of love and implements it in daily life.

His actions become competent in all areas of mental and psycho-social life.

He is always focused on the inner spirit in his decisions. Individuation is a way of life for him.

From the first systematic self-knowledge he grows until he is a living image of the archetype "circle-cross-mandala".

After that he lives his destiny.

Reflections and discussion

The main characteristics of the archaic human are:

☐ Denial of psychic life as the real life
☐ Rejection of the inner mind
☐ Beset by internal burdens that are repressed
☐ Without interior experience through dreams and introspection
☐ No holistic growth
☐ Only partially conscious formation of psychical forces
☐ Defence and repression of everything unpleasant, as far as possible
☐ Largely "unconscious" life, i.e. unconscious about the inner life
☐ Tendency for strong projections
☐ Anchoring life in ideologies and dogmas
☐ Comprehensive fixation on material goods
☐ Undifferentiated one-sided experience of love
☐ Highest value has external benefits

The evolutionary man is characterized by:

☐ Affirmation of the entire psychical life
☐ More and more free of the inner burden of the lived life
☐ Images in the subconscious that promote life constructively and progressively
☐ In all respects always in communication with the spirit through dreams
☐ Regular inner orientation through imagination and contemplation
☐ Conscious education of all psychical forces
☐ Integration of the unpleasant despite well-founded defence against circumstances
☐ More and more free from projections
☐ Anchoring life in the inner experience, especially in the spirit
☐ Shaping relationships, politics, economy from the individuation
☐ Dealing with nature and wildlife, the living environment with spirit and love
☐ Differentiated development and use of the power of love
☐ High flexibility and inner freedom towards material goods
☐ Highest value has psychical-spiritual achievements, characterized by the love

Discuss in a small circle the "evolutionary human" and draw a picture of the evolutionary social life:

Diagram 5.2.1: Individuation as evolution of human being

Diagramm OS1-4: Individuation als Evolution des Menschseins

English translation:

Integration of the psyche	> Affirmation and attention
Consciousness of inner life	> Discover, disassemble, understand
Order and structure	> Inner rebirth as base
Expansion in quality	> Spirit as principle of regime
Human care to life	> Love and spirit
Constructive progression	> Balanced growth
Differentiation of quality	> Individuation
Evolutive growth	> Inner transformation processes
Opening to new layer	> Union of contradictions
Dissolution of the archaic	> New regime principle
Dosing of quality	> Differentiation of quality
Realizing human being	> Unison inside and outside

Highest step of evolution   > Implementation main archetype

5.2.2. The first phase of individuation

The first phase begins with the gradual approach to one's own psychical life. These are first knowledge elements from psychology, which are used for self-knowledge and knowledge of human nature. Different practices of mental hygiene are to be learned.

The reflection on one's own actions and one's own feelings lead to the approach to the inner world. More and more the psychical life is accepted as reality.

In many ways, the psychical forces can then be reflected. Man, experiences thoughtfully: The thoughts, the feelings, the desires and plans, the conscience, the will, the responsibility and some virtues or vices. Systematically, all forces can be discovered and disassembled.

The goal is a deepened understanding: "That's me and through this way of life I have become."

The question "Who am I?" leads you into your own life story right back to the earliest childhood. Systematically, every phase of life has to be worked up. Unforgiven events, embarrassing moments, tragic events and also beautiful hours that you do not want to let go inside, have to be clear up and disbanded.

It also requires knowledge of human nature: "... that's why the other acted that way ...".

The dreams regularly bring material that bridges the gap from current events to the past. Many dreams say, "That's you" and continue to ask, "Do you want to stay that way?". These challenges the "I": "What do I want to become, in which direction do I want to change?"

Not always is the step into the past in the first place. Often it is enough to watch a "movie" about the past day.

This can "get under your skin" and make you want to grow: "I want to live more and more so that I can look after it without being ashamed, so that the spirit also finds it sage."

Responsibility grows through this, but not through a "higher conscience," which is anyway only the accepted inventory in the unconscious, but through the experience of the transcendence of the spirit. Gradually a new person unfolds inside.

It may take a good year or more for these first systematic efforts to create new life within.

This consists mainly: real basic needs, real feelings, conscious thinking, taking seriously the dreams and valuation of love.

If this first new life is strengthened, then the first phase is about to end.

Reflections and discussion

The first phase of individuation can be divided into three stages, each of which can be called a "transformation process":

1st stage: Interest, attention and affirmation of psychical life

2nd stage: Systematically discovering, disassembling and understanding

3rd stage: Rebirth of the inner human, i.e. of the new psychical life

In reality it is the case that every person has already made different steps to this entry:

☐ Partial knowledge of psychology and human knowledge
☐ Meditations and dream interpretation
☐ Practices in dealing with people, e.g. at work
☐ Experience in educational courses and in self-experience groups
☐ Psychoanalysis, psychotherapy or psychological counselling
☐ Self-help groups of all kinds
☐ Action groups on parenting, media education, environmental protection

The life story of each person is unique; heavy and tragic for many, harmless and loving for some.

This means that the first phase cannot be specified exactly in time. As a guide:

a) About 1 year for those who have already taken significant steps

b) About 2 years if there is little knowledge and experience

c) About 3 years, when the childhood or the later time is heavily loaded

The optimization of the duration of the first phase requires:

☐ Systematic work, every day with "psycho workbook"
☐ Part of the weekend and holiday season should be provided for this education
☐ Acquisition of comprehensive basic knowledge
☐ Optional phased advisory support
☐ Weekly at least two hours of group training (or monthly / quarterly), i.e. systematic training of relaxation, psycho-hygiene, reflection, dream interpretation, imagination and contemplation

Create a plan in the group that shows which steps and goals can be worked out in such time periods.

a) Weekly plan:

b) Monthly plan:

c) Annual plan:

Diagram 5.2.2: Characteristically employs in the 1st phase

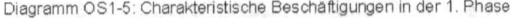

Diagramm OS1-5: Charakteristische Beschäftigungen in der 1. Phase

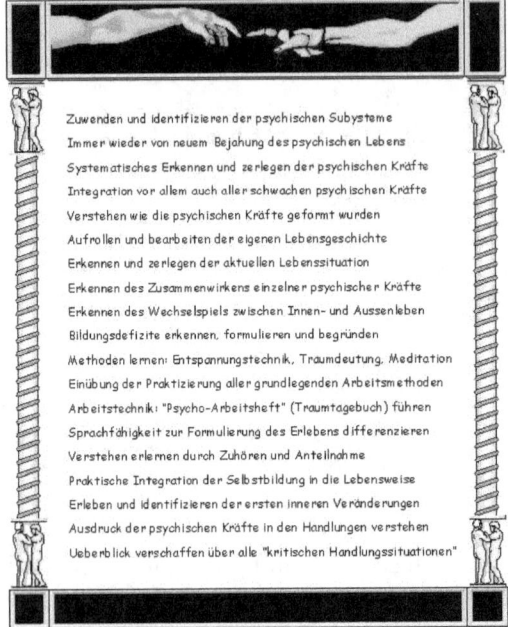

Zuwenden und identifizieren der psychischen Subsysteme
Immer wieder von neuem Bejahung des psychischen Lebens
Systematisches Erkennen und zerlegen der psychischen Kräfte
Integration vor allem auch aller schwachen psychischen Kräfte
Verstehen wie die psychischen Kräfte geformt wurden
Aufrollen und bearbeiten der eigenen Lebensgeschichte
Erkennen und zerlegen der aktuellen Lebenssituation
Erkennen des Zusammenwirkens einzelner psychischer Kräfte
Erkennen des Wechselspiels zwischen Innen- und Aussenleben
Bildungsdefizite erkennen, formulieren und begründen
Methoden lernen: Entspannungstechnik, Traumdeutung, Meditation
Einübung der Praktizierung aller grundlegenden Arbeitsmethoden
Arbeitstechnik: "Psycho-Arbeitsheft" (Traumtagebuch) führen
Sprachfähigkeit zur Formulierung des Erlebens differenzieren
Verstehen erlernen durch Zuhören und Anteilnahme
Praktische Integration der Selbstbildung in die Lebensweise
Erleben und identifizieren der ersten inneren Veränderungen
Ausdruck der psychischen Kräfte in den Handlungen verstehen
Ueberblick verschaffen über alle "kritischen Handlungssituationen"

English translation:
Turning to and identifying the psychical subsystems
Consistently new affirmation of the psychical life
Systematically recognizing and disassembling of the psychical forces
Integration mainly all weak psychical forces
Understanding who the psychical forces had been formed
Unrolling and processing of the own life history
Recognizing and disassembling of the actual life situation
Recognizing of the coaction of the single psychical forces
Recognizing of the interplay between inner and outer life
Recognizing, phrasing and justifying of deficits of formation
Learning methods: Relaxation techniques, dream interpretation, meditation
Rehearsing of the practising of all basic working methods
Working technique: Keeping a "Psycho working book" (dream diary)
Differentiating the faculty of speech for the verbalisation of the experiencing
Learning to understand by listening and sympathy
Practical integration of the self-formation into the way of life
Experiencing and identifying of the first inner transformations

Understanding the expression of the psychical forces in the actions
Procuring overview of all "critical act situations"

5.2.3. The second phase of individuation

The more human works with dreams in the first phase, and experiences the intelligent power of the spirit through meditations, the more the problem inflicts the "I", who its freedom is in relation to that inner guidance instance.

The second phase can only begin when human acknowledges this inner spirit as the spiritual principle (there are some concepts: the "spirit of God", the "higher life principle", the "cosmic spirit", etc.).

A stable, growth-oriented and holistic continuation is not possible without this step. Partly, individual psychical subsystems can be processed, e.g. clarifying complexes, reflecting on thinking, working on feelings, but an integrating, fundamental process cannot yet take place in this way.

The recognition of the spiritual regime principle includes various aspects. The "I" communicates with this intelligent power in order to transform itself, to find oneself, to plan one's life and to discover the "secrets of life".

Without the acceptance of this spirit, the overcoming of internalized images about mythological religion, about God, "heaven and hell" can hardly be achieved.

After this transformation step, various processes of transformation, which mainly concern the unconscious inventory, always follow the other psychical forces and daily actions.

All four areas of the unconscious have to be systematically worked through. Much is to be transformed in it. Because these images act as a "regime principle" from the unconscious ambush.

Just as this world of images will be transformed into a living inner reality, so do the needs and the emotions change.

The experiences often push for change of acting. This is to be re-learned and practiced step by step. At the same time, new life open and progressive images are forming in the unconscious.

If the new images are stronger than the old ones, only then can the inner spirit, as a new "regime principle", take on the growth process and the systematic integrating unfolding of life. Gradually, the inner contradictions dissolve. They disappear from the unconscious, and also from conscious thinking and acting.

This also applies to the emotional life, the needs and the relationship between the "logic" of thinking and the "principles" of the spirit.

Once all opposites have been dissolved, a new entity is formed: The psychical organism as a universally balanced entity.

Reflections and discussion

The second phase of individuation can be divided into three stages, each of which can be called a "transformation process":

4th stage: Recognition of the spirit as a guiding principle

5th stage: Transformation of all psychical subsystems and individual forces

6th stage: Dissolution of the opposites to a new comprehensive entity

The practical process contains many elements and variable progress, because:

☐ The order of the topics to be processed varies between people and can lead to the unconscious in the one case and the daily actions in another.
☐ Sometimes weaker forces can be strengthened until others can be processed.
☐ Life events can change the course and set new priorities, e.g. an intended marriage or divorce, a change of occupation or a death, an accident or illness, a "critical event".
☐ An irksome childhood and adolescence can be treated with complementary counselling, which sometimes helps to support it.

The duration of this phase depends on various factors, such as life history, "critical events", learning input and the person's environment:

a) About two to three years as a minimum, even for persons with previous experience

b) Three to four years with reasonably rapid progress and intensive work

c) Four to five years, if special factors slow down considerably, require special efforts or the use is temporarily limited

It should be noted that with 30, 40 or 50 years of life, different topics and quantities / types of life experiences have to be dealt with.

The goal of this second level of individuation is a significant value that has been rarely achieved and has not yet been addressed by science.

☐ Whoever has achieved this goal never wants to go back.
☐ Nothing in life can replace the value of this goal.
☐ People who achieve this goal have "highest value" to the community.

Discuss the description of this phase in the group:

a) What attracts interest?

b) What strengthens why defence?

c) What motivates you to live such a path?

Diagram 5.2.3: Characteristically employs in the 2nd phase

Konzentrierte Ausrichtung auf das Führungsprinzip des Geistes
Lebensweise, die einer Vertiefung der Selbstbildung Raum gibt
Zunehmend Halt aufbauen durch innenorientierte Erfahrungen
Resonanz der Träume auf die Lebensgestaltung beachten
Den inneren Geist als kooperatives Führungsprinzip bejahen
Erfassen der Menschen in der psychisch-geistigen Ganzheit
Dem Aufbau der Kraft der Liebe Aufmerksamkeit schenken
Konzentrierte Aufmerksamkeit auf die tägliche Wahrnehmung
Das gesamte Inventar des Unbewussten schrittweise bearbeiten
Das Denken, das wertende Urteilen und Reden reflektieren
Den Willen stärken durch Ziele und Entscheidung
Die Wirkungsweise der Abwehr erkennen und korrigieren
Die Projektionen erkennen und ihre Inhalte zurücknehmen
Immer differenzierteres und realistischeres Selbstbild aufbauen
Klare Identifizierung des Bewusstseins über die Menschen
Bewusstsein über den Lebensraum in Raum-Zeit-erweitern
Unterscheiden können zwischen Masken, Fassaden und Wirklichkeit
Die Kräfte, Neigungen und Begabungen formen und verwirklichen
Immer mehr die inneren Gegensätze versöhnen, umformen, auflösen
Die Grundbedürfnisse klar identifizieren und verwirklichen
Positive Gefühle aufbauen und generell Gefühle integrativ managen
Werte gemäss den inneren Erfahrungen leben und vertreten
Zyklisch alle Kräfte bis zur vorgeburtlichen Zeit klären
Das Leben zunehmend aus dem neuen inneren Sein gestalten
Fähigkeit zur Orientierung an den Archetypen entwickeln

English translation:
Concentrated orientation to the regime principle of the spirit
Way of living giving space to deepening of self-formation
Building support through inner orientated experiences
Respecting the reaction to the dreams on the life design
Affirming the inner spirit as cooperative regime principle
Perceiving the human in the psychical-spiritual wholeness
Paying attention to the designing of the power of love
Concentrated attention to the daily perception
Processing step by step the entire inventory of the unconscious
Reflecting the thinking, the valuing judging and talking
Strengthening the will with goals and decisions
Recognizing and correcting the effect of the defence
Recognizing projections and redeem its contents
Building more and more a differentiated and realistic self-image
Clear identifying of the consciousness about man
Amplifying the consciousness over the habitat in space and time
Differentiating between masks, facades and realities
Shaping and realizing the forces, aptitudes and talents
Reconciling, transforming, dissolving more and more inner opposites
Basic needs identifying clearly and realizing
Building positive feelings and in general managing integrative emotions
Values living and representing according to the inner experiences
Cyclically clearing all forces until the prenatal time

Designing life increasingly from the new inner being
Developing the ability to orientate on the archetypes

5.2.4. The third phase of Individuation

Those who have completed the second phase know the psychical life comprehensively, know the transformation processes as the "life secrets" and their powers "run smoothly". i.e. balanced on all sides.

Only now can the inner spirit, as the principle of psychic-spiritual life, be fully lived. That has to be practiced.

For this inner spirit grasps reality in a different way than thought, unlike "reason." The spirit experiences time and space in a larger context.

What is important to humans may have little weight for this power. Particularly important is the interaction of love and spirit. For love without spirit cannot be evolutionary.

With the newly found unity also the life determination forms. Every person finds his life task according to his abilities and talents. This forms in the context of the private situation and the occupational activities.

All actions that exceed the usual daily life are more and more thoughtfully incorporated into the principle of the spirit. This new way of life requires a lot of training. Often "you fall on the nose".

Everywhere are people who want to destroy the completion of this "great work".

The entire collective unconscious counteracts the final phase of individuation.

Politics, the economy, culture and religion are also outside of this target phase. If the inner work with the discovered unity is essentially completed, then it is now necessary to practice and enforce the new inner being.

There you have to do a lot of things, maybe go down deep or get away from the hectic gear of social life.

The external structure grows very slowly, quietly and carefully. "Fighting" cannot the person who lives in this phase.

May the world look different in decades, perhaps with many hundreds of thousands of people who have reached this stage, perhaps even with a school system that teaches individuation and a culture that nurtures individuation.

Today, this reality is still a "mystery" that has not been fully illuminated by either psychoanalysis or psychology.

Who then, after much experience of life, has created the complete wholeness, inside and out, knows:

It is unbelievable how many illusions are taught about it.

The human at the goal is closer to God than all the "highest dignitaries". He is a living image of the "circle-cross-archetype".

Reflections and discussion

The third phase of individuation can be divided into three stages of transformation:

7th stage: Complete turn to the spiritual leadership principle

8th stage: Finding harmony between inside and outside

9th stage: Completion of wholeness

The practical process is essentially more regular again and certainly always depends on the person's life situation. The levels are thematically homogenous, albeit multifaceted in life:

☐ Relationship life is given a special character and dynamic: Outside should become, what is processed inside.
☐ The professional life is also more and more centred around the subject of individuation for the people in general.
☐ The confrontation with the external reality can lead to considerable tensions and difficulties. An autonomous way of life facilitates the process.
☐ The daily meditation and the study of dreams is essential, because all forces are tested to the utmost.
☐ The challenges require that human completely relies on this spirit, and that the psychic-spiritual life keeps grounded, never the outer reality.

The author wants to comment personally on this:

☐ Very few people have reached this goal in human history
☐ The collective psycho-spiritual evolution is not feasible unless many people seek and achieve that goal
☐ If humanity does not go in the direction of this process, it will destroy itself; i.e. the accomplishment of individuation also has an opposite process, which is automatically realized more and more, if individuation is not collectively promoted and lived.
☐ Achieving this goal is a cosmic process and has special significance for the history of humanity.
☐ Who has reached the goal, cannot help but back to the people. But what people do with it is not his responsibility.

Formulate yourself in conversation with others your own questions:

Diagram 5.2.4: Characteristically employs in the 3rd phase

Diagramm OS1-7: Charakteristische Beschäftigungen in der 3. Phase

Lebensorientierung aus der Kommunikation mit dem Geist
Vielseitiges Wissen über alle Belange des täglichen Lebens
Training der neuen psychischen Kräfte durch aktives Handeln
Zentrierung aller wichtigen Entscheidungen in Geist und Liebe
Erleben eines stabilen Getragenseins in den inneren Bildern
Vollständiges Freisein von inneren Fesseln (bzw. Konflikten)
Detaillierte Bildung, da wo es noch nicht "rund läuft"
Erkennen und aufbauen der eigenen Lebensbestimmung
Verstehen des Kollektivs der Menschen aus innerer Sicht
Vernetzte Erfahrungen der archetypischen Prozesse
In allen Lebensbereichen das neue Leben aussen verwirklichen
Flexibles Umgehen mit den Masken und Fassaden der Menschen
Stabilität und Verlass entwickeln im inneren Geist
Fähigkeiten, die transzendierende Kraft der Liebe einzusetzen
Erleben des Abbildseins des Kreis-Kreuz-Mandalas
Alles äussere Leben baut sich systematisch aus dem Innern auf
Archetypische Prozeduren in Träumen zur Zielerreichung
Das Erreichen des Zieles vielseitig erkennen und festigen
Das Ziel als Anfang für das "neue Leben" umsetzen
Verstehen der Funktionsweise der psychischen Energie
Sich umfassend einfügen in einen eigenen "Schicksalsplan"
Jeder Halt basiert zunehmend auf der erreichten Individuation
Auch in sehr schwierigen Situationen innenorientiert leben

English translation:

Life orientation in the communication with the spirit
Manifold knowledge about all matters of the daily life
Training of the new psychical forces trough active handling
Centring all important decisions in the spirit and in love
Complete being free from inner bonds (resp. conflicts)
Detailed formation, where is does not "run around"
Recognizing and building the own life determination
Understanding the conflict of humans from inside view
Linked experiences of the archetypal processes
In all life areas realizing external the new life
Flexible handling with the masks and facades of humans
Stability and reliance develop in the inner spirit
Ability inserting the transcending power of love
All external life building up systematically from the inside
Archetypal procedures in dreams for the reaching of the goal
Manifold recognizing and strengthening the achievement of the goal
Transferring the goal as start for a "new life"
Understanding functionality of the psychical energy
Comprehensively fitting own self in the own "destiny plan"

Each support bases increasingly on the reached individuation
Also, in very difficult situations living inner oriented

5.2.5. Archetypes for orientation

Imagine: Sitting together a psychoanalyst, a behavioural therapist, a humanistic psychologist, a pedagogue, a social worker, a teacher, an adult educator, a philosopher, a priest, and a few more, all claiming:

"I know the way and the destination." As you know, many ways are touted. How can someone recognize which way leads to the goal?

One criterion is the model of the psychical organism: If only one subsystem is missing, then "the wheel can never run around". In particular, without the comprehensive processing of the unconscious and without dream interpretation, the goal is not achievable.

"Enlightenment" without comprehensive individuation is illusion.

Another criterion are the archetypes. Archetypes are supra-individual symbols, pictorial representations of basic characteristics of psychical powers or subsystems.

Various archetypes represent the transformation processes and stages from beginning to end.

The most abstract archetypes are the circle-cross-mandala, the hexagram, the ankh-symbol, the pyramid and the pentagram. Symbols activate and shape psychical energy.

By means of contemplation everyone can experience the energetic effect and above all the sense, i.e. what this archetype depicts. In this sense, the archetypes are guideposts in the process of individuation.

A concept without archetypes cannot lead to the goal.

The archetypes are also something like "tools" that can be used in meditations. They bring about relaxation, centring of the psychical energy, catharsis of the energy and above all they can be used for the transformation of the unconscious inventory.

In the active imagination, the images can thus revive, contrast and transform.

The grail story and many heroes epics represent the psychic-spiritual process.

It is always about the search for the "treasure", the "secret" and the struggle between the "good" and the "evil", i.e. the life-averted and the life-oriented forces.

Love and spirit are always the challenges of the "hero".

It always includes the internal forces and the external forces in life.

Learning processes have to be run through and passed "tests" until the "hero" has found the transcendence and his new wholeness.

Today we can use the findings of pedagogy, andragogy, philosophy and psychology to scientifically process and describe this educational process.

Reflections and discussion

The following criteria provide guidance for the assessment of which pathways lead to the goal of psycho-spiritual evolution:

☐ Wholeness of the psychical organism (at least in essence)
☐ The methods of dream interpretation, imagination, contemplation, reflection
☐ The handling of psychical energy
☐ The process as a multifaceted and well-founded transformation process
☐ The archetypes
☐ Archetypal stories as a reflection of the process

Archetypes are symbols about:

☐ The subsystems of the psychical organism
☐ Individual forces, as they can be shaped characteristically
☐ The wholeness of the psychical organism before individuation
☐ The wholeness of the psychical organism at the goal of individuation
☐ The process as a learning process with "exams"
☐ The relation between psychical inner world and the real outside world
☐ The processes of transformation as catharsis and constitution (education)
☐ The forces that can support the process

Archetypes are:

☐ Circle-cross-mandala (the highest archetype)
☐ Anchsymbol
☐ Hexagram
☐ Pentagram
☐ Pyramid
☐ Chalice (vessel)
☐ Grail (philosopher's stone)
☐ King / queen
☐ The good / the bad
☐ And many pictures representing basic patterns of human beings

Archetypes can be used in practical work:

☐ For contemplation
☐ For active imagination
☐ For psycho-energetic rituals (so-called symbol actions)

Create in the group a list of "routes" you are aware of and discuss them with the list of criteria listed.

Diagram 5.2.5: Archetypes of individuation (selection)

Diagramm OS1-8: Archetypen der Individuation (Auswahl)

English translation: (From left above to right below)

Circle-cross-mandala: Wholeness of human being, at once image of God, source of life, centring of energy, goal of individuation

Life journey: Way of individuation, inner discovery journey, searching the grail, discovering new life

Wise man / woman: Inner life guidance, inner formation of a folk, leading to liberation, messianic destiny, collective new orientation

Pyramid: Secret of life, secret of life, tightened energy structure, incremental way to God, openness in the cosmos, power source in the universe

Hexagram: Union earth-cosmos, penetration of both worlds, union of the opposites, integration of the invisible, connection psyche/spirit

Owl: Wisdom & life knowledge, spirit as guiding power, spiritual knowledge, clear-sightedness in the darkness, knowledge of the light

Yin & Yang: Dynamic of the basic principles, union masculine-feminine, reciprocity of the opposites, The active and the passive

Baby: Birth of the new human, inner psychical renewal, star of inner growth, the inner baby to form, hope trough transformation

Eternity of light: Spiritual energy, inspiration, spiritual view, love as life donator

Masks of humans: The life theatre, covered shadows, the calling unconscious, the many faces

Self-formation: Knowledge and awareness, life exams, life competences, spiritual asset of culture

Crown: The psychical king being, the spiritual regime principles, representative of God, goal of the individuation, being king of the grail

5.2.6. The dynamics of the psychical organism

The analysis of the subsystems of the psychical organism has revealed that every single subsystem pushes for development and expression in the lifeworlds.

Life forms these individual subsystems, and the formed has the psychodynamic tendency to reproduce itself.

The "I" experiences its own shaping as a little or hardly changeable reality. The internalized is the reality, for most people the only right and true reality.

What human has not appropriated and what has not produced any form of formation for him exists for him as something foreign, which he keeps away from himself. This applies to human expression as well as to beliefs.

The single subsystems always interact with other subsystems. Exemplarily formulated:

Those who live the power of love without using the intelligent functions cannot do much good.

Anyone who thinks he is free in his thinking underestimates the subliminal influence of the unconscious.

Anyone who has no conscious access to the inventory of his unconscious and has not work it up, cannot see that he (and how he) is fully dependent on this unconscious content.

Who does not interpret his dreams and cannot meditate properly, has no access to the spirit.

Who puts his intelligence - his mind - as the supreme principle undervalues his unconscious, his feelings and the spirit.

Individuation as a psychical-spiritual process of unfolding is beyond any idea in such a formed human being.

His learned religion is for this human truth and life-anchor; his communication with God and spirit is a projection.

His libido fixates itself in faith instead of in psychic-spiritual growth. He cannot recognize his so-being as archaic human being.

If people do not learn to form their psychic-spiritual being with the power of the spirit, they will destroy the earth and humanity.

Because man is the cause of the global destruction of nature and wildlife.

For in human, the instinct of destruction grows in proportion as he suppresses his vital instincts and does not build them up for an all-round balanced humanity.

Reflections and discussion

We recognize the interdependencies of the psychic subsystems, e.g. in order to:

☐ Those who do not use their intelligent functions in life with the power of love ultimately disrespect and destroy humanity.
☐ Those who do not perceive and realize their basic psychical needs do not live their human being authentically.
☐ Anyone who has no access to his unconscious, represses its contents and does not want to admit it in its effect, is chained to it and lives a life in constant reproduction of this content.
☐ Those who disdain or overestimate their feelings can never realize their human being in a balanced and real-life way.
☐ Without dialogue with dreams, access to inner humanity is limited. Individuation can never be carried out in this way - that is, for lack of dialogue with the spirit.
☐ The meditation opens the gates to the inner realities. Those who do not (or not properly) meditate, always live in a "being split", separated from his inner human.
☐ Those who cannot critically reflect on the contents of their consciousness and do not recognize them as products of the environment will tend to absolutize them.

Here are some questions that expand the perspectives:

☐ When fewer and fewer people form and live the power of love, where will that lead collectively?

☐ When fewer and fewer people live by the power of the spirit, where will this lead collectively?

☐ If people ignore individuation as an expression and theme of being, what kind of humanity will prevail in the future?

☐ If the reality of the psychical organism and the need to balance all subsystems around the world are negated by almost all people, then what is left for a human image?

☐ What is this religion (and politics) that disregards the reality of the psychical organism with all its subsystems - and thus individuation?

☐ How does man want to find "enlightenment", "redemption" and God, if he negates individuation as a process of growth towards this being?

Discuss the possible solutions in the group:

Diagram 5.2.6: The interaction in the psychical organism

Diagramm OS1-9: Die Interaktionen im psychischen Organismus

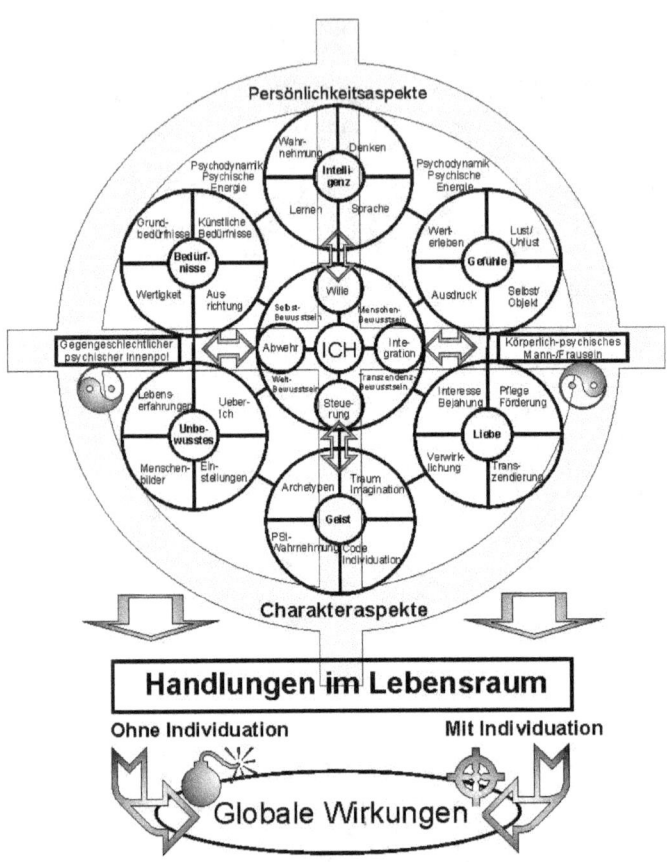

English translation: (From left above to right below)

Personality aspects / **Intelligence** (perception, thinking, learning, language) / Psychodynamics, psychical energy / **Needs**(basic needs, artificial needs, valence, orientation) / **Feelings** (experiencing value, lust / unlust, expression, self/object / Reciprocal sexual inner psychical pole / **"I"** (will, self-consciousness, human-consciousness, defence, integration, world-consciousness, transcendence-consciousness, control) / Physical man- / woman being / **Unconscious** (life experiences, super-ego, images of humans, attitudes / **Love** (interest / affirmation, care / encouragement, realization, transcending) **Spirit** (archetypes, dream / imagination, extra sensorial perception, code of individuation) **Character aspects** / **Actions in the habitat** / **Without individuation** / **With individuation** / **Global effects**

5.2.7. Working unit

5.2.7. Working unit - 1

1. a) How do you assess the difference between the 'evolutionary human' and the 'archaic man'?

1. b) Give three concrete aspects that fit the 'evolutionary human':

2. Give 7 short examples of what evolutionary might mean in society:

1) _____

2) _____

3) _____

4) _____

5) _____

6) _____

7) _____

3. Formulate an educational goal to promote evolutionary humanity:

4. a) Imagine your evolutionary psychical-spiritual state:

b) Your conclusion in one sentence:

5.2.7. Working unit - 2

1. a) What achievements of the first phase of individuation have not yet been performed?

1. b) What makes you feel particularly strong today (after completing the first phase)?

2. Describe what you achieved with the first phase of Individuation:

Describe how you transform your achievements for your private environment:

Describe how you transform your achievements for your societal environment:

3. Formulate an educational goal for you to complete Phase 1:

4. a) Imagine your unstable foundations:

4. b) Your conclusion in one sentence:

5.2.7. Working unit - 3

1. a) What are your outstanding experiences from the second phase?

1. b) Extend a transformation step with some knowledge elements (if available):

2. Comment and reflect on how you experience the description of this second phase:

a) What attracts way interest?

b) What strengthens why defence?

c) What motivates you to live such a path?

3. Formulate an educational goal that will complete the 2nd phase:

4. a) Imagine the internal forces that are still under-worked:

4. b) Your conclusion in one sentence:

5.2.7. Working unit - 4

1. a) How do you experience the description of the third phase of individuation?

1. b) Expand the target area with your own concrete expectations:

1. c) The 3rd phase of Individuation should bring me (benefit for me):

2. Describe the "goal value" for you:

2. a) Highest value:

2. b) Life-oriented value:

2. c) Mission value:

3. Formulate an educational goal that marks the third phase of your individuation:

4. a) Imagine the work on the third phase, which you still have to perform:

4. b) Your conclusion in one sentence:

5.2.7. Working unit - 5

1. a) What experiences do you have about archetypal symbols?

1. b) What is the "big problem" for you about the "right way and goal"?

2. Give 10 criteria when "holistic education" is fulfilled in an educational program:

1) _____

2) _____

3) _____

4) _____

5) _____

6) _____

7) _____

8) _____

9) _____

10) _____

3. Formulate an educational goal that helps to recognize the "right" way:

4. a) Imagine the role of archetypes in human education:

b) Your conclusion in one sentence:

5.2.7. Working unit - 6

1. a) How do you experience the interdependencies of the psychical subsystems?

1. b) What happens if you disregard the interdependencies? An example:

2. Answer as concrete as possible:
a) What does love have to do with intelligence?

b) How do you know if someone is integrating "spirit" into his life?

c) How do you see the expression of individuation in everyday life?

d) What happens when the wholeness of the psychical organism is ignored?

e) What does the transcendental reality have to do with humans?

f) What does "finding orientation in individuation" mean?

g) How can the educational achievements in individuation be promoted?

h) What is "enlightenment"?

3. Formulate an educational goal that includes the psyche-world interaction:

4. a) Imagine the consequences in society that promotes individuation:

4. b) Your conclusion in one sentence:

5.2.7. Working unit - 7

It would make sense if all priests (pastors) were so-called "individuates". Even education experts and teachers (educators, andragologists, education researchers) could (should) expect that. Justify with 5 points:

Multiple Choice Test

Choose the four correct answers:

10.1. Individuation as a psychical-spiritual development demand:
☐ a) The complete affirmation of the comprehensive psychical life
☐ b) The processing (education) of the entire own psychical organism
☐ c) The regular inner orientation (dream work / imagination)
☐ d) The comprehensive formation of the power of love
☐ e) The demarcation with respect to numinous internal forces
☐ f) The anchoring of life in clear beliefs

10.2. The first phase of individuation:
☐ a) Turning to, perceiving and identifying the psychical powers
☐ b) Recognizing the interaction of psychical forces and life
☐ c) Clear reduction of pleasure and joie de vivre
☐ d) Disclaiming goods and property of any kind
☐ e) Learn techniques (relaxation, dream interpretation, meditation, etc.)
☐ f) Rolling up and processing your own life story

10.3. The second phase of individuation:
☐ a) This is only for the "chosen" and "spiritually oriented"
☐ b) This leads to mysterious spiritual experiences
☐ c) Requires daily exercise of dream interpretation, imagination, reflection
☐ d) Leads through the central inner transformation processes
☐ e) Forms human to a very differentiated consciousness
☐ f) Requires the thorough processing of all psychical subsystems

10.4. The third phase of individuation:
☐ a) At this time, this phase is not for all people
☐ b) Here forms the living image of the main archetype
☐ c) Life is lived extensively in accordance with the spirit principle
☐ d) One's own determination of life is increasingly taking design
☐ e) The inner hold is based on the material life success through individuation
☐ f) The goal of individuation leads to "miraculous abilities"

10.5. Archetypes are symbols about:
- ☐ a) Wholeness of the psychical organism
- ☐ b) Transformation processes
- ☐ c) Key issues of existence
- ☐ d) Process forces
- ☐ e) Spirits and gods in the hereafter
- ☐ f) Everything that exists in life

10.6. The dynamics of the psychical organism. The self-destruction of humanity and the destruction of the earth is preventable, provided that:
- ☐ a) Many people fulfil the transformation processes of individuation.
- ☐ b) The experience of the archetypes of the soul becomes a spiritual orientation.
- ☐ c) People turn back to their Christian faith.
- ☐ d) Politics limits individual scope with military power.
- ☐ e) Politics too finds its orientation in the values of individuation.
- ☐ f) Worldwide, people want to live the love, the truthfulness and the spirit.